THE CASSON FAMILY IN NORTH WALES

The Casson Family in North Wales

A Story of Slate and More

Diana Devlin

First published in 2019

© Diana Devlin/Gwasg Carreg Gwalch

© Gwasg Carreg Gwalch 2019

ISBN: 978-1-84524-294-7

Cover design: Eleri Owen

Published by Gwasg Carreg Gwalch,
12 Iard yr Orsaf, Llanrwst, Wales LL26 0EH
tel: 01492 642031
email: books@carreg-gwalch.cymru
website: www.carreg-gwalch.cymru

For Gwyn and Gwenan,
who welcomed us back to Bron y Garth.

Contents

Acknowledgments

I started researching and writing about the Cassons in North Wales while attending Faber Academy: Writing Family History. I am grateful to its tutor, Andrea Stuart, who set me on the way, and to the loyal group who have stayed together, providing encouragement, support and fun: Clare Blatchford, Susie Gutch, Margaret McAlpine,Tracey Messenger, Barbara Selby, Vanita Sharma, Patrizia Sorgiovanni, Nicola Stevens, AnnieThompson, Clare Travers and Kristina Tzaneff.

I developed my work with the inspiring guidance of Professor Jon Cook, while attending The Guardian/University of East Anglia Masterclass: Writing the New Biography and its later manifestation as the Biography Group I thank all the members heartily for their enthusiasm and wisdom: Liza Coutts, Carrie Dunne, Monique Goodliffe, Lyn Innes, Barbara Pidgeon, Ted Powell, Jo Rogers, Barbara Selby (again), Ann Vinden, David Warren and Hephzi Yohannan.

I thank: Jane Aaron (for her advice), Griff Beale (for sharing information about our organ-building ancestors), Paddy Buckley (for sharing his research on William Turner and others), Alex Clatworthy (for Welsh translation), Paul Hale (for his expertise on Tom Casson's organ designs), Veronica Millington (for invaluable genealogical assistance), Siân Northey (for Welsh translation) and Harold Ogden (for his knowledge of the Seathwaite Cassons).

Staff at Archifau Gwynedd in Dolgellau and at Llyfrgell Genedlaethol Cymru have been unfailingly helpful.

Many members of the Casson family have encouraged me in the enterprise. In addition, Glynis Casson and Penny Pocock have accompanied me on field trips; David and Mark Leather have shared information and expertise, Janet Ritchie has supplied valuable family material. Liz Muldoon shared information about our Holland Thomas ancestors. My late stepfather, Ian Haines, safeguarded many family documents.

In Seathwaite, I received much help and hospitality from Felicity and Ed Hughes at the Chapelhouse, and Gail Batten at the Newfield Inn. In Llan Ffestiniog I was shown round the village by Bill Jones, and given valuable information by Moira and Neil Richards and by Diane Lea, who had lived at Plas Blaenddol and who shared its history. I visited Pengwern Hall with John Townsend and other members of Grŵp Dyddio Hen Dai Cymreig (Dating Old Welsh Houses Group), whose research has been useful. Gillian Smithson entertained me at Plas Penrhyn, Penrhyndeudraeth, and in Denbigh I was welcomed to Cae Derw by Alan Dorey. Vaughan Gaskell showed me round Betchton Hall in Cheshire. Special thanks to Michael Bewick at Llechwedd Slate Caverns, who arranged a magnificent tour of the Diffwys quarry.

I thank Myrddin ap Dafydd, Daniel Leeman and Mererid Jones for their patient work in preparing the book for publication.

Diana Devlin
Spring 2019

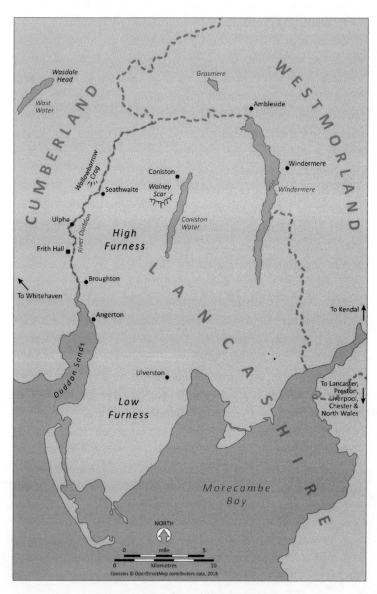

Furness, Lancashire in the 18th century

Chapter 1

Slate-getters of Walney Scar

There are two approaches to the Lakeland slate quarry
which was once familiar to my forebears. You can either take
the old road from Coniston, walking westwards over the fell,
past Coniston Old Man, or you can come at it from the
other side, setting off from the small village of Seathwaite in
the Duddon Valley. A few years ago, I took the second route,
on a quest to see where my family's story, as I knew it, had
begun. It was a pleasant spring day, but I was unused to such
a steep uphill walk. My companion and guide had to let me
pause several times on our way to the long-abandoned site.
I sat down on a pile of waste slate and looked around. The fells
and valleys of Cumbria stretched out for miles, grey and black
debris scattered around me, with rich greens and browns in
the middle ground, fading into grey-blue outlines on the
skyline. Two of my ancestors had worked here at Walney
Scar quarry.[1] They had eaten their midday meals in one of
the shelters that now stood roofless, a relic of a once active
industry, now home only to hikers and a few straying sheep.

The first of the family to work at the quarry was William
Casson. In about 1773, when he was twelve years old, he
finished his schooling and began as a 'slate-getter', as the
quarriers termed themselves, at Walney Scar. It was a career
that was to take him, years later, as an English immigrant, to
North Wales, a land that was his, in being part of Britain, yet
was as foreign as somewhere overseas; a career that would

11

Walney Scar

transform his fortunes, and those of his family, and contribute to the industrial development of his new homeland. I wanted to follow his story, and that of his brother, Thomas, from whom I trace my descent.

The father of these two brothers was what was known locally as a *'statesman'*, owning a smallholding in Seathwaite, where he cared for his flock of Herdwick sheep and managed his woodlands of birch and hazel, with a small acreage for oats, flax and vegetables. It was a family enterprise, providing sustenance, some income, and a status above that of peasant. In becoming a slate-getter, William brought in valuable supplementary income, and embarked on a new kind of work pattern, as an employee earning wages and reporting to an overseer, rather than answering to his father. The quarry where he worked had been in existence since the seventeenth century, providing slate for local needs.

The day when I walked up there, I was not only searching

for where William Casson and his brother Thomas had worked; I was testing out a tale that had come down the generations of my family. The story goes that, in the autumn of 1745, another ancestor, one of my great-great-great-great-great-grandfathers, a neighbour of the Cassons in Seathwaite, was apprehensive at the approach of Prince Charles Edward Stuart. 'The Young Pretender', as he was known, was intent on overthrowing King George II, the Protestant Hanoverian monarch, and restoring the pro-Catholic Stuart line. He had left France for Scotland and was coming south with a 6,000-strong army of Jacobites, having won the Battle of Prestonpans, near Edinburgh. English defensive preparations were so poor that in mid-November, the city of Carlisle, only sixty miles away from Seathwaite, surrendered, and the army marched on south. Like many others, my ancestor was concerned about his property as well as the safety of his family. Fearing that the Prince's army might ransack his village, he decided to protect his most valuable possession, his longcase clock. He carried it all the way up the fell and hid it in the quarry at Walney Scar. His fears were justifiable. Only when the Prince reached Derby, in December, was opposition strong enough to send him back. The retreating army came as close as Kendal, about twenty miles from Seathwaite, and continued to Penrith, about ten miles further north. The Clifton Moor Skirmish, which took place just south of Penrith, has some claim to be called the last battle on British soil. It was, one historian has commented, 'profoundly unnerving that a hostile army had been able to penetrate so close.'[2]

I wondered if the story of the clock could be true. From where I sat, surrounded by waste slate, there was little in the way of a hiding place. Soon my companion returned from further up the fell, reporting there were places where a clock could be concealed. I joined him, and we spent some time exploring, picking our way over fragments of slate, peering into dark caverns created by the original quarriers. It was quite possible. My ancestor could well have dismantled the clock, loaded its parts onto a cart, toiled up the way we had come, and stowed them deep in one of the caves. After a last look around, we returned to the village, and my companion suggested a drink at Newfield Inn, at one time the Cassons' farmhouse. There, he described our excursion to the assembled company, enhancing his account with a bit of fancy thrown in. 'I heard the clock ticking,' he assured the listeners. I protested, reminding them that the Jacobites had retreated to Scotland and were beaten at the Battle of Culloden. My ancestor had, in fact, fetched his clock back when the danger was over, and it has remained in the family ever since, an heirloom to be handed down through each generation. But everyone in the pub liked the idea of the ticking clock on the slopes of Coniston Old Man. No doubt it is part of local legend now.

Walney Scar cave

There are two approaches to telling the story of the Cassons who migrated to Wales and stayed for four generations. One is to trace those generations, with their sequence of births, marriages and deaths, ambitions and career choices, strokes of good or bad fortune, and individual character traits. I can unearth the wealth of information available to family historians. I can mine the miscellaneous items that make up the scanty family archive – a bundle of letters, a few portraits and photographs, a scrapbook, a memoir, a visitors' book, and the clock itself. I can read accounts and records of their friends, colleagues and neighbours. I can recall family legends that have been handed down, some of them verifiable, some of them not entirely believable.

The other approach is to place the family in their historical context, considering the developments in religion, war, local and national politics, economy, industry and engineering, social life and culture, that helped to shape their lives. Yet, just as the road from Coniston converges at Walney Scar slate quarry with the track from Seathwaite, so the family story blends with the historical background, as the Cassons both affected, and were affected by, developments in their native and adopted homelands.

The village of Seathwaite lies on the banks of the River Duddon, flowing for thirteen miles southward to the sea, its source high on the Wrynose Pass, at a point where once the three counties of Cumberland, Westmorland and Lancashire met.[3] It formed the western boundary of the area known as 'Furness', divided into 'Low Furness', a peninsula jutting out into the Irish Sea, and 'High Furness', to the north, part of the Lonsdale Hundred sub-division of Lancashire.

The first official record of the name 'Casson' dates back to 1510.[4] Legend has it that the family was of French extraction from Carcassonne in southern France, but there is little evidence to support this.[5] For the most part, the Cassons were born and bred in Furness and stayed there all their lives, different branches living within a few miles of each other. The women intermarried with local families as well as with their own cousins. At the beginning of the eighteenth century, the branch from which William and Thomas Casson sprang lived at Frith Hall. Its ruins still stand, imposing as a castle, silhouetted against the skyline, high on the fell above Ulpha, a little village a mile or so down the Duddon Valley from Seathwaite. Frith Hall was originally a hunting lodge. In the late seventeenth century, it became an alehouse, earning an unruly reputation. It stood on an old packhorse trail notorious as a smugglers' route from the port of Whitehaven, and the whole district was amply supplied with 'illegal brandy, rum, tea, tobacco, soap and other high duty goods illegally imported.'[6] Frith Hall itself was said to be a venue for runaway marriages.[7]

In the mid-eighteenth century, William and Thomas Casson's grandfather relinquished Frith Hall and brought his family to Seathwaite, acquiring a smallholding at Newfield, a more respectable property. In 1753, his only surviving son, Robert Casson, married Elizabeth Tyson from Wastdale, a few miles into Cumberland. By the time William was born in 1760, his grandfather had died, and his father owned the smallholding. William was the fourth of seven children, including Thomas, who was born in 1767. The Casson children were all educated by the curate of Holy Trinity Church, Seathwaite, the Reverend Robert Walker. Under his schooling, they learnt not only to read and write, and repeat their catechism, but enough arithmetic to form the basis for keeping accounts, enough geometry to undertake measuring and surveying of the land, and nature study, astronomy and geology. When not at school, the boys helped look after their father's sheep and tend the crops.

Some of the wool was taken straight to market in nerby Broughton, and some their mother and sisters spun and wove. The boys cut wood for charcoaling, bark for tanning, as well as timber for shipbuilding and local needs, and to feed the iron furnaces that were being established in the district.

When William began work at the slate quarry, it was run by Mr Thomas Rigg, whose father had obtained a lease in 1750 from the le Fleming family, Lords of the Manor of Coniston, to work all the quarries on their land. The manager at Walney Scar was Henry Turner.[8] Originally from nearby Troutbeck, Mr Turner had settled in Seathwaite and fathered thirteen children. His eighth child, another William, godson of the Rev Walker, and twelve years old at the time of his father's death, began working at Walney Scar. In due course, Thomas Casson, one year younger, began there too. William and Thomas Casson, and William Turner, formed an association which would last throughout their lives. It revolved around slate.

In the years to come, William Turner credited his schoolmaster and godfather with giving him his first knowledge of geology and familiarising him with the nature of slate. Although the Rev Walker would not have known the true age of the earth, nor had names for its geological eras, he knew that slate could be found throughout Britain, from Scotland, where the oldest slate was, through the Lake District, to Wales and then Cornwall, where the youngest could be found. We know that in the Coniston area where Walney Scar lay, volcanic lava and ash erupted about 450 million years ago, cooling to form the 'Borrowdale Group' of rocks. Fifty million years later, molten lava rose up, pushing and folding the rocks, re-orienting them from their original plane to form the fell range around Coniston Old Man. In the process, some of the rock metamorphosed into fine-grained layers. Where the re-orientation was consistent, the rock could be split cleanly along what is known as the 'cleavage plane'. This is slate, and this plane often lies at an angle to the original plane, splitting across the bandings in a piece of rock, rather than along them. Walney Scar slate, coming from what is known as the 'Silver-grey Band' in the Coniston area, has distinctive stripes of light and dark grey which can still be seen flagging the floors of what was once the Rev Walker's house, and in Newfield Inn, once home to the Cassons.[9]

No-one can set a date when slate was first quarried in Britain. There is some evidence of the Romans working it, but such skills as they brought disappeared with their departure. When the Normans arrived, they brought sophisticated building techniques for monasteries, priories, abbeys and castles, and so once again the working of slate became a necessary skill. The very word 'slate' comes from the Old French 'esclate', imitating the sharp sound of splitting rock. It is the ability to split or cleave slate into thin sections that characterises the rock, making it excellent material for roofing, flooring and decoration.

The Casson brothers and William Turner worked according to a long-established employment system said to have been brought to Britain with the Normans. A group of four or five men would form a company consisting of two *rockhands*, who worked the face, extracting the slabs or 'clogs'; two *rivers* (to rhyme with 'skivers'), who split the clogs into the characteristic thin layers; and a dresser, who shaped the slate to the required size – 'London' for the finest, then 'Country', then 'Tom' for the coarsest, leaving a small quantity known as 'Peg', which was used for slating walls. Perhaps 'slate-getter' was a generic term to cover all the levels of skill. Walney Scar was worked as an underground closehead; the rockhands bore shot holes into the rock, placed gunpowder to blast into the quarry at the best point of cleavage, then entered the cave that had been created. Whether you were a rockhand, a river or a dresser, you needed to develop a considerable degree of skill. Each company negotiated a price with the owner – or, in this case, with Thomas Rigg – for the amount of finished slate they would produce over a given period, taking into account the level of difficulty of extraction. This was the 'bargain' system, and it lasted well into the twentieth century.

On high days and holidays, or in the winter months when the quarry was snowbound, the Casson boys and their friends went fishing and shooting, hunting the hare and fox over the fells. There were seasonal fairs in Broughton and Coniston; at Whitsuntide, harvest and other festivals. They could compete in horse-racing, athletics, wrestling and traditional sports like climbing the greasy pole. As they grew older, there were more genteel amusements, such as the occasional assembly, where they socialised with their neighbours and danced. There was even a theatre in Barrow-in-Furness, but the most popular entertainment was cockfighting, a highly rated sport which most of the men and boys in the neighbourhood enjoyed watching and taking bets on.

Few visitors penetrated to the Duddon Valley, even though, as the boys grew up, some tourists were beginning to make the journey to Westmorland and Cumberland in the summer months, despite the hazardous conditions of the roads. Thomas West published a *Guide to the Lakes* in 1778, and most of those who came to gaze, sketch or write arranged their visits around the lakes, faithfully following the 'viewing stations' or viewpoints he suggested.[10] Only when the Seathwaite boys went further afield, to Coniston Water or Windermere, would they have encountered strangers, and perhaps wondered what they were about, with their pencils and books, sometimes presenting a comic aspect when they viewed the landscape backwards, through a mirror.[11]

For the first decades of their working lives, William and Thomas Casson, and their friend William Turner, earned good wages. In 1792, one local landowner commented:

> The farmers of Slate Quarries are getting large quantities of slates, and the demand for them is so great, that there are scarce any on hand, I have had many applications to open new Quarries, which I have refused, as the present Quarries employ all the labourers in the neighbourhood at high wages. Some of those who are expert at riving and chopping slates making £50 or £60 a year each.[12]

There was no reason for the boys to think that they would need to look further afield to earn a satisfactory living, but times would soon change. In 1793, the revolutionary government in France declared war on Britain. In 1794, the Prime Minister, William Pitt the Younger, needing to raise money for the war, imposed a tax on coal and slate carried by sea. This had a devastating effect on the local slate industry. Slate from Walney Scar was normally carted to the coast and then shipped to Lancaster. Now, a duty of 10 shillings per ton of slate was to be levied, which amounted to £20 for every £100 of value. Thomas Rigg and other quarry owners appealed to Pitt and tried to interest the politician William Wilberforce in their plight, but to no avail. The industry declined drastically. By 1796, the local slate merchants had discharged more than half of their workmen and had 'quantities of slate on hand which they ... [could] not sell.'[13] The following years brought incessant rain and poor harvests. It was not a happy time.

At the end of 1796, another change affected some of the local men. The chief constable for the district drew up a list of thirty-three Seathwaite men liable for service in the militia, the force raised locally for national defence, to take the place of soldiers fighting in the French Revolutionary Wars. The list included the names of Thomas Casson and William Turner, among other slate-getters, husbandmen and tradesmen. William Casson had already been balloted.[14] New militia regiments were being formed, one of which became the 3rd (Militia) Battalion of the Loyal North Lancashire, based in Preston.[15] If balloted, William Turner and Thomas Casson would need to engage in twenty days of training at Preston, and in whatever duties that battalion was undertaking, whether dealing with social unrest or with national defence. It was possible to buy yourself out, or to find a substitute. Thomas may have stood ready to serve, should his name be drawn, but William Turner's thoughts turned towards the idea of leaving Seathwaite.

At this point in the story, different versions are told. One account is from a memoir, written many years later by William Turner's youngest son, remembering what he had heard in his childhood:

My father … was sorely troubled by the feeling that his mother must be very much hampered by so large a family … At length, he made up his mind to quit the nest that he felt contained too many birds, and try his fortune elsewhere … My father, having heard that the Welsh hills contained beds of slate, determined to make a walking tour through the northern mountains, and told his brothers who, as in my case were much his seniors, what he intended to do, and that he would take whatever they chose to give him and go and seek his fortune. They asked him what sum he required, and he said he would leave it to them, and they gave him £500.

Back then, £500 was an unbelievably large sum, worth tens of thousands of pounds now, casting some doubt on the accuracy of the tale. The memoir recounts how William Turner found a vein of slate in the neighbourhood of Llanrwst, in the county of Conwy, and negotiated with the owner, Mr Holland Williams, a landed proprietor who ived in a mansion near Bae Colwyn, to start quarrying there:[16]

> After working this quarry on a small scale without any loss, my father came to the conclusion that it would not pay, and that it would be a waste of time to go on ... Having made a careful examination of miles of mountains he at last hit upon a splendid vein of slate at Dyffwys [Diffwys], near Ffestiniog. The place was for sale, but he had not enough money to purchase and work it. He accordingly wrote to two friends in Lancashire, Mr Thomas and Mr William Casson.[17]

William Turner and his two Lancashire friends did indeed purchase Diffwys Quarry near the village of Ffestiniog in Meirionydd. Exploring how and why they did so, I uncovered a more complicated story than this account suggests. The preliminary agreement for the purchase, drawn up in October 1799, shows that William Casson was already in Wales, and involved from the beginning.[18] It was between 'William Wynne of Peniarth', who owned the land, and 'William Casson and William Turner of Trefriw in the County of Caernarvon [Caernarfonshire].' Both men were probably working at the slate quarry Clogwyn y Fuwch, near Trefriw, on the Caernarfonshire side of the river Conwy.[19] It was worked in a manner that was 'redolent of Lakeland practice.'[20] The agreement begins: 'On payment of £100 [about £5,800 in 2019], William Wynne assigns them the

Title to the Messuage, Tenement and Lands with the Slate quarry and appurtenances hereinafter mentioned.' The lands are further described as being 'called Gelli with the Slate Quarry, Hereditaments and Appurtenances thereto belonging situate in the parish of Festiniog [Ffestiniog] in the County of Merioneth [Meirionnydd] and now or late in the occupation of Owen Richards & Partners.' To complete the agreement, William Turner and William Casson were to pay 'on or before the twelfth of May then next ... £900 of lawful money.'

What was the history of this quarry? How did William Turner and William Casson come to hear about it? When did Thomas Casson join the venture? What made them take the decisive step from being slate-getters to becoming quarry owners?

As in other parts of Britain, the early history of slate in North Wales is hazy. It was formed 500 million years ago, when layers of mud, sand and pebbles gathered to a depth of 13,000 feet and then subsided, leaving fine-grained deposits which were then covered with volcanic lava, creating a thick accumulation of sediment. As in the Lake District, heat and pressure caused sedimentary and volcanic rock to be folded and thrust upwards, forming the mountain range of Snowdonia ('Eryri'). The sediment metamorphosed, forming cleavable slate, which lay in three belts, one to the north-west of Snowdon ('Yr Wyddfa'), one to the south-east, and one passing through central Wales. The slate varied in colour and quality from quarry to quarry, that of Ffestiniog being blue-grey, with the fine grain which William Turner had observed when he first inspected it. Slate was used at Segontium, the Roman fort near Caernarfon. It was also used to roof some of the medieval castles; Llywelyn the Great, the last native Welsh prince, had his hall moved from Conwy to Caernarfon, where its roof was slated by Henry le Sclatiere.[21] The medieval Welsh word for 'slate' was '*ysglatus*', having the same derivation as the English word, but later the word '*llech*' replaced it, a generic word used for other kinds of rock as well.

One of the earliest areas to be quarried was at Cilgwyn in the Nantlle valley, Caernarfonshire. Another area was on the Penrhyn estate, also in Caernarfonshire. There, in the first years of the eighteenth century, the owners established standard sizes for the finished slate: '*Singles*', '*Doubles*' and '*Double doubles*'. But in 1738, General Hugh Warburton, co-owner of the estate, made a significant and colourful contribution to the development of the slate industry, by introducing larger slates, with a new terminology. He created a hierarchy of female nobility, with the largest, over thirty inches long, being called '*Queens*', preceded by '*Countesses*', '*Duchesses*' and '*Ladies*' (*Double doubles*). The names soon caught on and began to be used in other quarries.

Diffwys Quarry is said to have been discovered by Methusalem Jones, who at one time worked the quarry at Cilgwyn.[22] He claimed to have dreamed that there was a rich vein of slate near Ffestiniog, and he came in search of it. He struck his pick into a crag, revealing 'Slate that scintillated like a jewel and glistened like a mountain lake.'[23] He certainly came to Diffwys at some point between 1750 and 1765 and was a tenant of the Gelli land in 1771. He did not stay long, but he did bring men from Cilgwyn. These men leased the land, with its farm and quarry, on a year-by-year basis. By 1799, Mr Owen Richards was in charge and living at the farm.

The owner of the land on which the quarry lay, was William Wynne V. His family held the large Wern estate, with land in Caernarfonshire and Meirionydd. His grandfather, William Wynne III, bought Gelli in 1748, but when he died in 1766, he passed on a mass of debt to his son, William Wynne IV, who nevertheless bought even more land, and gained another estate through marriage, at Peniarth in Meirionydd. To redeem his debts, he mortgaged all the Wern estate around 1776. William Wynne V inherited the estate and the debts in 1796.[24] By that time, he was an officer in the Ancient British Fencible Cavalry, one of the voluntary regiments raised to defend Britain against invasion (the word 'fencible' being derived from the word 'defensible'). This regiment had been raised in 1794 and was led by Colonel Sir Watkin Williams Wynne, from another prominent Welsh family, connected through various marriages with the Wynnes of Wern and Peniarth. The regiment was most active in Ireland, where the Society of United Irishmen, led by Wolfe Tone, rebelled against British rule in 1798.

The Irish connection is important because there are several accounts claiming that William Turner, contrary to his son's account, did not go directly to Wales when he left Seathwaite, but spent some time at Cronebane in County Wicklow, working either in a copper mine or a slate quarry.[25] He might have met William Wynne in Wicklow, heard about Diffwys Quarry, and stored the knowledge in the back of his mind. Perhaps the rebellion was a sufficient disincentive to remain in Ireland, and so he took the ferry to Holyhead ('Caergybi'), and perhaps walked his way across Anglesey ('Ynys Môn') to the Menai Strait ('Afon Menai'), and then on from Bangor to Llanrwst.

By the beginning of 1799, Wynne was in desperate financial straits. He put the whole of the Wern estate on the market, including the Gelli land, in order to redeem the mortgages and acquire some cash. The sale advertisement appeared in February 1799 and included 'the very valuable Slate Quarry ... at Ffestiniog [which] lies within a very convenient Distance of a Navigable River, where the Slates are sold for Exportation.' Owen Richards and his partners wanted to buy. According to local accounts, they 'tried to collect money from their friends in Caernarfonshire, but some held back to see if the quarry would be offered cheaper.' A second auction was advertised to take place at Penmorfa in April, but 'while the Welsh were hesitating, the place was bought.'[26]

There was considerable local resentment that Englishmen, rather than Welshmen, were buying the Ffestiniog quarry. Several legends about the sale spread through the neighbourhood. One story was that a man from Owen Richard's company set off for Penmorfa but was wrongfully persuaded that he did not need to go until the following morning, as there was no danger of anyone else buying it. The next day he started out but turned back before he left the house, because he was told *'Mae hi wedi ei gwerthu'* (It has been sold).[27] The humble circumstances of the purchasers were as much a matter of comment as the fact that they came from England. William Turner's son once met a man who told him that 'a great number of years before, a tramp who was going through Wales purchased the quarry for some tobacco, and made a large fortune out of his bargain.'[28] His account continued: 'the fact of a stranger coming into the country and possessing himself of tracts of slate beds under the noses as it were of the inhabitants, created an amount of animosity and jealousy on the part of many[,] who complained that a tramp who walked over the country and got what ought to have been theirs, was unbearable.'[29]

It seems clear that William Turner made a private offer which was accepted in March or April of 1799. The signing of the formal agreement had to wait until October because Wynne was still serving in Ireland. It is not known when

William Casson joined William Turner in Wales. At the time the agreement was signed, William Casson was thirty-eight years old. Both Turner and he were unmarried, and free to look for new possibilities when the work at Walney Scar was drying up. He left Seathwaite, perhaps in 1798, and joined Turner at Trefriw. It may be that they already had it in mind to go into partnership together, and the opportunity to purchase the Gelli land was a stroke of luck. They paid the £100 in October 1799 but had only a few months to raise the considerable sum of £900 to complete the purchase. At that point, they involved Thomas Casson, another experienced slate-getter, in the venture. If he became an equal partner, they would each need to raise £300 (over £17,000 in 2019), and Thomas would need to contribute his share of the first £100.

The two Williams had to persuade Thomas that the three of them could make a success of Diffwys Quarry, though he could see that Walney Scar was failing. There was still a duty imposed on seaborne slate. It would be just as much of a burden in Meirionydd as it was in Furness, since Owen Richard and his men were used to boating the slate down the 'Navigable River' (included in the advertisement), and then shipping it out from Bae Ceredigion. They would be working in a land that the two Williams had already discovered was more foreign than either of them might have expected. William Casson soon set about learning the language spoken by the quarriers, but William Turner was less willing to make the effort. There were two main incentives that would convince Thomas to make the move: the quality of the slate and the prospect of the three men being their own masters.

William Turner, who was the leading spirit, despite being younger than William Casson, was an enterprising and persuasive man. He had succeeded in driving a good bargain.

Once he visited Gelli, he knew that, dream or no dream, Methusalem Jones had struck on a source of potential wealth. The blue-grey vein of slate in the Diffwys gorge had a finer grain than any he had seen before. Perhaps he convinced himself that, once the war was over, the slate industry would prosper as the British population grew and more industries were established. He trusted his old neighbour, William Casson, and he knew other Seathwaite men who would be willing to work with them, as well as his old schoolmate, Thomas Casson. They had known each other all their lives. While sharing their midday meal on the western slopes of Coniston Old Man, they had no doubt nurtured childhood ambitions of leaving the valley and making their fortune. Here, in a strange land, was an opportunity to exploit what his knowledge of quarrying told him was rich treasure lying on and below the Meirionydd slopes.

Perhaps Thomas Casson was pleased, too, to think that leaving Lancashire would free him from the militia ballot. But if the three potential partners thought they would be more distant from the French Revolutionary Wars by leaving England, they were wrong. The threat of invasion was more real in Wales than in Lancashire. Only two years earlier, in October 1797, an 'invasion' of sorts had actually occurred, when the French landed at Fishguard ('Abergwaun') in Pembrokeshire ('Sir Benfro'), as part of an attack on Britain in support of the Irish Rebellion. William Turner related to his son the famous story, of how the Earl of Cawdor, heading a troop of cavalry, had concocted a clever device:

[The Earl of Cawdor began] sending messages to the various upland farms and cottages for the women to assemble in something like martial order and parade on the hills with the tall hats and red cloaks of their Sunday attire; and thus the French were led to imagine that a large military force was concentrating on the hills ready to march to join the troops below.[30]

Before Thomas Casson could make up his mind to leave his home and risk all his savings in the purchase of Diffwys Quarry, he had another matter to settle. There was a young woman in Seathwaite he had set his heart on. If she would agree to marry him, he would bring her to Wales and join his brother and friend in their new venture.

Sketch of Duddon Valley

Notes

[1] Now known as Walna Scar.

[2] Colley, Linda, *Britons: Forging the Nation, 1707-1837*, 2009 edition, p. 87

[3] The county of Cumbria was formed in 1974, comprising former Cumberland, Westmorland and a part of North Lancashire.

[4] Russell, Margaret M., *The Family Forest*, 2000, p. 137. This book has extensive genealogies of local families.

[5] Referred to in a letter from Thomas Casson (1842-1910), 1893.

[6] HMS Customs Board, Whitehaven, quoted www.duddon. valley.co.uk, *History of the Valley*

[7] Cooper, J. C., *Duddon Valley History*, undated pamphlet, p. 16

[8] His gravestone records him as 'undertaker' of Walney Scar, though his burial record has him as 'slate-getter'.

[9] Cameron, Alastair, *Slate from Coniston: A History of the Coniston Slate Industry*, 1996, p. 103

[10] Thomas West's guidebook makes no mention of Seathwaite, nor the Duddon Valley, although his *Antiquities of Furness*, dedicated to the local lord, George Cavendish, has two incidental references to Seathwaite.

[11] The 'Claude glass' was a convex mirror popularised by Thomas Gray in *Journal of His Visit to the Lake District*, 1769.

[12] Letter of J. N. Robinson to Lord John Cavendish, a local landowner, quoted in Marshall, J. D., *Furness and the Industrial Revolution*, Barrow-in-Furness, 1958, p. 43. According to www.moneysorter.com, £50 in 1800 was equivalent to £3,000 in 2019.

[13] quoted Marshall, p. 44.

[14] Copy of the list for Seathwaite, drawn up by the Chief Constable, 15 December 1796

[15] www.lancashireinfantrymuseum.org.uk/the-royal-lancashire-militia

[16] According to Llewelyn Turner, his father went into partnership with Holland Williams, but his account, written when he was in his 80s, usually errs on the side of heightening his father's early fortune and status.

[17] Turner, Llewelyn, *The Memories of Sir Llewelyn Turner*, ed. J. E. Vincent, 1903, p. 15

[18] Tanymanod and Gelli Estate Papers: No 239, LlGC/NLW

[19] Caernarfonshire and Meirionydd now part of the county of Gwynedd, were separate counties from 1536, when the

administration of Wales was joined to that of England. The combined county was formed in 1974, based on the old Welsh kingdom.

20 Richards, Alun John, *Gazetteer of Slate Quarrying in Wales*, 2007, p. 93, although this belies a different account which states that the Lancashire men did not secure any work there, and were at Conwy, on their way home, when they heard there was a quarry in Ffestiniog and found work there. See Williams, G. J., *Hanes Plwyf Ffestiniog*,1882, p82, translated for the author by Alex Clatworthy

21 Lindsay, Jean, *A History of the North Wales Slate Industry*, 1974, p. 19

22 My main source is *Pioneers of Ffestiniog Slate*, by M. J. T. Lewis & M. C. Williams, Snowdonia National Park Study Centre, 1987, and even they admit that local historians give conflicting accounts.

23 quoted in Richards, Alun John, *The Rails and Sails of Welsh Slate*, 2011, p. 78

24 Peniarth Family Estate records, LlGC/NLW

25 *Pioneers*, p 19 and Buckley, John, *William Turner in Ireland?*, unpublished

26 *Pioneers*, p. 9

27 Williams, p82

28 Turner, pp. 58-59

29 ibid

30 Turner, p. 18

Chapter 2

The Walker Family

The young woman Thomas wanted to marry was the granddaughter of his schoolmaster and pastor, the Rev Robert Walker. His wooing of her was successful. They were married at Holy Trinity Church, Seathwaite, in April 1800, and set off on the journey to Wales soon after.

The bride signed her name 'Esther Walker', raising questions about her birth. She was the daughter of the Rev Walker's youngest daughter, Ann Esther, baptised in the church at Seathwaite in 1753. In September 1780, 'Ann Esther Walker, spinster', married 'George Wilson, bachelor' at St Philip's Church, Birmingham.[1] I have found no record

Sketch of Old Seathwaite Chapel

of young Esther's birth or baptism. According to the ages she recorded for the Census many years later, she was born between April and the beginning of June 1779, over a year before Ann Walker was married. This date, combined with the fact her signature used her mother's maiden name, suggests that she was illegitimate.

Ann Walker was fortunate, in that she was left unmarried for less than eighteen months. If George Wilson was Esther's father, it was a hard though temporary abandonment, leaving her mother to support the child on her own. But if he was *not* her father, it was a generous act to marry her. In one Census, Esther Casson's birthplace is stated as 'Liverpool'; one of Ann Walker's sisters lived there. Perhaps Ann got off with a sailor, who deserted her. But her ties with Birmingham were strong, so it is not surprising that she got married there.

Ann Walker's oldest brother, Zaccheus, was one of the significant few who left High Furness. Originally apprenticed as a tanner, he was then encouraged by his father to seek out opportunity in the wider world. He went to Birmingham, armed with an introduction to Matthew Boulton, the successful toy manufacturer. 'Toys', in those days, meant small metal objects, such as cane heads, snuffboxes, watchchains, buttons and buckles. Zaccheus became close to the Boulton family, and in 1765 married Boulton's sister, Mary. That year, Boulton built the Soho Manufactory, a magnificent warehouse with an impressive Palladian front. There, he expanded his business. Zaccheus Walker rose swiftly up the ranks, as a clerk, an accountant and then handling the marketing side of the business.

Mary Walker's (née Boulton) children were all born in Seathwaite, where Zaccheus sent her to be cared for by his family. Ann Walker would have known them as babies. Mary died in 1769, soon after the birth of her third child.

Not long afterwards, one of Zaccheus' brothers joined him in Birmingham. Ann, sixteen years old by then, may have joined her brothers to look after her nieces and nephew in the house in Snow Street, Birmingham, where Zaccheus lived. He was part of a lively community; Matthew Boulton ran an annual music festival, helped to found a theatre, and was a member of the Lunar Circle, which met for philosophical discussions and was at the forefront of scientific and intellectual thought. In 1775, Zaccheus remarried. Perhaps his sister Ann stayed on to help with the children of her new sister-in-law. Four years later, in Birmingham, or in Liverpool, or in some place yet to be identified, she gave birth to her daughter, who was given her middle name, Esther.

All that is known of Esther's childhood is that she 'resided much during her infancy with her grandfather.'[2] Robert Walker and his wife must have taken in their daughter's child, and cared for her, keeping her in their home even after Ann Walker became the wife of George Wilson.[3] Contemporary and later accounts of the Rev Robert Walker provide a vivid picture of life in a Lakeland parish in the eighteenth century, and of a remarkable man, who had a strong influence on Esther's character and upbringing, and on the man she was to marry.

At the time of Esther's birth, Robert Walker had been the curate of Holy Trinity Church, Seathwaite, for over forty years. He was born in Seathwaite in 1709. His parents found enough money to send him away to be educated. He became a schoolmaster and studied towards ordination. There was not enough money to send him to university, but in those days it was considered desirable, but not essential, for a priest. He was a working priest, appointed deacon at Buttermere, in Westmorland, where he was paid in kind, with no stipend and no lodging. He taught school during the day and eked out his living by labouring before school and in the evenings. One of his great-grandsons later recorded what he had heard about his life there:

> In summer, he rose between three and four o'clock, and went to the field with his scythe and his rake, and in harvest time with his sickle. He ploughed, he planted, he went upon the mountains after the sheep; he sheared and salved them; he dug peat – all for hire. In the winter he read and wrote his sermons and did many tasks usually considered women's work ... He knit and mended his own stockings, and made his own shoes. In his walks he never neglected to gather the wool from the hedges and bring it home. He was also the physician and lawyer of the place; he drew up all wills, conveyances, bonds ... wrote all letters and settled all accounts; and frequently went to market with sheep, wool ... for the farmers.[4]

When Robert Walker was twenty-four, he was ordained as a curate, and the following year he heard that there was a vacancy back in his native parish of Seathwaite, with an annual stipend of £5, and a cottage to go with it. He could now propose to Ann Tyson, whom he had met in Buttermere.[5] They were married in January 1736, anticipating the event by many months, as their oldest child, Zaccheus, was born that February. Perhaps this contributed to their acceptance of Esther into their household over fifty years later. Within a year or so, the couple had acquired their most valuable possession, a longcase clock, perhaps a gift, perhaps bought out of the £40 Ann Tyson had brought to the marriage. This was the clock that, according to family tradition, he carried up to Walney Scar in 1745, to keep it safe from the army of 'Bonnie Prince Charlie', bringing it back down to the Chapelhouse when it was safe.

The Walkers had nine surviving children, Esther's mother being the last. Robert Walker continued to live the industrious life he had established at Buttermere, increasing his small income through labour on his small glebe land and helping with such tasks as sheep shearing in the valley. His clipping stone still stands outside the church. Seathwaite was a remote village with no amenities. His wife claimed, with some exaggeration, that she thought it had never before been inhabited before her arrival: 'No roads, no bridges, no woods, no meadows, no neighbours.'[6] It was said that a visitor, returning from a stroll while dinner was being prepared, explained that he had walked 'As far as it is finished.'[7] Another described the landscape as 'wild, barren and dreary.'[8]

Having fathered more children than could easily be sustained at home, the Rev Walker encouraged his daughters, as well his sons, to go out into the world to earn their living. He had sent his second daughter, Mary, to Liverpool when she was quite a young woman, to make her own way in a town far away, and very different from her childhood home. No doubt, like her brother Zaccheus, she was provided with some kind of introduction to give her a start. She was apprenticed to a milliner, a respectable job for a curate's daughter (although sometimes 'milliner' was a polite name for bawd). Her older sister, Elizabeth, lived in Scotland during her first marriage to John Bamford, but returned to Furness as a widow, married a local man, Thomas Robinson, and ran the Black Bull Inn, in Coniston. Thus, Esther learnt as a child that a woman worked outside as well as inside the home, and that she might, at some point, need to leave her childhood home, either moving to a neighbouring parish, or much further away. The lesson stood her in good stead when Thomas Casson came calling.

Her daily life was busy. In the mornings, there was water to be drawn, animals to be fed, eggs to be fetched, oatcakes to be baked, butter to be churned, not to mention schooling, which her grandfather conducted in the chapel, with other children from the village and outlying houses. In the winter months, there was spinning of flax and wool, weaving, knitting and sewing, mending shoes, cooking, and making the rush candles which they used in the evenings, except at Christmas, when tallow candles were lit. The meals were simple: oatmeal pottage in the morning and evening; midday dinner was vegetables, bread, milk and cheese in the summer, dried beef and bacon in the winter. On Sundays, there was meat – and two church services. After the morning service, her grandparents provided beef, potatoes and broth to farmers who had come long distances and were staying for the afternoon service.

The Rev Walker instilled a strong Protestant faith in his family, in the schoolchildren and in his congregation, some of whom came from miles away to hear him, and sometimes had to stand outside the chapel at festival times. He was a devout Anglican, proud of the fact that there were no

Sketch of Robert Walker

Dissenters in his parish. His pupils, including the Casson brothers and William Turner, as well as his granddaughter, were better taught than many children of their time. As well as teaching them reading, writing and arithmetic, he was interested in the natural world, taking the children out to study the earth and sky. On Saturday afternoons, the only leisure time he had, he read a newspaper, and he kept a range of books on the slate shelves he had built in his study. He had practical skills as well. A stout wooden chair that he designed and built still stands in Coniston Museum.

The Chapelhouse was the social centre of Seathwaite. There was no inn in the village and, amongst his other numerous occupations, the Rev Walker sold ale, even though, strictly speaking, this was against Church of England regulations; his daughter Elizabeth held the licence. Family, friends and neighbours gathered there. Esther could listen to stories of families in the valley, some of whom had been in the region, generation after generation, for hundreds of years. There were stories of sprites and fairies, said to live in caves in the fells. The tradition of legend and local history that she would learn in Meirionydd lay in the distant future.

Nothing is known of Esther's mother. There is no indication whether Esther made visits to her family in Birmingham, wrote regularly, discussed her future or the circumstances of her birth. Only the fact that she would later name one of her children 'George' suggests that she had some filial loyalty towards Mr Wilson. All that is known of him is that someone of his name was listed as a 'factor commerce' in Birmingham.

All through her childhood, Esther would have known the Casson family, but for Thomas, already twelve years old and ready for work when she was born, what interest would he have taken of her as a baby and then as a little girl? But in

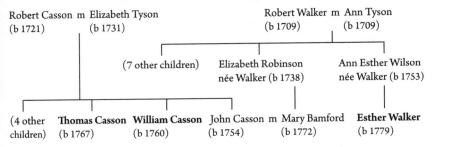

The Casson and Walker families 1795

1795, Esther's cousin, Mary Bamford, married Thomas' oldest brother, John Casson, bringing the two families close together.

There must have been a time when Thomas first looked on Esther and saw, instead of a child, a young woman he would like to marry. But four years were to pass between his brother John's marriage and his own. Perhaps he procrastinated, waiting for some decisive turn of events that would prompt him to speak. The pressing invitation to join the partnership with his brother and William Turner was his chance. Although the war was creating hardship for many, with the ongoing blockade limiting opportunities for trade, those two believed in a future for slate. Turner had invited a local quarrier, George Penny, known to them all, to join them. Thomas would not have wanted to see George Penny riding away towards North Wales, leaving him behind. At Walney Scar, more men had been laid off; there was much hardship to endure, much grumbling and threats of protest. The idea of leaving the valley and making his way in a part of Britain he had never set eyes on was daunting. And could he persuade Esther to uproot from Seathwaite and accompany him, like Ruth in the Bible, into an alien land?

The fact that he did persuade her, and in a short space of

time, suggests that Esther was already attracted to him. He proposed, but there was a difficulty, for Esther's grandmother was failing. She died at the end of January 1800 and was buried on 1 February, the day before Candlemas. Esther's grandfather was desolate. He was ninety years old by then and almost blind. Instead of leaving the women at home, as was customary, he wanted them as pallbearers, so three of his daughters, Elizabeth Robinson, Mabel Atkinson and Mary Borrowdale and John Casson's wife Mary carried the coffin as it was borne into the chapel, while he followed behind.[9]

If it were not for Thomas' hopes and plans, Esther was the obvious person to take charge of the Chapelhouse and look after her grandfather, but the Rev Robert Walker put nothing in the way of the marriage. After his wife's death he rarely led a service again, yet there was one he wanted to perform himself. On the 5 April 1800, he conducted the marriage ceremony for Thomas Casson and Esther Walker, with John Casson, and Jane Gunson, a neighbour and friend, as witnesses. The date itself suggests urgency, for it was still Lent, a time when canon law normally forbade marriage. Perhaps the date was brought forward once Thomas heard that the agreement on the quarry land was to be signed early in May; his future partners needed him to be there with his precious £300 contribution.

There were plenty of people from their combined families to wish them well and share bride-ale and cake in the Chapelhouse. Now the couple had to prepare for their journey to Wales. The prospect must have seemed less fearsome considering that many in the community they were leaving were now hungry, restless and unhappy. Just before their departure, there was an uprising, when men from Coniston and nearby Tilberthwaite marched into Ulverston, in Low Furness, and opened a storehouse there.

Some called it a 'riot', but others stoutly maintained that the men had been well organised and caused no trouble.[10] These troubles were now no affair of Thomas and his bride. Esther Walker's origins, whatever they were, lay all behind her. Now she was 'Esther Casson' and her future fortune would unfold with that of her husband.

Notes

[1] In his will, Robert Walker wrote '[to] my daughter Ann Esther Wilson', '[to] her husband George Wilson' and '[to] my granddaughter Esther Casson', thus confirming part of the genealogy.

[2] quoted in Parkinson, Richard, *The Old Church Clock*, Fifth Edition, 1880, ed Evans, John, p. 43, with no attribution beyond a pious reference to 'one who, from his near connection [with the Walker family], has had ample opportunities of forming a correct judgment of their characters and merit'.

[3] There was a George Wilson, son of John Wilson, born in Seathwaite in 1753, the same year as Ann Walker. There was a John Wilson in Birmingham known to the Walker family, as evidenced in a letter to Zaccheus Walker in Birmingham, from his son in Seathwaite, reprinted in *The Old Church Clock*, op. cit., p. 196.

[4] Bamford, Robert, in a paper originally in the *Christian Remembrancer*, October 1819, reprinted in *The Old Church Clock*, p. 34.

[5] There were Tysons throughout the Lake District who married into many local families.

[6] Bamford, p. 35.

[7] Wordsworth, William, *The Poetical Works of Wordsworth*, (New Edition), 1960, Notes, p. 711

[8] Bamford, p. 34

[9] Notes made by Dorothy Wordsworth, quoted Hughes, Felicity, *William Wordsworth and Wonderful Waker*, 2004, p.41

[10] See Gibson, A. Craig, 'The Last Popular Uprising in the Lancashire Lake County', *Transactions of the Historical Society of Lancashire and Cheshire, New Series Vol IX*

Chapter 3

Interlude: A Journey into North Wales
1800

There is no record of how Thomas and Esther travelled to Wales in the spring of 1800, except a family story that they came all the way on horseback, with Esther riding pillion. It was a momentous and arduous journey for a young bride at the beginning of her marriage, taking perhaps two weeks to complete. The route took them first on the road from Seathwaite, with a last glance at Wallowbarrow Crag which loomed over the village, down past Dunnerdale Fell to Broughton Mill, and on to Ulverston in Low Furness, along

Wallowbarrow Crag

roads that were little more than tracks. From there, they had to be guided across the treacherous sands of Morecambe Bay, to join the great road towards Lancaster. Then on through Preston, with its thriving cotton-mill, and the market town of Ormskirk, sometimes staying in inns, sometimes relying on farmhouse hospitality, until they reached the great metropolis of Liverpool, where they had a chance for a few days' rest with Esther's aunt, Mary Borrowdale, who lived with her sea captain husband and daughter in 'Sailors Town', near the Old Docks.

From Liverpool, the likely route was by ferry across the Mersey to Netherpool, then along the path beside the Ellesmere Canal, opened three years earlier, to link the Mersey with the river Dee. Their last night in England would have been in Chester, from where there was a packhorse trail they could follow into Wales.

For the first time, the language they heard spoken was unknown to them, but the first town they reached was Corwen, where they could find people who spoke English to set them on the next part of the journey and suggest where they might stay. A drovers' route led them through villages with unpronounceable names, though the land itself was not unfamiliar. At first it was mainly flat, like Low Furness, but ahead they could see the ranges of Caernarfonshire, with the top of Snowdon, no doubt wreathed in cloud. When they reached the river Conwy, a wooded track led north to Llanrwst, where they crossed an ancient stone bridge, saw the rooftop of Castell Gwydyr on their left, and then took a narrow trackway northward, arriving within a mile or so at a small slate quarry in the hillside beside a river. This was Clogwyn y Fuwch, on the river Crafnant, where William Casson and William Turner had taken a lease. Esther now met them for the first time as Thomas' wife. They could all stay in the village of Trefriw, until it was time for the men to ride down south to Dolgellau, the county town of Meirionydd, to meet Mr Hugh Jones, the solicitor and agent for the sale. There, Thomas could hand over the £300 he probably carried in coin (since notes from a Kendal bank might have been looked on askance), while the two Williams could have paid their share in notes obtained in Holywell ('Treffynnon'), at the only bank in the district. When the men returned, they could all set out on the last part of the journey.

The track from Trefriw to the Gelli land they now owned was the roughest and most precipitous that Thomas and Esther had yet encountered, all the horses picking their way downhill, through rocky woodland, past a lead mine bustling with activity. They crossed the drovers' road from Corwen at the village of Betws-y-Coed, where the river Conwy met two other waterways. Some of the track was along an old Roman road, now barely passable. They followed a riverbank to Dolwyddelan, where the outline of an old castle stood out against the sky. At last, they climbed up to Gelli farmhouse, and they either stayed there or went on down to the village of Ffestiniog, where they could take rooms at one of the inns and begin their new life

Chapter 4

Ffestiniog: A New Home
1800–1802

We came to Festiniog, a village in Merionethshire [Meirionnydd], the vale before which is the most perfectly beautiful of all we had seen. From the height of this village you have a view of the sea. The hills are green and well shaded with wood. There is a lovely rivulet which winds through to the bottom; on each side are meadows, and above are corn fields among the sides of the hills; at each end are high mountains, which seem placed there to guard this charming retreat against any invaders. With the woman one loves, with the friend of one's heart, and a study of books, one might pass an age in this vale, and think it a day.[1]

So wrote George, 1st Baron of Lyttelton, on a journey into Wales in July 1756. A politician and patron of the arts, Lord Lyttelton was one of the first Englishmen to appreciate the beauty of the landscape of Wales. Over forty years later, Thomas Casson saw Ffestiniog and its vale for the first time, in the company of the woman who had just become his wife; of his brother; and of the great friend whose enterprise had drawn him there. He was to pass the next forty years there, but not with a study of books.

Life in Meirionydd was a struggle for many. The area was remote, with poor communications, especially in the

The Vale of Ffestiniog

mountains. The few roads were rough, and often impassable in winter. Farming was at subsistence level. There was a cottage-based woollen industry; some mining and quarrying had already begun, but for most of the eighteenth century there was little investment and the 1790s had brought a series of harsh winters and poor harvests. When the Cassons arrived in Ffestiniog, it was a village of just over sixty inhabitants, yet there were no less than three inns. The most lucrative trade of North Wales was driving cattle from the lowlands of Anglesey and the Llŷn Peninsula ('Penrhyn Llŷn') towards England, and the route passed through Ffestiniog. But while the cattle drovers had to speak and understand English, there was no such necessity for the local inhabitants. According to the first history of the village, there were only two people who could converse with the Cassons when they first arrived.[2] One was Morgan Prys, a descendant of Edward Prys (the sixteenth-century rector of St Michael's Church in Ffestiniog, later Archdeacon of

Meirionydd). The other was Miss Martha Owen, daughter of the village blacksmith, who ran a public house, 'Yr Efail' (The Smithy), also known as the 'Pengwern Arms'.[3]

Perhaps it was through Martha Owen that Thomas and Esther were able to take over the running of another inn, Ty Uchaf (Upper House), also known as 'The Eagle'. This provided them with an income and a roof over their heads. Like her aunt, Elizabeth, in Coniston, Esther became an innkeeper. Unlike her aunt, she could not at first converse with her customers. Some of the first words she added to her vocabulary were *'cwrw'* for 'barley ale', *'bara'* for 'bread', *'caws'* for 'cheese', and *'ceiniogau'* for 'pence'. Meanwhile, the two bachelors, William Casson and William Turner, took up residence in the Gelli farmhouse, close to the quarry, and set about finding a housekeeper.

The new partners soon had to face the fact that the payment to William Wynne V had used up all their resources. There was no money to hire men or equipment. As experienced slate-getters, they could make a start in the quarry using their own tools, but that would be a poor beginning, and give the wrong impression to the local men, already suspicious of the English incomers who had gone over the head of Owen Richards to acquire the quarry. 'William Turner & Company', as the business was called, would need capital from the start if they were to make it as prosperous as they intended. If they could hire some of the men from the old Welsh company, they might begin the task of winning hearts and minds. So, they needed to find someone else to buy into the company.

Turner, always resourceful, knew of a man in Talsarnau, down by the coast, who might invest. However, this man, John Richards, a wealthy farmer who had expressed some interest, turned down the invitation. Instead, they asked Hugh Jones, the solicitor, to come in with them. This was a provocative action, for it immediately raised the suspicion in the neighbourhood that Mr Jones had deliberately negotiated a low price for the purchase, with the idea of becoming part-owner himself. Fortunately, they could demonstrate that the offer to John Richards had been made in good faith, and no legal action was taken against them. Hugh Jones became a sleeping partner and a good friend. But resentment against him, and to some extent against the three Englishmen, festered for some time to come amongst some of the local businessmen. Years later, a Mr Griffith Parry of nearby Penmorfa still bore a grudge, referring to the 'sham publick sale' offered by Hugh Jones, and the subsequent private sale offered to the 'poor labouring Quarrymen' who 'had not One Pound between them to pay for this Purchase.'[4]

One of the first challenges, therefore, was to win local approval. Amongst the men who had worked for the Welsh owners, several were prepared to swallow their disappointment and work for the Englishmen. One was Thomas Williams, an experienced quarryman who could show his new masters the great potential of Diffwys. They soon appointed him manager.

Three practical tasks confronted the new working owners at Ffestiniog: quarrying, splitting and dressing the slate; transporting it; and marketing it. William Turner's main task was seeking out purchasers, leaving the first two tasks to the Casson brothers. This meant that, of the three men, he was the only one who never learnt to speak Welsh fluently. William and Thomas began, with their first workmen, to quarry the outcrops of slate which lay near the surface, covered with a thin layer of rock. They bought gunpowder from David Lloyd (who kept the only shop in Ffestiniog) and created controlled explosions to free large blocks without shattering them. They hewed out the blocks and split them along the cleavage line, '*yr hollt*'; with a heavy wooden mallet, '*y rhys*'; against an iron edge, '*y trafal*'. Then they used a small knife, '*y gyllell fach*', to dress the slate on the spot. They sawed larger slabs, to be used for flooring, or gravestones. Boys carried the waste away in wheelbarrows and threw it onto the hillside. They piled the roofing slates into panniers, ready to be transported. Sharing the work with the Welshmen, William and Thomas learnt the necessary vocabulary quickly. A mixture of Welsh and English filled the air. Eager to build up a good stock of slate from the start, they sometimes had the men working well into the evening during the summer, knowing winter hours would be much shorter. Soon, there were quarrying stories being told, first in Welsh, then perhaps translated by someone for the benefit of the Cassons:

You heard about William Morris and William Williams, did you? They were standing atop a rock and wanted to get down. They had a rope with them, but they couldn't work out how they could both use it to get down the steep slope. 'Well,' says William Morris, after considering the matter, 'You hold it for me, and I'll hold it for you.' So, William Williams stood on top of the rock, and held on to the rope, and William Morris climbed down it. When he reached the bottom, he dug his heel against the rock, held on to the bottom of the rope and shouted for William Williams to come down. Not giving it a thought, William Williams made a start! He rolled all the way down the slope, while William Morris, ran off, shouting, 'WAR!' in English.[5]

Since the men were paid by the load, the Cassons soon found there were various ruses being used to inflate the number of loads. Harri Shôn, a lame old man, was in charge of counting. He would put a number of stones into his left-hand pocket. As each load went past him, he transferred a stone to his other pocket, and so kept score. The Cassons had to be on the lookout for anyone who slipped a stone into Harri's right-hand pocket, and for any pannier that looked full but was only half filled. In due course, a more reliable system was introduced, scoring each load by marking down a stroke, with a crossed stroke to mark every twelfth, so that the dozens could easily be counted at the end of the day. William Casson seems to have had a soft spot for Harri Shôn. He was so poor that William took to giving him his old clothes, but as Harri was a much smaller man, they hung on him like a tent.[6]

The next stage was transport. This presented a challenge, as there was no road up to the quarry. The men had to load the panniers of slates on to packhorses and mules, which picked their way down the gorge, lying about 1,300 feet above sea level, then uphill along a stony track, for about a mile, until they reached the nearest road, where the panniers were loaded on to carts. This was a slow, laborious and inefficient procedure. The first innovation that the new partners made, drawing on the capital Hugh Jones had invested, was to replace the track with a road, providing a direct route to the existing road. From then on, carters could come all the way up to the quarry, load the dressed slate straight onto the carts, and then descend. It was a rough route even then, for the existing road was in a poor state, and became worse through their use of it. At Ffestiniog village the carts joined a better, turnpike road, and continued down into the vale until they reached the river.[7]

The river Dwyryd, about six miles in length, began where the river Goedol, tumbling down from the north, joined the river Teigl, flowing from the east, about sixty feet above sea level. The Dwyryd flowed westwards, down through the vale of Ffestiniog to the sea. The old company had leased a

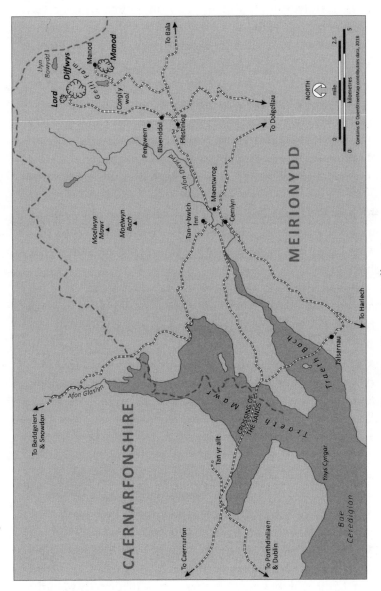

From Ynys Cyngar to Diffwys Quarry c. 1800

quay on the river. The Cassons arranged to lease the same wharf, Cemlyn Quay, which stood on a bend in the river, conveniently close to the road. Here, the slate was unloaded from the carts and piled up along the quay. Ellis Williams, the wharf clerk, had it counted and loaded onto boats, which travelled down the river and out to sea. Then the boatmen steered north-west, past Traeth Bach and Traeth Mawr, to reach Ynys Cyngar, an outcrop of rock where the water was deep enough for sea-going ships to anchor. Originally an island, sand dunes had built up behind it, so that it was now joined to the mainland, except at high tide, and gave some shelter. Ellis Williams oversaw the transfer of the slate from the boats to the ships, where they were packed in straw, to minimise breakages. These were so frequent, however, that every order had to be oversupplied, to take account of the shortfall.

William Turner, in charge of merchandising, travelled through the rough roads of Wales and England and to Ireland, getting their first orders. Getting payment was a challenge in itself. Once, William Casson and he met a slate merchant in Bangor who offered to buy a load. The slates were duly cut and loaded at Ynys Cyngar, but the merchant never took delivery. Undaunted, Turner accompanied the slate across the Menai Strait to Anglesey, took ship from Holyhead and crossed the Irish Sea to Dublin, where he sold it. He then took the ferry back to Holyhead, the crossing taking him more than seven hours each way. From there, he carried the money all the way back to Ffestiniog, a journey of over fifty miles. Later, they met the same merchant, who wanted to place another order. He managed to convince them that he was genuine, and they arranged another deal. This time, they put some pressure on him to pay up front. He paid them £500, and they agreed to send the slate directly to him.[8]

Despite that successful sale, the first year or so in

Ffestiniog was a struggle. The war with France held back trade in Wales just as much as in England. Added to that, they lost the lease of Cemlyn Quay. The estate on which the quay stood was owned by Owen Poole, a lawyer from Caernarfon, who had been leasing it to Hugh David, who had sublet to the old company and now to William Turner & Company. But less than eighteen months after the Cassons arrived, Hugh David surrendered 'the Wharf or Landing place' back to its owner, in order to reduce his rent. When the Cassons applied to Owen Poole for a new lease, he refused it, because, in keeping with what one historian has called 'the Machiavellian slate politics of the [Ffestiniog] valley', he was using the wharf as a bargaining tool, being in negotiation with one of the great landowners of the district, Lord Newborough.[9] This gentleman was from a branch of the Wynne family whose main estate was at Glynllifon, in Caernarfonshire. He also owned land near Diffwys on which lay a quarry which Owen Poole was interested in leasing. It had hardly been worked until now, but Lord Newborough was thinking of managing it directly and would need the use of a wharf. The enterprise of the in-coming Englishmen evidently touched off his competitive spirit. 'It is my wish,' he wrote, 'to obtain from Mr Poole the same Indulgence for my Quarry, as he grants to the other Quarry [Diffwys] ... and upon the same Terms. The Proprietors of the other Quarry being Strangers, Mr Poole's Countrymen will I doubt not receive from him at least similar Assistance.'[10] This last part was an appeal to Poole's Welsh patriotism. For eleven weeks, the Cassons were without a quay, but as Lord Newborough had no intention of leasing out his quarry, Poole's advantage in controlling the quay was of no use to him. He negotiated a new annual lease with the Cassons, while Lord Newborough went on exploring the potential of his quarry. These were days of struggle, but at least Thomas Casson had some income from the inn.

What of Esther? She had to unpack their few possessions and find places for them in public and private rooms at Ty Uchaf. She had to make up a straw-stuffed mattress for their bed and explore the kitchen with its baking oven and open fire. She would have made her oatcakes, patting them into shape on a sheet of slate, boiled her puddings tied up in linen and suspended over the hearth, and beaten eggs to make a custard. Within a few days, she would have discovered where the village women did their washing and enquired in shaky Welsh about food supplies: '*Lle mae blawd?*' (Where is there flour?) She learnt how to order ale and porter to be delivered. Only a few weeks after the Cassons' arrival, there was the excitement of a local fair, in mid-June, the week after Trinity Sunday.[11] The babble of incomprehensible gossip was overwhelming, yet this immersion in the Welsh language was also useful in familiarising her with the local vocabulary, as everyone bartered over woollen goods and farm produce. Except for the language, life was unexpectedly similar to what she had known in the Duddon Valley. The same flowers grew along the hedgerows, the same birds sang, the baaing of sheep sounded the same, and she even heard a Welsh shepherd counting in the same way they counted in Lancashire, the same way she had been taught to count her knitting stitches: '*Yan, tan, tethera, methera, pimp, sethera, lethera, hovera, dovera, dick*'. One surprise, though, was to see the Welsh women sharing farm labour with the men, even driving the plough, as well as the duties she herself had been used to in Seathwaite, like milking and caring for poultry.[12] Soon after their arrival, Esther was indisposed. If Martha Owen asked her '*Yn feichiog yn barod, Mrs Casson bach?*', she perhaps understood well enough to answer '*Ydw*' (Yes). She was expecting a child.

In the late summer, activity at the quarry slowed down as the men peeled off to attend to the harvest. And then came the drovers. Coming back from blackberry-picking, when she was well on in her pregnancy, Esther might have heard the rumour that they were near and hurried back to welcome them. Soon she would have heard the shouts, 'Heiptro ho!', warning the local farmers to rush their own livestock out of the way, unless they wanted them to be part of the cavalcade bound for the south. And then she saw them. A slow-moving stream stretching back half a mile. Not just cattle – the little black Welsh runts that thrived on poor Welsh pasture – but sheep, pigs, geese and even turkeys, all moving along as if on their way to some giant Noah's ark, while corgi dogs ran around barking, keeping them together. The drovers rode on Welsh ponies. Other men journeyed with them, travellers seeking protection from brigands on the road, boys being sent as apprentices to London.[13]

Ffestiniog – standing where herds converged from north, south and west – was suddenly like a great fairground. Esther had never been so busy, needing all the extra help Thomas and William could muster, to cater for this invading but friendly army. Some of the top drovers and older men required accommodation, but the younger men slept alongside the cattle. Dafydd Owen, Martha's blacksmith husband, set up extra shoeing stations. Not only for the ponies, for the cattle too needed protection for the long journey ahead; they wore cues – twin arcs of metal for their cloven hoofs. Even the pigs wore little woollen socks with leather soles, and the geese had protection too, their claws covered with tar and sand, or crushed shells. In the evening, there was entertainment: fiddle-playing, boxing and wrestling. And then, as suddenly as they had arrived, they were gone, embarked on the three-week journey that would take them to the markets of Essex and Kent, where the animals would be fattened, and the cattle sent up to Smithfield. Weeks later, drovers straggled back through the village in twos and threes, returning to their other occupations, and paying out for the sales they had made. Ffestiniog returned to its quieter times, and Esther prepared for her baby's arrival.

The first Christmas in their new home, William Casson proposed a toast 'To all old friends round Wallowbarrow Crag', thinking of the crag overlooking Seathwaite and the toast became a family tradition that continues to this day. Esther's baby was born in January 1801, and christened 'Robert', after Thomas' father and her grandfather. It must have been an ordeal to bear her first child in a new home, without mother, aunt or a woman friend at her side. The first published history of Ffestiniog was written by a man, so perhaps it is not surprising that there is no information about childbirth arrangements. There was no doctor, but the blacksmith's wife, Alsi, mother of Martha Owen, was said to treat children's illnesses, so she may also have been the local midwife.[14] It is to be hoped that Esther's Welsh was good enough to understand such advice as she was given as she went through her first labour, and to appreciate when neighbours congratulated her on a safe delivery, or brought gifts. Someone, no doubt, told Thomas '*Mae mab gyda chi!*' (You have a son!), and he could rejoice and plan a great future for his first boy. But it was not to be, for in August, the baby died, the cause unrecorded, bringing the first phase of their marriage to a sad end.

Later that year, the French Revolutionary Wars ended, or so people thought. In March 1802, the Treaty of Amiens was signed. Napoleon Bonaparte was made Consul for life and ceased to be thought of as the bogeyman he had been before. Perhaps times were looking up. William Turner clearly thought so, for he chose this time to get married. His wife, Jane Williams, came from a Protestant family in Ireland. She probably met Turner there, for her home was near Dublin, a mile from where he is supposed to have worked before coming to Wales. She had lived through tumultuous times during the Irish Rebellion. She had Welsh connections and met Turner again while staying at Maes-y-Neuadd, a large estate near Harlech, owned by a branch of the Wynne family, though whether she was there as a guest or a domestic is not clear. Turner travelled back and forth between Dublin and Holyhead while courting, married her some time that year, and brought her back to Gelli. By that time, Esther was pregnant again. It would have been a great comfort to her, having an English-speaking woman added to their little circle. In July, she gave birth to her second son, who was christened 'George', a hint that regardless of whether George Wilson was her biological father, she regarded him as a parent. But pleasure at the birth was soon overshadowed by the news that the Rev Walker had died, just two weeks before his newest great-grandson was born.

He was ninety-two and had been curate at Seathwaite for over sixty-six years. In his will, sealed just two days before he died, he remembered his children, his grandchildren and his great-grandchildren. Several bequests were offset by loans he had made, including £200 to Esther's mother, which was to take into account £100 lent to George Wilson – whether to fund some business enterprise, or to pay off debts, he did not record. Esther herself received £80, the largest sum bequeathed directly to a granddaughter, reflecting her close relationship with him. His goods, chattels and personal effects were to be divided between his eldest son Zaccheus, in Birmingham, his four daughters Elizabeth Robinson, Mary Borrowdale, Mabel Atkinson and Ann Wilson, and one of his grandsons. One of these must have taken possession of the longcase clock.

Robert Walker's death was a special cause of grief for Esther, nursing the new-born son her grandfather would never know. The Casson brothers and William Turner decided his gravestone should be made from Diffwys slate. Perhaps they chose and hacked out the slab themselves and dressed it. It was transported all the way to Seathwaite, where it still has a prominent place in the church-yard.

Notes

1   Lyttelton, George 'Account of A Journey into Wales in Two Letters to Mr Bower', *Works*, Dublin 1775, p. 553

2   Williams, G. J., *Hanes Plwyf Ffestiniog*, 1882, translated for the author by Alex Clatworthy, p. 71

3   Bradley, Lonna, *Ffestiniog Yesterday and Today: a history of our village*, Federation of Women's Institutes Project, 1998, p. 66. She states that Martha Owen was sixty-two in the Census of 1851, which would make her only eleven when the Cassons arrived. A precocious young lady, or perhaps she reduced her age for the Census.

4   Peniarth C3/28, LlGC/NLW

5   drawn from Williams, p. 101

6   Williams, pp. 102-103

7   *Pioneers*, p. 25

8   Williams, p. 83

9   Lewis, M. J. T., *Sails on the Dwyryd*, 1989, p. 18

10 *Sails*, p. 26

11 Bradley, p. 76

12 See Aaron, Jane, *Nineteenth-Century Women's Writing*, 2010, pp. 14-15

13 See Toulson, Shirley, *The Drovers' Roads of Wales*, 1988

14 Williams, p. 70

Chapter 5

The Cassons of Ffestiniog
1802–1809

A late traveller approaching Maentwrog, the neighbouring village to Ffestiniog, on a moonlit night, after the Cassons' arrival, might have witnessed a vivid scene: at a bend in the river, by Cemlyn Quay, the outlines of men stood out, silhouetted against the opposite bank. The full tide flowed inland, snaking up the river. A line of small craft, some rowing boats, some with square sails, rocked in the water lapping against the quay along one bank. Some men carried lanterns. There were shouts of instructions, some in Welsh, some in English, the creaking of oars, the scrape of wood against stone. The belly of each boat was filled, the boatmen manoeuvred it round and set off downriver, following the trail of moonlight towards the sea, carrying slate to Ynys Cyngar.

When Hugh Jones, agent for William Wynne V, had set about arranging the sale of the Diffwys Quarry, he had advertised that it 'lay within a very convenient Distance of a Navigable River.'[1] What he omitted to say was that, for most of the time, this river, the Dwyryd, was too shallow for boats. The only time when they could come any distance up was at the springtides, occurring just twice a month, a couple of days after the full moon and again after the new moon. At first, as the Cassons and Turner began working the quarry, their business was small. Twice-monthly river journeys were frequent enough to fulfil such orders as they had gained. But within a year or so, their fortunes began to turn and to flow as fully as the springtides. The peace in Europe had not lasted, and when war broke out again in May 1803, Turner gained a valuable government contract, to supply slate for roofing naval barracks. Over the years, they had orders to provide slate for barracks at Portsmouth, Plymouth, Dublin and Cork.[2] While war brought trade almost to a standstill in much of Britain, William Turner & Company began to flourish. To fulfil their orders, they sometimes worked through the night, loading boats with slate already piled up on the quay.

In what other ways did the war affect them? There was now a greater fear than before that Napoleon Bonaparte might invade. William Pitt stressed the cause of determined resistance in Churchillian terms: "'It is for our property, it is for our liberty, it is for our independence, nay for our existence as a nation; it is for our character, it is for our very name as Englishmen, it is for everything dear and valuable to man on his side of the grave.'[3] Pitt's exhortation did not include the Welsh, the Scottish or the Irish; nor did he say 'British', even though 'The British Grenadiers' was already the marching song for several regiments. Like others before and after him, he used the word 'Englishmen' to cover all the inhabitants of Great Britain. Many native Welsh people described themselves as 'English', especially when it was a question of fighting the French.[4] Yet Wales had made a distinct contribution to the war in fending off the threatened invasion in 1797. According to historian Jenny Uglow, a rumour spread that Bonaparte was 'hiding in the mountains in Wales.'[5] Lord Newborough, who owned land on Anglesey [Ynys Môn], built forts and installed cannon to guard the entrance to the Menai Strait.[6] One version of family history has it that Thomas Casson went off to fight, but there is no record of his joining the Army or the Navy, and it seems unlikely that he would have wanted to be drawn away from Ffestiniog and the quarry. Nor was he balloted for the militia, but he and his brother may have joined one of the volunteer forces that sprang up all over the country.

The most likely regiment for the Cassons to join was the Cader Idris Volunteers, named after the mountain on the south side of Dolgellau, commanded by Sir Robert Vaughan, local landowner and Member of Parliament (MP) for Meirionydd. Their duties would have been light, involving twelve to twenty-four days each year; route marches from Dolgellau to Cader Idris and back, sporting a smart uniform of red jacket, white breeches, black boots and a fine cocked hat. As a warning of invasion, the order was to light beacons as a signal. Colonel Sir Watkin Wynne, in command of the militia in Denbigh ('Dinbych'), and prominent among the military men in North Wales, pointed out that no signal-keeper could live on the topmost peaks of the Welsh mountains, and even if they could, the signals would often be concealed by clouds.[7] Today, in the safe knowledge that no invasion took place, it is tempting to look on these preparations as a little absurd, like an early version of *Dad's Army*, but until late in 1805, the threat was very real.

While talk in the Ffestiniog inns must inevitably have turned to the war, local matters were equally important. William Turner & Company had quickly become a significant enterprise in the district. The number of employed men grew. On average, during the first decade of the century, seventy quarriers were employed, mainly gathered from the surrounding district.[8] With their wives and children, they made a noticeable addition to the population of the village. The company built houses for some of the families near the quarry. Early on, George Penny, an experienced quarrier from Furness, had joined them. Another name that appeared in Ffestiniog records was that of John Tyson, who has also been traced back to Furness.[9] These English incomers soon learnt enough Welsh to make themselves understood, but the natives must have become familiar with the sound of English spoken by the Lancashire men, different in accent and dialect from that spoken by great landowners like Sir Robert Vaughan, who were used to frequenting London society. William Turner's wife Jane, like the Cassons, learnt to speak fluent Welsh, but added an Irish brogue to the English being spoken when the two families met at the Gelli farmhouse, or at Tŷ Uchaf.

More carts rumbled through Ffestiniog on the way to Cemlyn Quay. The carters were usually farm labourers, supplementing their income by supplying, as one writer put it, 'One cart, one man, one horse' to carry 'one ton.'[10] The boatmen, too, had other occupations, but formed more of a united group. These men, combining work on land and water, became something of a legend, and acquired the nickname '*Philistines*'. No-one knows the origin of the term, which they learnt to carry with pride. Perhaps it was because they sometimes worked on Sundays, instead of treating it as a day of worship. Perhaps the name characterised them as fierce seafaring men like the original tribe, steering their boats down the surging river waters on their twice-monthly journeys, and out over the notorious 'bar', a treacherous sandbank dangerous to mariners, before reaching the point where the sea-going brigs were anchored. They had to be strong: their boats, manned by two men, could carry six tons of slate, which they had to load and unload. At busy times, they made the journey twice a day, sometimes returning at the next springtide to complete the loading. They also carried goods upriver, bringing supplies such as salt, onions, beans, ale and porter for the village; iron, saws and sand for the quarry.[11] November to February, when few ships arrived, were the quietest months, though the carters could still make their journey in most weathers, stocking up piles of slate along the quay. Most of the Philistines owned, or part-owned, their own boats, which bore a mixture of English and Welsh, heroic and homely names: *Hector, Alexander, Samson, Delila, Mackerel, Peli-can, Wenci* (Weasel), *Llanc Eryri* (Snowdon Lad), *Cynffon Twrch* (Pigtail), and *Nain* (Granny).[12]

Other men, seeing how William Turner & Company was beginning to prosper, recognised that possible riches lay in the Ffestiniog mountains. Lord Newborough reopened his quarry, which in honour of his nobility was known as 'Chwarel Lord', but his quarriers worked it in a somewhat desultory fashion, and after he died, in 1807, it was not worked again until his son came of age. John Richard, the man who had turned down the offer of a share in Diffwys, joined forces with Owen Poole, owner of Cemlyn Quay, and obtained a lease on Manod Quarry, which lay to the south-east of Diffwys. They poached a foreman from Diffwys but did not make a success of it at that time, though they did, like the Cassons, build a road down from their quarry to the parish road.[13]

For some years to come, despite the acknowledged quality of the slate, William Turner & Company remained the only Ffestiniog quarry that was thriving. What was the secret of their success? Turner himself was an ambitious and determined man, whose energy, commitment and courage were crucial, and the Casson brothers worked hard to support him. As partners, they had the motivation to succeed that working for an employer, or taking out a lease, did not provide. Yet all three had themselves been slate-getters in their time, with the practical experience that Lord Newborough lacked. Once the initial opposition to Englishmen taking over the quarry was overcome, the workforce would have recognised, even if grudgingly, that the bosses knew what they were doing.

The women were kept busy, with Esther taking on most of the responsibility of running Tŷ Uchaf as an inn as well as her home, while Jane Turner supervised the farm work at Gelli. Both households could afford at least one servant, probably more – a farmhand at Gelli, a barmaid at Tŷ Uchaf. Before the winter set in, when the track to Llanrwst was impassable, they would stock up with enough provisions to last until spring, and set about spinning, knitting, sewing and candle-making.

In the winter of 1806, when her son George was three and a half, Esther gave birth to her first daughter, Elizabeth, named after Thomas' mother. There was to be a similar interval of three or four years between the births of each of their next three children. There is no information about these gaps. Whatever the reason, they made her life easier, with pregnancy and childbearing taking up less of her time and energy than was the case for many other women. By the time Esther's first daughter was born, Jane Turner had produced a son and daughter, and was expecting her third child. She would go on to have eight more.

The incomers began to impose their presence in their new community. In 1806, William Turner bought a farm estate just outside Ffestiniog: Blaenyddôl, meaning 'in front of the meadow'.[14] It was well known in the village, having twice, in the eighteenth century, been occupied by a High Sheriff of Meirionydd. The villagers knew its single-storey farmhouse as 'Cefn Crach', 'dail crach' being the Welsh name of foxgloves, which grew there in abundance. It lay in a slight dip below the road leading from the quarry and was within easy reach of the village.

In 1807, William Casson married Catherine Evans, the daughter of Sylvanus Evans, proprietor of Tŷ Isaf, an inn that stood lower down the village from his brother's. He was forty-seven and she was nearly twenty years younger. Little is known of her. She signed the wedding register with a cross, evidence that they were unequally matched in terms of both age and education. Being the daughter of a publican meant that she had at least a smattering of spoken English. A year later, she bore him a son.

The couple lived at Pengwern Hall, a historic mansion a few fields away from Blaenyddôl. Originally built in the fifteenth century, it had been the home of the constable of Castell Harlech, where he was said to have given shelter to King Henry VI and the Queen during the Wars of the Roses. Substantially altered in the seventeenth century, the house had passed down a junior branch of the Wynnes of Gwydyr. By 1800, the Wynnes were no longer resident and had split the property into tenements, each wing housing a different family.[15]

Thomas and Esther continued in residence at Tŷ Uchaf. In 1808, Thomas and his brother purchased a property together, though not to live in. Cynfal Fawr was a farm lying in a valley south of the village, across the field from a spectacular waterfall. It had been vacated by the Rev John Gryffyddh, who was instead provided with a rectory near Maentwrog. The Casson brothers' prosperity was reflected in the purchase price. They paid just under £3,000, almost three times what they had paid for the land that was beginning to make them wealthy. Tenants' rent added to their income. This estate, too, had a lengthy history, being associated with Huw Llwyd, a legendary fifteenth-century bard and magician. In the nearby river Cynfal stood a huge columnar rock known as 'Pulpit Huw Llwyd', onto which the bard was said to ride his white horse and summon up the Devil.[16] The acquisition of these properties embedded the Cassons and Turners firmly in Ffestiniog. They were no longer strangers but part of village life, contributing to its ongoing story. They, in their turn, began to understand that the principality they now lived in had its own history and identity, distinct from that of England.

Coming into Wales, they had encountered a society which was, in terms of government, no different from what they had always known. The same laws prevailed, the same Parliament enacted them, the same form of jurisdiction enforced them. But this legal framework had been put in place much more recently than in England. The Act of Union, passed in 1536, in the reign of King Henry VIII, had aligned English and Welsh administration for the first time. For some years after that, there was still the Council of Wales and the Marches. Only when that was abolished in the late seventeenth century, did the administration of England and Wales become one.

There was no-one left alive in Meirionydd from the days when Wales held separate power, and no political will, at that time, to restore it. Nevertheless, the sense of nationhood remained strong, expressed as a conscious pride in the nation's independent past. There were monuments of Welsh history all around, such as Castell Dolwyddelan, standing on top of a grassy hill a few miles north of Diffwys Quarry. It had been the last stronghold of Llywelyn the Great, thirteenth-century ruler, defeated by the English King Edward I. Out of what had originally been the Kingdom of Gwynedd, King Edward created the counties of Meirionydd in which Ffestiniog lay, and of Anglesey and Caernarfonshire. Other reminders of the past lay nearby. When the Casson brothers accompanied the boats down to the Dwyryd estuary, they could see Harlech on their left, where one of King Edward's defensive castles stood sentinel, commanding the coastline to the north and south.

The landscape around Ffestiniog became familiar to the

Cassons. The outlines of the nearest mountains, Moelwyn Bach and Moelwyn Mawr, were imprinted on their minds as clearly as Wallowbarrow Crag, Scafell, Bowfell and the Langdale Pikes had been, back in Lancashire. As they learnt more of the language and the environment, they heard the local myths and legends that gave the region its identity, still told by the bards and rhymers in and around the village. Pengwern Hall, where William and Catherine Casson lived, was said to have its own ghost. The tale was told of a young woman who, on the eve of her wedding, sat at the window waiting for her bridegroom, who was to come up the Vale of Ffestiniog from Maentwrog. She waited and waited, but he never came. A pressgang had caught him and carried him off to the wars. The years went by and he never came back, but the bride sat by the window on the stairway, waiting for his return. She waited there for the rest of her life, and it was said that on moonlit nights, she could still be seen sitting there.

From Cynfal Fawr, the Cassons could walk up to the old Roman road, Sarn Helen, and in a mile or so reach Llyn Morwynion, ('lake of the maidens'), named after a story from the 'Fourth Branch' of *The Mabinogion*, the collection of oral tales first written down in the fourteenth and fifteenth centuries. A local man, William Owen Pughe, born in the foothills of Cader Idris, had translated some of these tales into English, but the Cassons could just as easily have heard the story from bards in Ffestiniog. It concerns a young man called 'Lleu', of whom it was foretold he would never have a human wife, so his wizard uncle created Blodeuwedd for him, a woman made out of *blodau* (flowers). But she fell in love with a nobleman, Gronw, and they plotted to kill Lleu. The wizard transformed Lleu into an eagle and then pursued Blodeuwedd, who escaped with her maidens. The maidens kept looking back over their shoulders, and all of them except Blodeuwedd fell into the lake and drowned. Eventually, Lleu killed Gronw and succeeded to the throne of Gwynedd.[17]

There is another story explaining the name, telling how the men from Ardudwy – the region west of Ffestiniog – had a dearth of women. They raided the vale of Clwyd, which lay about forty miles north-east of Ffestiniog, and carried off their maidens, like the Romans who carried off the Sabine women. The men had just reached Bryn-y-Castell, a hillfort by the lake, when they were overtaken by the men of Clwyd, who killed the captors in a fierce battle. The women climbed onto a rock and threw themselves into the lake, devastated because, like their later counterparts in *Seven Brides for Seven Brothers*, they had fallen love with their captors (but if someone from Clwyd was telling the story, the reason they jumped was said to have been their shame at having left their husbands).[18]

Learning these stories, told by the bards during evenings in the inns, and seeing the places they commemorated, anchored the Cassons more firmly in the neighbourhood. Their fluency in Welsh developed through immersion, as William was now married to a native speaker, while Thomas and Esther heard and conversed in the language every day at Tŷ Uchaf. If they needed more formal instruction, Hugh Jones was on hand, and the same man who translated some of *The Mabinogion* had published his *Welsh and English Dictionary* in 1803.

The slate workings at Diffwys were gradually changing the look of the landscape. Soon there was another incomer to the area, bent on creating a local transformation of his own, which would greatly alter the Cassons' neighbourhood. He was William Madocks, the son of a prosperous London barrister. Unlike the Cassons and Turners, he had some Welsh ancestry. He enjoyed his

Welsh connection so much, that when he was in his early twenties, he acquired some land near Dolgellau, built a house there, and enjoyed hosting parties for his friends, where their entertainments included outings to Snowdonia, travelling up to Maentwrog and dining at the Tan-y-Bwlch Inn in the vale of Ffestiniog.[19]

Two years before the Cassons arrived in Ffestiniog, Madocks, then an energetic young man of twenty-five, had bought a property in Caernarfonshire, at Penmorfa, on the banks of the river Glaslyn, which flowed down from Snowdon and through Traeth Mawr to the sea. At once, he set about having an embankment built, to reclaim some land for farming, and on this reclaimed land he converted a cottage, Tan-yr-Allt, into an elegant villa where he could continue to entertain his friends. He began to build a town around this house, envisaging it as a staging post on a major route from Dublin. In 1800, the Act of Union had linked Ireland with the rest of Britain. Travel from there to England and back grew more frequent and necessary. Madocks planned a canal from Penmorfa to Ynys Cyngar, where the Cassons' slates were loaded. If these plans came to fruition, it would greatly simplify some of the journeys William Turner took. By the summer of 1808, Madocks' new town was finished, complete with church, chapel, hotel and a manufactory for the woollen industry. He called it 'Tre Madoc', 'tre' for 'town', and 'Madoc' being a Welsh version of his own name, which also carried a pleasing association with Madoc, legendary son of Owain Gwynedd, the twelfth-century Welsh ruler. Later, it came to be called 'Tremadog'. The Casson brothers and Turner would have met William Madocks on occasion at the Tan-y-Bwlch Inn. No doubt impressed by his enthusiasm, they would have taken their families to visit the new town. In 1806, Madocks held a summer fair at Tremadog; in 1807, he organised horse races; and in 1808, he mounted an amateur performance of Richard Sheridan's *The Rivals*.

Madocks had more schemes in his head. The route that he envisaged from Dublin would start at Porthdinllaen, on the north coast of the Llŷn peninsula, run to Penmorfa, cross the Traeths and continue through Maentwrog, Ffestiniog and Bala to England. This, he believed, was better than the rival route from Holyhead on Anglesey, which involved ferrying across the Menai Strait to Bangor on the mainland; and his road, of course, would come right through Tremadog. The scheme would necessitate developing a proper harbour at Porthdinllaen. More ambitiously, he also began to consider an embankment across Traeth Mawr, a vast undertaking. At the time, the two Traeths could be traversed only at low tide, like Morecambe Bay, though not so treacherous. The idea of an embankment had been mooted as long ago as the seventeenth century, with other schemes put forward in the eighteenth century, but none succeeded. However, Union with Ireland meant that the benefit of improving travel and the mail service between Dublin and England was clear.

In the summer of 1807, Madocks succeeded in a parliamentary petition to build an embankment across Traeth Mawr, and by the following summer, the project was underway. By this time, he was a Lincolnshire MP, only in Wales periodically. His agent, John Williams, from Anglesey, began hiring men and purchasing stone, which they laid out from starting points on the Caernarfonshire and Meirionydd shores. The task was to create a dam which would eventually meet in the middle. Early in 1809, a major problem arose. The Glaslyn still flowed into the middle of the estuary. When it met the unfinished embankment, it worked its way to the sluice gates constructed at the Caernarfonshire end, beating against the bank and continually eroding it. Madocks sent a directive out: 'Apply to Turner and all Mines & Quarries in the Neighbourhood in my name in this emergency to get a sufficient Gang to turn the river with all possible Expedition.[20]

William Turner was preoccupied at this time, embarking on a new project himself. The main quarry in Caernarfonshire was Lord Penrhyn's, centred on the village of Bethesda, on the west side of Snowdon. Another great landowner, Thomas Assheton-Smith of Vaynol Hall, who had been leasing out his quarry at Dinorwic, on the east side of Snowdon, decided to take a more direct interest in the business. In 1809, he formed a partnership with two of the men holding the lease and involved Hugh Jones, the Dolgellau solicitor who was the sleeping partner in William Turner & Company. Knowing Turner's abilities, Hugh Jones persuaded Assheton-Smith to lure him from Ffestiniog to join the partnership. It was a difficult decision, especially as Jane and he had just lost their four-year-old daughter in February of that year. Nonetheless, he accepted, uprooted Jane and his three sons, and embarked on rebuilding a large house on the Bangor road outside Caernarfon, to house his growing family.

Neither Turner nor Hugh Jones gave up their stake in the Diffwys Quarry. The company there continued to bear Turner's name and the Cassons continued to use his agent, Turner's brother-in-law, George Ford, who acted as their London merchant. However, the day-to-day management was now entirely in their hands. While the two families continued to be close in friendship, they were no longer within walking distance. Esther had recently given birth to their second daughter, Ann, at Tŷ Uchaf. Thomas and she took over Blaenyddôl from the Turners and established their first real family home. The Cassons were now the foremost residents of Ffestiniog.

Notes

1   *Salopian Journal*, 16 January 1799, quoted in *Sails on the Dwyryd*, p. 21

2   Lindsay, p. 80

3   Uglow, Jenny, *In These Times, Living in Britain through Napoleon's Wars, 1793-1815*, 2014, p. 340.

4   Aaron, pp. 1-3 for example

5   Uglow, p. 366

6   Morris, Jan, *The Matter of Wales*, 1986, p. 229

7   See Owen, Hugh J., *Merioneth Volunteers and Local Militia during the Napoleonic Wars* (1795-1816)

8   *Pioneers*, p. 11

9   Buckley, John, 'Another Cumbrian at Ffestiniog', www.windycreek. plus.com

10 Hughes, Henry, *Immortal Sails*, 1969, p. 24

11 *Sails*, p. 97

12 ibid, p. 78

13 *Pioneers*, p. 20

14 *Pioneers*, p. 11

15 www.britishlistedbuildings.co.uk/wa-4699-pengwern-old-hall-ffestiniog and Davies, William Lloyd, 'Pengwern, Ffestiniog', *CCHCSF/JMHRS,Vol 1*, pp. 180-184

16 Robinson, Kate, *History of St Michael's Church Ffestiniog*, private publication, 1998, p. 38

17 http://en.wikipedia.org/wiki/Math_fab_Mathonwy

18 Bradley, p12

19 Beazley, Elisabeth, *Madocks & the Wonder of Wales*, 2nd Edition, 1985, p53

20 ibid, p. 149

Chapter 6

Denizens and Visitors
1810–1815

One August day when the sky was grey and the cold summer rain poured down, the mountains were hidden in cloud and the slate-clad houses in the main street of Ffestiniog looked dark and unwelcoming, I pushed open a heavy gate, and walked into the churchyard of St Michael's, now a redundant church, to look at the gravestones. Amongst the Casson memorials, I read this inscription:

> To the memory of CATHERINE
> wife of WILLIAM CASSON
> late of Pengwern Hall, yeoman[1]
> She departed this life on the 14th day of
> November 1809 in the 30th year of her age.
> Likewise CATHERINE their infant daughter
> who died on the 8th January 1810
> Also
> WILLIAM their son who died on the 7th day of February
> 1810 aged 17 months and 3 days

From these bleak words, I first learned that after only two years of marriage, William Casson had lost his wife and both his children, making them the first of the Cassons to be buried in Ffestiniog. The cause of these deaths is unrecorded.

How did William deal with the sudden loss of his new family? The Rev John Gryfyddh, rector of St Michael's, no doubt preached about fortitude and resignation. Some may have uttered a virtuous prayer that William bear his loss with patience, but they might also have wondered if he had offended some bad spirit who was punishing him, for superstition and Christian faith still mingled at this time in rural Wales. Outside the village was Ffynnon Mihangel ('St Michael's Spring'), thought to have healing powers. There was a legend telling how Edmund Prys, rector of Ffestiniog and Maentwrog, whose hymns and psalms were sung in St Michael's Church, conjured up ox's horns on the head of Huw Llwyd, the famous bard of Cynfal Fawr, and how Huw Llwyd retaliated by setting demons on him. Some in Ffestiniog remembered '*Mari y Fantell Wen*', (Mary of the White Cloak), a woman from Anglesey who claimed she was betrothed to Jesus Christ and celebrated her marriage to him in St Michael's, and held her wedding feast in one of the Ffestiniog inns. An itinerant preacher, an early Methodist, heard raucous singing and dancing coming from inside the inn. Invited to join the guests and meet her groom, he replied 'No, I'll go to the chapel to see if the young man comes there.'[2]

Gradually, these wilder manifestations of Christianity died out as Nonconformism gained influence. The first Methodists to arrive in Ffestiniog used to meet at Tŷ Uchaf, some years before Thomas and Esther lived there. Later they built themselves a chapel. Esther's grandfather had boasted that there were no Dissenters in his parish; he had taught the Cassons to put their trust in the established church, which they did. No-one then knew that 'chapel' would become the main moral and religious force in Wales.

William Casson now made his home with his brother's family at Blaenyddôl. He concentrated on the operation of the quarry, more pits being opened up, more waste slate piling up on the Diffwys slopes. The company now provided employment for 180 men, some of whom married and settled their families in Ffestiniog. The Diffwys partners subscribed to a parish school in St Michael's Church, where George Casson could join the other village children and learn his letters, chalking them on writing slates from his father's quarry.

While William and Thomas Casson could pride themselves on bringing greater prosperity to Ffestiniog, there were other Englishmen who came to be there from different motives. Some of the tourists who had 'discovered' the Lake District were also eager to explore North Wales. In the last years of the eighteenth century, the cult of the 'picturesque' had brought artists such as J. W. Turner to paint a mixture of 'the beautiful' and 'the sublime', arousing a kind of 'agreeable horror' at the wilder aspects of the landscape.[3] Previously, as in the Lake District, the wildness had been off-putting, and the area inaccessible because of the poor roads. One early traveller had described the Welsh landscape as 'the very Rubbish of Noah's Flood.'[4] But since Baron Lyttelton's letters of 1775, many had published accounts of their Welsh travels, the best known being Thomas Pennant's *A Tour in Wales*, first published in 1779. Visitors to Wales not only admired the landscapes, some also took an interest in its history, inspired by the activities of organisations in London. The Honourable Society of Cymmrodorion ('earliest natives') was founded in 1751, one of its aims being to promote Welsh history and literature.[5] Some of those who explored the remoter parts of Britain began to recognise that British 'antiquities' bore comparison with the classical antiquities they learnt about in school and university. Thomas Pennant compared the Vale of Ffestiniog to the Vale of Tempe in Greece, mythic haunt of Apollo and the Muses; he also described many of the historic monuments, legends and myths of Wales.

By the time the Cassons arrived, well over thirty accounts of tours into North Wales had been published and republished, often with illustrations. In 1809, Mrs Piozzi, friend of Samuel Johnson, wrote that her daughter had gone "to make the fashionable Mountain Tour of North Wales: – the Ton folk *do* so now o'Days; that they may say next April in London, at what Distance they pass'd their Summer from the Metropolis."[6] Although the village of Ffestiniog was not on every traveller's route, tourists were a familiar sight, clutching their sketchbooks and journals, some making their way on foot, some on horseback, and some by carriage, although the rough state of the roads did not make for a comfortable journey.

One visitor to Meirionydd was a young poet, Thomas Love Peacock, inspired by his love of Welsh folklore and mythology. He arrived at the beginning of 1810, via Tremadog, and moved on to Maentwrog, on the river Dwyryd, just four miles down the vale from Ffestiniog. The Cassons would have encountered him as he walked the neighbourhood. He wrote enthusiastically to a friend:

> This is a delightful spot, enchanting even in the gloom of winter: in summer it must be a terrestrial paradise … My sitting-room has a bow-window, looking out on a lovely river, which flows through the vale. In the vicinity are many deep glens, along which copious mountain streams of inconceivable clearness roar over rocky channels, and numerous waterfalls of the most romantic character.[7]

He became so enamoured of the neighbourhood that he stayed for over a year and fell for the charms of the Rev John Gryffyddh's daughter. Most visitors, however, hardly concerned themselves with the local inhabitants. The artists did not exhibit in Wales, and the writers were not recording their experiences for the locals; they came as observers, their accounts to be shared with family, friends, and a wider reading public, just as modern tourists post on *Facebook* or start a blog. None of those recording their travels had much to say about the slate industry. One writer did describe the works at Penrhyn, Caernarfonshire, intrigued by the aristocratic nomenclature of *Duchesses*, *Countesses*, etc., but he wrote much more about 'the noble mansion of Penrhyn', and disparaged the higher wages offered by the mining industry which 'tend[ed] to corrupt the morals of the lower classes.'[8] Mrs Piozzi's daughter was critical of the people she encountered. She found them 'uncivilised' and complained that, while she was out sketching, she was surrounded by 'dirty little Children all chattering Welch.'[9] The only people she met who could understand her were the post boys or the maids at the inns. To her, Wales was a foreign country, whereas the Cassons, having left England nearly ten years earlier, now identified with the community, were personally acquainted and conversant with any children that they met on the roads around Ffestiniog, and took an interest in the development of the area.

Slowly, work on William Madocks' embankment across the Glaslyn estuary progressed. The Cassons shared his optimism that this feat of engineering would greatly ease local travel. But Thomas Love Peacock was more concerned with what would be lost. In his most famous publication, the satirical novel *Headlong Hall*, completed after he had left Wales, he described two of the characters walking through the Aberglaslyn pass in Caernarfonshire looking at the embankment before it was finished, conveying a vivid picture of before and after:

The tide was now ebbing: it had filled the vast basin within, forming a lake about five miles in length and more than one in breadth. As they looked upwards with their backs to the open sea, they beheld a scene which no other in this country can parallel, and which the admirers of the magnificence of nature will ever remember with regret, whatever consolation may be derived from the probable utility of the works which have excluded the waters from their ancient receptacle. Vast rocks and precipices, intersected with little torrents, formed the barrier on the left: on the right, the triple summit of Moelwyn reared its majestic boundary: in the depth was that sea of mountains, the wild and stormy outline of the Snowdonian chain, with the giant Wyddfa towering in the midst. The mountain-frame remains unchanged, unchangeable: but the liquid mirror it enclosed is gone.[10]

The conflict between conservation and development had begun, the Cassons more appreciative of the 'utility of the works' than regretful for the 'liquid mirror.' Their own works were already tearing up the Meirionydd hills to provide roofing, employment and financial reward. In the autumn of 1810, Madocks' embankment was so nearly complete that people could walk across it. In July 1811, it was finished, a firm road running across Traeth Mawr carrying carriages, carts and pedestrians for a full mile between Ynys Tywyn, the rocky outcrop on the Caernarfonshire side, and the promontory that separated the two Traeths on the Meirionydd side. Madocks set out to celebrate his achievement appropriately. By then, there were two regional newspapers which could publicise the event, the *North Wales Gazette*, which had been published in Bangor since 1808, and the *Carnarvon and Denbigh Herald*, from 1811. These English newspapers indicated a growing number of people who could read the language. An account of the event in the *North Wales Gazette* reflected both patriotism and local pride:

> We congratulate the public at large on the completion of a work which stands unrivalled in the history of the world ... We felt particularly happy in witnessing so full an attendance of our Cambrian Nobility, Clergy and Gentry.[11]

The Cassons shared in that pride, beginning to identify themselves with Cambrian gentry.

Madocks celebrated his achievement in a distinctly Welsh fashion, by organising an *eisteddfod* as part of his 'Jubilee'. With a history dating back to medieval times, the *eisteddfod* was promoted by the Gwyneddigion Society, another of the London societies dedicated to Welsh history and culture. The first 'modern' revival had been in Bala, in 1789. Two years later, Edward Williams, an antiquarian from Glamorgan, arrived in London, founded Gorsedd Beirdd Ynys Prydain (the Community of the Bards of the British Isles), gave himself the bardic name of 'Iolo Morgan', and developed an elaborate ceremony which he claimed had its origins in Druidry. Later, his rituals would turn out to have little basis in historical truth, but they were nevertheless adopted as a tradition worth following. In due course, the Gorsedd became an integral part of the *eisteddfodau*. The first revived *eisteddfod* close to Tremadog had taken place in Penmorfa in 1796, two years before Madocks bought his land there. At his *eisteddfod* in 1811, a local bard, Dafydd Ddu Eryri, opened the event with a reading of a poem entitled 'Y Cob' (embankment).[12]

But Madocks' triumph was short-lived. On a winter's night in February 1812, barely five months after the celebrations, the Casson family sat round the hearth at Blaenyddôl, listening to the wind. A heavy gale blew from the south-west. There came a hammering at the door, and a muffled shout: *'Mae'r cob wedi torri!'* ('The bank has broken!'). News had quickly spread around the village. The springtides, battering against the middle of the embankment, had breached it. The Cassons could only bar the doors and windows and lie in bed waiting for the gale to subside. On the morning after the breach came an urgent note from John Williams. He desperately needed fresh stone, men, carts and teams of horses. Riding down to the south end of the embankment to see what help was needed, William and Thomas Casson would have seen how the tide had now receded, but the river Glaslyn, still not turned to flow straight through the sluice on the northern end, was raging through the breach. Water had met water with devastating effect.

From all over the nearby counties, farmers and landowners did what they could to help. The men originally hired to build the embankment had long since departed. The iron rails laid down to carry the stone had been lifted; everything had to be loaded on carts and sledges. Madocks himself was absent at this crucial time. Only his agent knew he was in such desperate financial straits that bailiffs were threatening him, and that he was in negotiation to sell his personal estate. Right through the equinoctial March tides, the men struggled to build a bridge across the gap and stop it from growing bigger. John Williams circulated a printed appeal to his fellow countrymen, asking for manual labour, horses and carts, and appealing to their patriotism:

> Though you are distant from this spot where this catastrophe has taken place ... yet I still have that confidence, that any Friend to the country which has

given him birth, will not accuse me in taking this liberty.'[13]

The Casson brothers, not being native-born, would have responded out of neighbourly spirit, sending materials and tools, releasing men and horses when they could spare them. Slowly, the repairs progressed.

Meanwhile, the Cassons' priority remained the quarry. Their London agent, George Ford, found plenty of outlets for the slate produced at Diffwys. He suggested they should describe some of the slate as 'writing slates', since they were free of duty, but Ellis Williams, the wharf clerk, knew that if the evasion was discovered, the whole cargo might be confiscated.[14] Still, there were other ways of reducing the tax load; there was often a difference between 'the Quantity Shipped and the Quantity Duty was paid for'.[15] Ford continued to send goods on the ships returning to Wales. He noted that 'Mr Casson's Candles and Soap' were in the *Athalia*, and on another occasion, he sent a writing desk ordered by William Casson.[16] He also sent corn, but only if it was cheaper. 'Please to let me know,' he wrote once, 'when your market gets up, but at present corn is full as high heare [sic] as it is with you.'[17]

National news reached the Cassons through press reports, or through drovers and other travellers. It was nine years since the short-lived peace in Europe, but as Napoleon had long ago dropped any invasion plans, the volunteer regiments had been disbanded. The battles that Arthur Wellesley, Duke of Wellington, fought in Spain, during the Peninsular War, seemed distant affairs. Because of the King's illness, the Prince of Wales was now Regent. The Prime Minister, Spencer Perceval, did not instil much confidence; and the Orders of Council kept trade stagnant. Although Napoleon had raised the embargo on the export of corn, prices remained high and there was economic distress in many parts of Britain. In May 1812, the Government and the whole country were shocked at the assassination of Spencer Perceval.

In Ffestiniog, national news soon paled into insignificance, when a brutal attack only four months later brought violence much nearer to home. One September day, a maidservant at Penrhyn Isa farmhouse, near the south end of the embankment, was hacked to death with a pair of sheep-shears, while the family was out harvesting in the fields. The murderer was quickly identified as Thomas Edwards, known as 'Hwntw Mawr', or 'The Great Southerner', who had come down from the Parys copper mine on Anglesey to work on repairing the Cob. The maid had interrupted him as he was ransacking the dresser for money. Trying to make a getaway, he plunged into the river Dwyryd, where pursuers followed him, holding him until the constable arrived. Hugh Jones, the Cassons' business partner, was sent for as Deputy High Sheriff. By nine o'clock that evening, an inquest had been completed, and six special constables accompanied the accused to the Tan-y-Bwlch Inn, where he would stay until taken to Dolgellau the next day. Unfortunately, he escaped the constables, but gave himself up the next morning, and was taken to the gaol at Dolgellau, where he remained until his trial five months later. The day after Good Friday, he was hanged. It was the last public hanging in Meirionydd.[18]

The murder reminded local inhabitants that violence and brutality might break out at any moment, though in reality, such an event was rare. Only a month or so before, the *North Wales Gazette* had congratulated its readers on their immunity from the Luddite riots which were breaking out in other parts of the country.[19] But a few months after the local murder there was another dramatic incident, when a tenant of William Madocks, living at Tan-yr-Allt, was apparently attacked. He was twenty-year-old Percy Bysshe Shelley, not yet a published poet, but known to be an atheist and to have radical political opinions. He arrived in November 1812, with his sixteen-year-old wife, Harriet, and her sister. At first, he was delighted with his new surroundings, writing enthusiastically about 'wild Cambria', but within weeks, he was declaring that 'Welsh society is very stupid ... They are all aristocrats or saints.'[20] He particularly antagonised the Hon Robert Leeson, an Irishman who owned a quarry supplying stone for the Cob, when he openly criticised the way local labourers were treated and circulated inflammatory literature. One night, in February 1813, Shelley was attacked by an intruder, or so he said, describing how he had aimed a blow at the assailant, how a servant rushed into the room and the man escaped. A shocking tale, but the next day, a rumour began to spread that the attack had been dreamed up by Shelley so that he could leave the neighbourhood without paying his bills. 'This they believed,' wrote Harriet, after they had fled from Wales, 'and none of them attempted to do anything towards his discovery.' The man who started the rumour was none other than the Hon Robert Leeson, who, Harriet wrote, 'had been heard to say that he was determined to drive us out of the country.'[21]

For Madocks, a source of income had dried up. He was threatened with bankruptcy and for the next couple of years was unable to continue with any further enterprises in Wales. Yet much had already been achieved. The Cob transformed travel between Meirionydd and Caernarfonshire, as carts, carriages, riders and pedestrians made their way across Traeth Mawr. Once the river Glaslyn was diverted to run through sluices at the north end of the embankment, a whole tranche of land that had been underwater was drained, ready to be turned over to agriculture. And as it swept through sluices, it scoured out a deep channel, dumping the sand at Ynys Cyngar, which gradually silted up. The Cassons moved their shipping place to this newly formed channel between the mainland and an offshore island, Ynys Tywyn.[22]

The Cassons' lives progressed more steadily than that of William Madocks, and they settled further into Welsh life. In September 1813, Esther Casson gave birth to another son, who was named William, after his uncle. George, the oldest of the children, was now eleven years old. He may have been a pupil at the grammar school in Dolgellau. The two girls, seven-year-old Elizabeth, known as 'Betty', and Ann, who would be five in January, would have gone to the village school. That winter was unusually cold, but there were plenty of logs to keep fires blazing. At Christmas, the custom was to make treacle toffee on Christmas Eve, and then carry candles to the church, for *Plygain*, a service starting in the early hours, when the village men sang unaccompanied carols in harmony.[23] The Casson children were well used to switching from Welsh to English, according to who they were with. At home, Uncle William raised his glass as usual and toasted family and neighbours in their old home: 'To all old friends round Wallowbarrow Crag.'

At the end of February 1814, the thaw set in after a severe winter, and the war at last appeared to be coming to an end. In April, the Duke of Wellington's victory at Toulouse ended the Peninsular War. Prussian, Russian and Austrian armies advanced on Paris. Emperor Napoleon abdicated and was banished to Elba. Although there were celebrations marking peace, and the slate duty was reduced, the Cassons found that the market was stagnant, and prices were falling. Within the year, Napoleon escaped and started the

Hundred Days that ended with the Battle of Waterloo in June 1815, and the restoration of King Louis XVIII. But at the very moment of Napoleon's final defeat, George Ford wrote from London that the slate trade was 'very flat and no money to be got.'[24] The Cassons' prosperity was under threat.

Notes

[1] Perhaps the word 'yeoman' was used simply because he was a landowner. Thomas Casson styled himself 'gentleman' at this time.

[2] Williams p. 30, translated for the author by Sian Northey

[3] The terms drawn from Edmund Burke's *Philosophical Enquiry into the Origin of Our Ideas of the Sublime and Beautiful*, first published in 1757

[4] quoted in Andrews, Malcolm, *The Search for the Picturesque: Landscape Aesthetics and Tourism in Britain, 1760-1800*, 1990, p. 109

[5] Another aim of the Society was to support a Welsh charity school, and London Welsh people in distress, since there was a sizeable immigrant population.

[6] quoted Uglow, p. 590

[7] Letter to Edward Hookham, 20 January 1810, quoted in Felton, Felix, *Thomas Love Peacock*, 1973, p. 58

[8] Evans, The Rev J, *A Tour through part of North Wales in the year 1798 and at other times*, 2nd edition, 1802, p. 233 and p. 381

[9] Uglow, quoting Sophie Hoare, of the banking family, op. cit. p. 589

[10] Peacock, Thomas Love, *Headlong Hall*, written 1815, published 1816, ed. Richard Garnett, 1891, pp. 106-107

[11] quoted Beazley, p. 160

[12] Eofion, Alltud, trans Jack Kidd, ed Richard Walwyn, *The Gestiana*, 2013, p. 178

[13] Beazley, p. 177

[14] George Ford to William Turner, 20 Oct 1812, quoted Lindsay, Jean, 'Call them all rags: some complexities of the Early Slate Trade', *CCHCSF/JMHRS* 7, p285

[15] ibid

[16] George Ford to William Turner, 19 October 1811, Lindsay, p. 187

[17] ibid

[18] Account drawn from Jones, E Vaughan, 'A Merioneth Murder', *CCHCSF/ JMHRS* Vol 6, pp 66-100

[19] Dodd, A H, *The Industrial Revolution in North Wales*, 1933, p. 398, ref *North Wales Gazette*, 23 July, 1812

[20] quoted Beazley p. 195

[21] Holmes, Richard, *Shelley: the Pursuit*, 1974, p183

[22] *Sails* p. 69

[23] https://museum.wales

[24] Lindsay, Jean, 'Call them all rags' op cit

Chapter 7

A Woman's Part
1815–1816

In October 1815, Napoleon Bonaparte began his exile on the island of St Helena. Peacetime worsened the economic depression throughout Britain. The slump was felt in agriculture, in mining, and in the textile industries. According to one historian, the Caernarfonshire quarries were not too badly affected, 'but Ffestiniog suffered as badly as anywhere.'[1] There was a huge national debt, as well as unemployment through post-war economic stagnation, population growth, the influx of Irish labour, and the demobilisation of 300,000 soldiers and sailors. There was no further need for war manufactures and the Tory government cancelled many contracts. They also brought in new Corn Laws, restricting the import of foreign corn to protect British farmers and landowners. The hardship this created was not helped by catastrophic weather and a series of failed harvests, so corn was scarce as well as expensive. 1816 was known as the 'Year Without a Summer' and was an agricultural disaster. (It would later be recognised that the eruption of Mount Tambora, in Indonesia, in April 1815, was the origin of this climate catastrophe which caused famine throughout Europe.)

The people of Ffestiniog struggled on. Sixty years later, when the writer of the first history of the village was gathering stories, he learnt how Thomas Williams, manager of Diffwys, went across the Cob to the more fertile land on the Llŷn Peninsula, where he had heard there was oat flour to be had. He bought a load, and agreed that it would be sent to Tremadog on market day, where a wagon from Ffestiniog would be to meet it. Many of the villagers waited eagerly for the wagon, but it returned empty; the townspeople in Tremadog had locked up Thomas Williams' load, protesting that they did not have enough flour to supply their own needs. The next day, the Diffwys men met at work and decided to go and fetch the flour themselves. William Casson was on his way to the quarry when he met them, and asked the first man: '*I lle yr wyt ti yn myn'd bod-y-gun?*' (Where are you going like this?). When he understood their mission, he tried to persuade them to return to work, assuring them that he would send to London for a load of rye. But their hunger was more persuasive than their master's words, and on they went. However, they were law-abiding men, so they first paid a call on Mr William Gryfydd Oakeley of the Tan-y-Bwlch estate, High Sheriff that year, to ask how they could act without leaving themselves open to punishment. The High Sheriff assured them that they could insist on having the flour, that they could even break the locks of the warehouse, but he advised them not to create any kind of disturbance. So, when they reached the Cob, they lined themselves up in fours, leaving a good distance between each rank, and marched along, hoping they would give the impression of being a sizeable army. This had the desired effect. By the time they reached Tremadog, the townspeople were frightened enough to give them the keys to the warehouse. They walked back to Ffestiniog, each with a thirty-pound sack of flour on his back.[2]

The Cassons were pleased to have avoided any kind of riot, but distress and hardship continued. Business slackened alarmingly. No orders came through from

London, nor from anywhere else. The brothers surveyed the blank order book with dismay. Not only their own livelihoods but those of their men were at stake. Having spent years working as quarriers themselves, they had set out to be responsible employers, giving fair wages, making sure their workers had cottages to live in. Now they would have to lay off many men. While some were single men, prepared to walk away and look for work elsewhere, many had by this time established their lives and families in and around Ffestiniog. The Vestry, the committee of ratepayers that met at the church, had been accustomed to supporting paupers in the village through the poor rate, but the parishioners were now wary of being drawn into support for all the incomers who might be in need. The Rev John Gryffyddh had died, and the new incumbent was more conspicuous by his absence than for any pastoral work he undertook. The Cassons, as leading members of the community, and the chief employers, felt responsible, but they could no longer keep more than a skeleton workforce and had to let those who were laid off fend for themselves.

At this point, according to family tradition, Esther Casson played a key role in the future of Diffwys by persuading her husband and brother-in-law that they should keep the quarry open and stockpile the slate until there was an upturn in trade. No contemporary evidence exists for her intervention. Late in the nineteenth century, local historians began to write down stories from the people who had lived through the early years of the Ffestiniog slate industry, and historians of the twentieth and twenty-first centuries uncovered documentation and studied the industrial archaeology. None of them mentions Esther Casson. But her husband and children gave her the credit for their survival through the difficult years of the depression. One historian has confirmed that 'production was kept up and the slate stockpiled against better times.'[3] Like the story of the quarriers' march on Tremadog, Esther's reputation depends on oral history, passed on, in this case, by members of her family. Her grandchildren, the oldest of whom was twenty years old at the time of her death, would have heard their parents, uncles and aunts talking about those difficult times, as well as Esther herself, and shared the tale with their own children.

I was told, from an early age, that Esther was a woman of achievement. I set out to find out more about her but was disappointed to find nothing written about her role until over a hundred years after the fact. In the 1930s, a journalist reported an interview with my grandfather, in which he gave his own colourful account of his ancestor: 'My father's family,' he explained, 'had started the slate-quarrying industry in North Wales.'[4] Methusalem Jones got no mention in this version, nor those who were already quarrying in Caernarfonshire: 'Throughout the Napoleonic Wars,' he went on, 'my grandmother, who was a remarkable character, managed the quarries herself.' Esther was his *great*-grandmother, but his rapid speech, noted by the journalist, may have been the cause of the error. It would have been most unusual for a woman to take on a management role, and surely worthy of record. He continued: 'When the slate trade slumped during the Napoleonic Wars, and most of the quarries shut down, she kept the Casson quarries going by rigid economies.'[5] Again, there is some doubt about the accuracy of his account; the real downturn was after the wars, rather than during them, and the Caernarfonshire quarries did not close down, nor did the other Ffestiniog quarries, since none of them was properly up and running by that time. Still, the bones of the story remain, that Esther persuaded her husband, her brother-in-law and William Turner, still an active partner, to keep the quarry open during the depression. They had to lay off the Philistines but kept on the quarriers, while carters continued to carry the loads. Slate piled up along the side of the road from the quarry and down to the river. When business picked up, the Cassons would be ready to meet orders rapidly and make a swifter recovery than if they had to recruit new quarriers and start up activities from scratch.

Another family story recounts how Esther set up soup kitchens to feed the community. Again, there is no contemporary record, but a historian has confirmed that 'relieving hardship in bad times was frequently done by owners' wives.'[6] With wages cut back and disastrous harvests, the inhabitants of Ffestiniog were in considerable distress. The idea of providing soup as food relief for the poor was attributed to the Anglo-American inventor, Sir Benjamin Thompson, who had introduced soup kitchens in Bavaria, where he was honoured as 'Count Rumford'. His cheap, nutritional recipe was known as 'Rumford's Soup', and it was based on barley, dried peas, vegetables and sour beer. His influence spread through Britain, with soup kitchens being set up from the end of the eighteenth century onwards.

Whether or not Esther knew about Count Rumford, she would have remembered the hospitality offered by her grandfather, at the Chapelhouse, after Sunday services, to all who had travelled distances to be there. It was a small step to start doing this on a more organised basis. My grandfather asserted, that she involved 'the whole community including the family and the workpeople.'[7] She would have known every wife, mother and child whose husband or father worked at Diffwys. 'Cawl' (broth) was a standby for all the wives and mothers. Pooling their resources, they could make it cheaply and distribute it not just to the quarrier families, but to others in the parish who were in need. Most families had a little plot where they could grow vegetables: leeks, potatoes, swedes, parsnips and turnips. The soup could be flavoured with bacon, cured in her own kitchen, or with mutton, and thickened with barley, potatoes or dried peas, as in Count Rumford's recipe. It was filling, nutritious and cheap. She and her team of cooks, helped by the children, could prepare great pans of soup, ladle it into basins and carry it to the cottages.

During the first months after the war ended, Esther was pregnant. In February 1816, she gave birth to another son. Her main work for the community is likely to have been from the spring of that year onwards. While the post-war slump and the poor harvests brought misery to many, the Casson slate stacked up from the Diffwys Quarry all the way down to Cemlyn Quay on the river Dwyryd, awaiting the recovery of the trade; and Esther's soup kept hunger in abeyance.

There were accusations that might be made against what she was doing. For one thing, she was going against Providence. Didn't the Bible say, that the poor are always with us? Wasn't it tampering with God's purpose to set up against an acceptance of His will? And those who followed the principles of Thomas Robert Malthus believed that it was futile to give charity to the poor, as it would lead to unsustainable population growth. Others believed that it was wrong to create dependency.[8] But Esther had been brought up to share what she had, however frugal. The prosperity of the quarry had introduced her to a higher standard of living than she had known before, but she remembered very well how to cope in leaner times. Her legendary intervention in the business of the quarry and the life of the village brought her out of the conventional domestic sphere of women.

Esther's husband Thomas owned a book which

prescribed how daughters should be educated. It contained two works: *Letters on the Improvement of the Mind*, by Mrs Chapone; and *A Father's Legacy to his Daughters*, by the late Dr Gregory. Mrs Chapone was a highly educated woman, a member of the Bluestockings, the eighteenth-century group of intellectuals who centred around Elizabeth Montagu. She wrote letters for her fifteen-year-old niece. When published, they became one of the most popular 'conduct' books of the period. Dr Gregory, author of the second work, was a Scottish doctor, who also taught mathematics and philosophy. He and his wife lived in London for some years, and they too joined the circle around Elizabeth Montagu. He wrote his treatise in 1761, after his wife had died, intending it to be read privately by his children. After his death, his son decided to publish, and it soon became as popular as Mrs Chapone's work.

Mrs Chapone's work makes stern reading, consisting of chapters on 'The First Principles of Religion', 'The Study of Holy Scriptures', 'The Heart and Affections', 'The Regulation of the Affections', 'The Government of The Temper', before we get to 'Economy', 'Politeness and Accomplishments', 'Geography and Chronology', and 'Reading History'. While advocating a thorough education for her niece, Mrs Chapone had no doubt that its purpose was to fit her for the role of virtuous gentlewoman. She was to avoid 'intimacy with those of low birth and education'; she should be 'amiable and faithful in friendship, except when it goes against your judgment.' For example, she would have to dissuade a friend from 'a marriage unsanctioned by parental approbation', even to the extent of telling the parents if necessary. The chapter on 'The Government of The Temper' indicated the range of a woman's role:

The principal virtues or vices of a woman must be of a private and domestic kind. Within the circle of her own family and dependants lies her sphere of action; the scene of almost all those talks and trials, which must determine her character, and her fate, here and hereafter.[9]

The subjects which Dr Gregory addressed, and the chapters of his work, are: 'Religion', 'Conduct and Behaviour', 'Amusements', and 'Friendship, Love and Marriage'. He wrote that he considered the female sex 'not as domestic drudges, or the slaves of our pleasure, but as our companions and equals', but he went on, 'as designed to soften our hearts and polish our manners; and as James Thomson finely says:

To raise the virtues, animate the bliss,
And sweeten all the toils of human life.[10]

Both writers defined the role of the 'gentlewoman'. Neither allowed for women to stray far outside the house. But in Ffestiniog, work inside and outside the domestic hearth overlapped. In the early years, Esther had helped to run Tŷ Uchaf. After they moved to Blaenyddôl, long before the post-war depression, farm work took her out of the house more than a townswoman might have ventured. She had a dairy and may have supplied villagers with cheese and cream. She may have supplied medicinal remedies outside the home, as many gentlewomen did. She exercised a greater freedom than her more refined urban contemporaries, extending her role in ways that, as we have seen, established her as something of a pioneer.

How did their father's conduct manuals affect Esther's daughters, as they grew up? Her older daughter, Betty, was nine years old in 1815, while Ann was six. Did they, perhaps, begin to envisage a more genteel life than that of their mother? Or did they appreciate the wider sphere in which she had always operated, and hope to emulate her? Some romantic novels of the period endorsed an idea of Welsh liberty. Perhaps, if they read such works, Betty and Ann would have enjoyed exploring the contrast between town and country that such stories presented. One heroine, who left Wales for London, complained that young women there were kept on 'leading strings' with every 'spark of independence' destroyed: 'I have breathed the free air of my native mountains, and my actions have been as free as that.'[11] Another proclaimed: 'In the wild regions of Wales, I had imbibed a love of liberty with the air I breathed. From my childhood I could remember clambering from rock to rock, rapidly descending the steepest sides of the mountain, fearless of danger.' She compared this freedom unfavourably with life in the metropolis: 'confined within that stated circle of perambulation which the votaries of fashion had marked out.'[12]

On the other hand, Thomas Love Peacock bewailed the lack of intellectual life in Wales:

But can the son of science find
In thy fair realm, one kindred mind,
One soul sublime, by feeling taught
To wake the genuine pulse of thought,
One heart by nature formed to prove
True friendship and unvarying love?
No – Bacchus reels through all thy fields
Her brand fanatic frenzy wields
And ignorance with falsehood dwells
And folly shakes her jingling bells.[13]

It was true that there were no circulating libraries, no

gentlemen's book clubs, no learned societies, no public lectures, no theatres or concert halls in Meirionnydd. Nevertheless, the Casson family could only have felt affronted if they knew Peacock was dismissing all the local people as nothing more than a bunch of drunks. Unlike him, the poet William Wordsworth wrote affectionately of those who, like Esther, were of stout Lakeland stock. One of Wordsworth's poems is likely to have entered the Casson home. In the summer of 1814, he had published a long work, *The Excursion*, which included a description of a local priest identifiable as Esther's grandfather. Wordsworth knew of Robert Walker from soon after the old man's death. In 1804, he and his sister visited Newfield in Seathwaite, which by that time was run as in inn by Mary Casson, Esther's cousin. The Wordworths talked to Mary about her grandfather.[14] In 1811, Wordsworth visited again, with his wife. He spoke to former pupils and parishioners who still bore 'affectionate testimony to the benign influence in their lives of the saintly old man.'[15] A few months later, his interest was further piqued when he met one of Robert Walker's great-grandsons, Robert Walker Bamford, a nephew of Mary Casson. This young man was head boy at Ambleside Grammar School. In the spring of 1812, when he was not yet seventeen, he went as a temporary schoolmaster to Grasmere School, where he taught Wordsworth's son and spent time in his home.[16] Bamford was well placed to give Wordsworth a fuller account of his great-grandfather. It became clear to the poet that the Rev Robert Walker was his ideal of what a country priest should be, and he introduced him into 'Book VII' of *The Excursion*.

The Wanderer, one of the main characters, describes a virtuous priest living in a nearby vale, and praises his temperance, his industry, his self-denial, his 'charity in deed and thought', and his spiritual graces. The Pastor, another main character, recognises the portrait, supplementing the description so that the subject is clearly identified, for anyone that knew him, as the Reverend Robert Walker, curate of Seathwaite:

'Doubt can be none,' the Pastor said, 'for whom
This portraiture is sketched. The great, the good,
The well-beloved, the fortunate, the wise, –
These titles emperors and chiefs have borne,
Honour assumed or given: him, the WONDERFUL,
Our simple shepherds, speaking from the heart ...'

From then on, Robert Walker was frequently referred to as 'Wonderful Walker'.

Wordsworth had *The Excursion* printed in two volumes in quarto. It is unlikely that the Cassons bought a copy, for it cost the princely sum of two guineas, and only 300 copies of the 500 printed were sold. Still, Robert Bamford's close association with the poet ensured that Robert Walker's descendants knew about the passage. Wordsworth's tribute was a public acknowledgment of the moral standards Esther had learnt from her grandfather, and which had also informed the teaching he gave to William and Thomas Casson, and to William Turner. Although none of them had undertaken further schooling than what he had provided, that did not mean their lives were culturally barren. The occasional *eisteddfod* kept Welsh culture alive, as well as more informal bardic recitals, while church sermons offered some food for debate, and newspapers informed them of current affairs. Most entertainment took place in the home or in the public house. Esther and her family would have had entrée to the Oakeleys of Tan-y-Bwlch, the chief English-speaking family in neighbourhood, but their main social life revolved around Hugh Jones and his family, a ride away in

Dolgellau, and the Turner family at Parkia, near Bangor, far more accessible than before, once the Cob was built.

If Esther kept a household journal, as many gentlewomen did, it has not survived, nor has any vestige of her correspondence. Yet, letter-writing would have been how she kept in touch with those in more far-flung places. With the completion of Thomas Telford's Waterloo Bridge in 1816, bridging the river Conwy at Betws-y-Coed, mail coaches could come as far as Betws, private carriers then covering the twenty miles or so to the Tan-y-Bwlch Inn. Esther would have exchanged an abundance of news, rumours, advice and gossip with family and friends in Seathwaite, Liverpool and Birmingham. She must have clung to the comfort such letters could bring, trying to keep her family's spirits up as they hoped, like much of the population, for an upturn in their fortunes.

Notes

1   Dodd, p. 383
2   Williams trans Northey, pp. 111-112
3   *Pioneers*, p. 11
4   Roberts, Glyn 'Lewis Casson – Welsh Actor Plays Part of Welsh Prince', *Western Mail*, March 1935.
5   Casson, Lewis, 'A Famous Welshman greets CABAN', undated cutting from a quarrier's magazine, and oral transmission
6   Richards, Alun John, e-mail to author, 23 May, 2012
7   Casson, Lewis, op cit
8   The Poor Law Amendment Act of 1834 would outlaw soup kitchens for that very reason.
9   Chapone, Mrs (Hester), *Letters on the Improvement of the Mind*, (1773), 1812 edition, p. 64
10 Gregory, Dr (John), *A Father's Legacy to his Daughters*, (1774), 1812 edition, pp. 62-63
11 Hutton, Catherine, *The Welsh Mountaineer*, 1817, quoted in Aaron, p. 36

[12] More, Olivia, *The Welsh Cottage*, 1820, quoted in Aaron, p. 36

[13] from *A Farewell to Meirion*, written 1812, quoted Madden, Lionel, 'Beauteous Merion', *CCHCSF/JMHRS*, Vol 10, see Felton pp. 73-74

[14] Hughes, Felicity, p. 41. On p. 46, Hughes quotes a letter from Dorothy Wordsworth to her friend Lady Beaumont, telling her of the hospitality they received: 'Excellent cream and delicious bread and butter – broiled Char straight out of the Tarn to supper, 'the total bill, including what their horse ate, being 4s 6d.

[15] Moorman, Mary, *William Wordsworth: A Biography, Vol 2: The Later Years*, 1965, p. 379

[16] Southey, Robert and Charles Cuthbert, *The Life of the Rev Andrew Bell*, vol ii, 1854, p. 425

Chapter 8

Growth and Expansion
1818–1829

In February 1818, the city of Boston, Massachusetts, passed 'An act to secure the town ... from damage by fire.' It included an ordinance that augured well for the Cassons and all slate proprietors:

> Be it enacted by the Senate and House of Representatives in General Court assembled and by the authority of the same, That ... no house or building of any kind whatsoever, which shall be ten feet high from the ground to the highest point in the roof thereof, shall be erected within the town of Boston ... unless the roofs of all such houses or buildings shall be entirely covered with slate, tile or some incombustible composition.[1]

Here was an example of a public body endorsing the use of slate for roofing. Not only was post-war recovery well advanced in Europe, but the slate industry was poised for unprecedented growth, with the building of new factories and the expansion of many cities at home and abroad. The Cassons had survived three years of poor trade, helped by collaborating over prices with the two largest Caernarfonshire quarries, Penrhyn, and Dinorwic, where William Turner and Hugh Jones were partners. When the upturn came, the slate that was piled up along the road and wharf ensured they could meet new orders swiftly, thankfully refilling their coffers. The London agent, George Ford, had died, but his successor continued to seek out business for them. William Turner & Company did not in fact trade with America, but sent shipments to Dublin, Sligo, Gloucester, Lancaster, Liverpool and up the east coast of England as far as Lynn.[2]

The Casson family in Ffestiniog was now complete. Esther had given birth to her sixth child at the time when their prospects were at the worst. Although she was still in her thirties, at an age when many modern women first plan motherhood, there were no more children, and no discoverable reason. Thomas and she called their youngest son 'John', after the oldest Casson brother, who had died some years earlier. His widow, Mary Casson, had stayed on at Newfield Inn, Seathwaite, but died three months before the new John was born. William and Thomas Casson were now the only surviving brothers in their branch and generation of the family. Their parents had died during the war; they had a sister and brother-in-law, a widowed sister-in-law, and numerous nieces and nephews in and around the Duddon Valley, all of whom William, in particular, kept track of.

Of Esther's family, her cousin Zaccheus Walker II led the most exotic life. Son of the first Zaccheus, he had prospered in Matthew Boulton's company in Birmingham. He travelled to the United States, where he encountered Robespierre, who subsequently saved him when he was arrested in Paris during the Revolution. He later represented Boulton's company in St Petersburg.[3] The other Walker sons remained in High Furness; Esther's three aunts were all widows. The oldest, Elizabeth Robinson, remained in Coniston, running the Black Bull Inn. Esther's mother was also widowed; she left Birmingham and joined her sister Mary Borrowdale in Liverpool, as did their other sister, Mabel Atkinson. These three sisters provided a welcoming halfway house between Seathwaite and Wales for any Walkers or Cassons who passed through. Family tentacles thus spread through Ffestiniog, High Furness, Liverpool, Birmingham and beyond Britain, confirming the fact that while many remained in the same neighbourhood all their lives, others in the early nineteenth century emigrated short or long distances from their childhood home.

Eighteen years after the death of Esther's grandfather, William Wordsworth wrote of him again. In 1820, he published *The River Duddon*, a series of thirty-four sonnets, one of which, 'Seathwaite Chapel', praised its curate:

> Whose good works formed an endless retinue:
> A Pastor such as Chaucer's verse portrays;
> Such as the heaven-taught skill of Herbert drew;
> And tender Goldsmith crowned with deathless praise!

He added lengthy notes, including a memoir of Wonderful Walker. As his verse gradually achieved popularity, so the fame of this character he admired spread more widely. At some point, Esther acquired a more material reminder of her childhood home: her grandfather's longcase clock. Robert Walker had left his goods and chattels to be divided between his daughters and one grandson. Elizabeth Robinson, as the oldest, had the greatest claim to the clock; and she died in 1820. Perhaps the three widowed daughters in Liverpool had no space for it and offered it to the family in Blaenyddôl. By whatever means the clock arrived, George, Betty, Ann and young William soon heard the story of its concealment at Walney Scar. Once it was reassembled and set going again, Esther could rejoice that one of the earliest sounds her youngest child grew to know was the ticking of the clock in the hall at Blaenyddôl.

As the children grew up, Ffestiniog did not stand still. For nearly twenty years, the Cassons' company had been virtually the only show in town. But soon after the Boston ordinance, another Englishman began to consider the possibility of making money from Ffestiniog slate. Samuel Holland was a Liverpool merchant whose main interests were in lead and copper mining. He had already undertaken the sale of slate from Penrhyn Quarry and was subleasing Cefn Du, a small quarry in Caernarfonshire. While there, he heard that Ffestiniog slate was very fine and went over to visit William Gryffydd Oakeley of Tan-y-Bwlch (the man who, as High Sheriff, had advised the Diffwys quarrymen not to make trouble when they marched to Tremadog to get their grain). Mr Oakeley owned Rhiwbryfdir, a quarry north-west of Diffwys which had hitherto been worked only for local use. Samuel Holland was impressed; he obtained a three-year take-note, giving him liberty to quarry there. He appointed a local foreman, sent for a man from Liverpool to act as clerk of the works, and made occasional visits himself. When the three years were up, he took on a full lease and sent for his son, Samuel Holland Jr, to superintend. Mr Oakeley is said to have remarked, 'I don't expect there will ever be any royalty.'[4] He was wrong.

Young Samuel Holland had been working in his father's office in Liverpool. He set off from there in March 1821, at the age of seventeen. His later account of the journey gives a vivid idea of what that entailed, travel in North Wales being far from straightforward.[5] He took the steam packet, *Cambria*, to Bagillt, travelled by coach to nearby Holywell, and then walked ten miles to St Asaph ('Llanelwy'). The next day, carpet bag on shoulder, he walked another twelve miles or so to Llanrwst and enquired the way to

Dolwyddelan. There was still no proper road, so he took the long way around via Penmachno, where he spent another night, in a rat-infested room. On the final part of the walk, a man on a pony, who turned out to be the village baker, took pity on his weariness and let him ride the pony into Ffestiniog, where Martha Owen welcomed him into the Pengwern Arms, fed him and pointed the way to the quarry.

He soon settled into his new life. He first found lodgings with the widow of the Rev John Gryfyddh, and then rented a cottage from Mr Oakeley, found a maidservant who was then working at the Tan-y-Bwlch Inn, and began to offer hospitality to friends and family. Like the Cassons, the first improvement he needed to make at Rhiwbryfdir was to build a road that could take one-horse carts. And like William Turner in the early days at Diffwys, he travelled all over Britain, seeking out slate merchants. Young Mr Holland did not record when he first met the Cassons, but early in his residence, he was involved in a dispute with them, when he proposed to build a shorter road from Rhiwbryfdir which would pass through the Cassons' land. He was willing to pay the value of the land, but the Cassons refused his offer, so he boldly took the matter to the Quarter Sessions at Dolgellau, where the magistrates took his side. The Cassons eventually made money from the agreement, so any hard feelings soon dissipated.

Young Samuel Holland's path inevitably crossed that of George Casson, who was little more than a year older, but there is no evidence of their becoming close. George did not manifest the same kind of enterprising spirit as Samuel, who was given *carte blanche* by his father, in the management of his quarry. George had few opportunities to use his own initiative, since his uncle and father were very much in command of Diffwys, and William Turner still nominally the head of William Turner & Company. The quarry itself was thriving. For some time, most of the slate on the surface had been carved out. Under the Cassons' instruction, mining had begun, creating underground chambers such as they had made, years before, at Walney Scar. George enjoyed the pleasures and responsibilities of belonging to a leading local family. His family's long residence in Meirionydd meant that they now had more diverse concerns than slate. There was the farm to run, and other Casson properties, such as Cynfal Fawr, to oversee. They began to invest in ships, too, joining with Turner in building a brig, *Jane*, at Traeth Bach, and taking shares in two more.[6]

Meanwhile, William Madocks was still a force in the wider district, despite his earlier financial setbacks. He proposed to create a new port out of the natural harbour created at Ynys Tywyn, to connect with the canal he had built from Tremadog. It was to be called 'Port Madoc' and he planned to levy duty on all goods imported or exported there. For that very reason, there was opposition, most particularly from the guardians of young Lord Newborough's estate – for work had by that time recommenced at Chwarel Lord, his Ffestiniog quarry at Bowydd. The Cassons, too, were firmly opposed. Madocks' Bill failed at first, but passed on his second attempt, and although there was some delay in starting, the port was eventually completed early in 1824, and soon became known as Porthmadog.

Samuel Holland (henceforth the name refers to the son) was the first quarry director to use Porthmadog, renting a wharf.[7] Lord Newborough had come of age by that time, and he too capitulated, but the Cassons stood out. John Williams, Madocks' agent, who was now styled 'Director of Works in the Harbour of Port Madoc [Porthmadog]', arranged to meet with them, and Madocks instructed him to 'to exemplify to them the material advantages of Port

Madoc, its superiority over anything Ynyscyngar could have been or any place in either Traeth.' He pointed out that once the river boats rounded the point at Penrhyn, 'the South West wind is all in their favour, and blows them into Port. You may also tell them they would have a quay and landing place assigned to them exclusively'; and a fortnight later, he added, 'With respect to the dues, I trust you will bring Casson round as you did Turner. *Where* can they load out of the limits of the Port, as they threaten?'[8]

Eventually, William Casson accepted the inevitable, and began, reluctantly, to arrange for ships to use the new harbour and pay dues for the privilege. But he did not rent a wharf. He was now fifty-eight years old, and not eager to make changes in arrangements which had been perfectly satisfactory for the last quarter of a century. And in fact, the wharf at Porthmadog was not long enough to accommodate all the river boats; instead, the Philistines brought their boats to ships that were loaded not in, but near the new harbour.[9] Nevertheless, the creation of the harbour showed that the Ffestiniog slate industry was developing in ways that the Cassons had never envisaged. For the first time, speculators from London began to take an interest in the region.

In December 1824, Nathan Meyer Rothschild, the financier, and Thomas Hamlet, a wealthy London jeweller, decided to stake a claim on the rich mineral resources which they suspected lay below ground in much of the Crown land in Wales. They applied to the Board of Commissioners of Woods and Forests, in charge of those lands, stating that they were: 'desirous of working the Mines and Quarries situated in Wales, which we presume to say will be of great benefit, not only to the Revenue, but also to the poor inhabitants of that part of the Principality by the introduction of skilful Miners and other experienced persons.'[10] They were granted a thirty-one-year lease, formed the Royal Cambrian Company, and appointed an agent to begin surveying Crown land around Ffestiniog. He was Richard Smith, who, with his younger brother Benjamin, was to become well known to the Cassons. Like them, the Smith brothers came from England. They were the sons of Thomas Smith, a rich coal and ironmaster from Staffordshire. Richard married the daughter of Sam Fereday, considered 'the most important Black Country industrialist.'[11] The post-war slump brought a severe drop in iron prices, and the partnership he had with his father-in-law went bankrupt. How he met Rothschild and Hamlet is not clear, but by June 1825, he was actively engaged around Ffestiniog. He soon ran into difficulties with the local landowners, first Lord Newborough, who served a notice on him, prohibiting him from working certain lands because they were 'anciently enclosed', and then William Gryffydd Oakeley, who claimed Smith was encroaching on his land.[12] Rothschild and Hamlet withdrew their claim, but by that time, Smith had found a vein of workable slate on the saddle of land between Moelwyn Bach and Moelwyn Mawr. His brother Benjamin became supervisor.

When he first started working for Rothschild, Richard Smith called on the services of yet another Englishman, James Spooner, a surveyor from Worcestershire. He had come to Meirionydd in 1818, working for the Ordnance Survey. Instead of moving to Ireland, when the survey began there, he had stayed in Wales and settled in Maentwrog, with his wife and three children, working as a freelance surveyor, and producing three more children. The Smith brothers and the Spooners all settled locally. With more English neighbours, the Cassons' social life became busier. After Mr Oakeley had put paid to Nathan Rothschild's plans, he made his chief residence in England, leaving his estate in the hands of his nephew, also called William Oakeley. William Madocks, being often away from Wales, rented out his Tremadog house, Tan-yr-Allt, to the Spooners, while young William Oakeley and his wife took over their old Maentwrog house, and enlarged it.[13]

There were more development plans afoot for Ffestiniog. While the first work that James Spooner did for Richard Smith was to prepare a map of the site over which William Gryffydd Oakeley was disputing, he also surveyed the land around Moelwyn for another purpose. Rothschild had applied to Parliament for a Bill to allow a railway to carry slate from his quarry to Porthmadog. William Madocks had already conceived the idea that the rail track originally laid across the Cob for carrying stone should be developed as the first stage of a rail connection with the quarries, to carry the slate to his new harbour. He tried to bring in his own Bill for a railway that would run along a different route, from Newborough and Oakeley land, and from Diffwys, well to the south of Rothschild's route. Partly because of the rivalry between the two Bills, neither was successful, and the railway project stalled for the time being.

Samuel Holland sold the lease of Rhiwbryfdir, retaining the upper part, which he later worked. Like Rothschild and Hamlet, the purchasers were speculators. They formed the Welsh Slate, Copper and Lead Mining Company, its first chairman being Lord Palmerson, soon to become Secretary at War. Its directors had no knowledge or experience of slate, and originally planned to sell on. However, after a difficult start, the company began to prosper. Rothschild's Moelwyn Quarry lasted for only two years, and his company was not heard of again. Richard Smith moved on, to manage a coal mine in Nova Scotia, Canada. His brother Benjamin may have gone there with him, but he was soon back in Wales.[14] Like James Spooner, Benjamin Smith decided to stay in Wales and moved to Caernarfonshire, to work in a quarry in the Nantlle valley.[15]

On the one hand, the Casson brothers could feel a sense of pride. The entrepreneurial spirit which had brought them to Wales had led not only to prosperity and fulfilment beyond their expectations, but it was helping to make the Ffestiniog quarries a recognisable seat of enterprise. The whole district was now abuzz. On the other hand, there was now competition from Samuel Holland's quarry, Lord Newborough's Chwarel Lord, and the Welsh Slate Company. New wharfs opened up on the river. Carters and boatmen could seek employment from other managers. Esther, who once knew all the quarrier families, now often walked past streets of cottages where she barely knew the inhabitants.

In the spring of 1825, another great development in the infrastructure began, to build a bridge across the dangerous and turbulent Menai Strait, linking Bangor to Anglesey. The road between Shrewsbury and Bangor had already been rebuilt by 1819, under the supervision of Thomas Telford, by then known as one of the greatest civil engineers of the day. The Government had funded the works, through country consisting of 'a succession of rocks, bogs, ravines, rivers and precipices.' According to the select committee overseeing the project, the new road 'surpasses anything of the same kind in these countries.'[16] But mail and stagecoaches, drovers and cattle, riders and walkers still had to be carried by ferry across the river at Conwy, and then across the Menai Strait. Telford now designed a spectacular suspension bridge that would allow ships to pass underneath. Many considered the project no more than a castle in the air, but the first chain carrying the bridge was successfully hoisted in April 1825, to the celebratory sound of the fife. The first traffic passed over in January 1826.

'Menai Bridge,' commented one onlooker, 'appeared more like the work of some great magician than the mere result of man's skill and industry.'[17]

That same year, Thomas Casson expanded his concerns, taking a lease on a new quarry, at Cwmorthin, just north of Ffestiniog village, in partnership with two other men. They worked it for some years, opening what was ever afterwards known as 'Twll Casson' ('Casson's Hole'). But although the slate was of good quality, extraction was difficult, and after a few years, they gave up and sold the lease on. No matter, for this was the peak year for Diffwys, when over 6,400 tons of slate were shipped out from Cemlyn Quay. The quarry manager, Thomas Williams, had worked for them from the very beginning, but now handed over to Richard Williams, son of another quarrier who had come to the Cassons from the old company.[18] Change was in the air. The very next year, the output from the Welsh Slate Company overtook that of Diffwys, and the year after that so did Chwarel Lord.[19] From then on, the Cassons had always to take note of the rival companies working away on the Ffestiniog slopes, sometimes with different aspirations for the industry from their own.

But if their dominance over the local slate industry could no longer be assumed, the Cassons' standing in the county was considerable by this time. They were as well known in the neighbourhood as William Gryffydd Oakeley, though without his Welsh credentials.[20] In 1826, William Casson was appointed 'High Sheriff of Merionethshire'. Two years later, it was the turn of Thomas, carrying the title for the year 1828/9.

The position of High Sheriff was one of two Royal appointments in the county. The Lord Lieutenant (at that time Sir Watkin Williams Wynne, 5th Baronet) was the representative of the Sovereign in charge of military duties, and a permanent appointment, while the High Sheriff was appointed for a single year and had judicial duties. He entertained High Court judges when they were out on circuit in the county; he was responsible for issuing writs, preparing the court, the prisoners and the juries, and ensuring the sentences were carried out. He was also responsible for running the election of the MP representing Meirionydd. He was appointed on a recommendation to the Sovereign from judges in the Court of Great Sessions (established in Wales at the time of the Act of Union), from a list offered by the incumbent High Sheriff. By custom, the name of the next year's High Sheriff was normally second on the list presented to the monarch, who traditionally pricked the top name with a bodkin.

The men who served immediately before William Casson's Shrieval year were from established Welsh families, as was Thomas Hartley, who served during the year between the two brothers' tenure. The Cassons' appointments were a mark of how far the family had been integrated into their adopted country, and how well respected these English incomers were in the higher echelons of Welsh society. Their partner, Hugh Jones, a Meirionydd man born and bred, had been High Sheriff in 1806,[21] and William Turner had already served as 'High Sheriff for Caernarfonshire' in 1823/4, and would in due course serve in Meirionydd as well.[22]

The Casson children must have enjoyed watching their uncle, and then their father, dressing in the ceremonial uniform the position carried – a dark velvet coat with steel-cut buttons, breeches, a lace jabot, a cocked hat and a sword. The Quarterly Assizes were held in Dolgellau, with much attendant formality.[23] The High Sheriff escorted the judge to the courts, with the chaplain and the javelin men – his ceremonial retainers who kept order in the court – and other dignitaries. After the formal opening of the court, there was a church service, and the next morning, the judge took his seat and swore in the grand jury, selected local dignitaries, who considered whether or not there was sufficient evidence in the cases put before them. The High Sheriff then prepared the bills of indictment; the judge delivered the charges, together with any comments of his own, and the grand jury retired to review the bills, with the High Sheriff in attendance. The prisoners were then brought into the court and formally charged, in front of the petty jury (those members of the public sworn in for that day), and the trial commenced.

As well as dealing with these formalities, the High Sheriff's main duty was providing hospitality – at his own expense – not only to the judges but to all the people who expected to be included. A surviving note from William's tenure lists items purchased by the housekeeper, who was looking after the judges, ranging from mops, brushes and rushes, to beef and oysters, veal, mutton, herrings, cider and bottled porter, as well as gloves, stockings, Irish linen, payments to the tailor, the surgeon, the glazier, the shoemaker and carriage costs. For Thomas' tenure, a part of his account book survives, showing the level of entertainment he was providing, including dinner at the Golden Lion, Dolgellau, for the judges and one hundred gentlemen, 'Tea and Supper for the Ladies and Gentlemen amounting to 105 [guests]', food for the javelin men, and the expenses of a ball. He also paid for lodging each judge and his entourage, and for 'a Chaise and Drivers and Turnpikes.'[24] An item of 'clothing for 18 men' suggests that retainers, whether javelin men or waiters, had to be outfitted. No wonder the appointment was for a single year.

During William's Shrieval year, he ran the general election held in June 1826. The result was a foregone conclusion. Sir Robert Vaughan, Tory, had been representing the county since 1792. The seat was uncontested, and Sir Robert returned to a House of Commons that had an increased Tory majority. There was little in the way of election fever. Political change was not yet in the Meirionydd air. The year after the election, George Casson was balloted for the militia. While there was no threat to national security at this time, there was always the fear of internal disturbances, especially when times were hard. Unlike his father thirty years earlier, George would have been in a position to buy himself out if he so wished. However, as the requirement for Meirionydd's militia was twenty-eight days' training in Dolgellau, it would not have been very arduous if he did undertake it.

As prominent members of Meirionydd society, the Casson brothers were now less involved in the day-to-day running of the quarry. Nevertheless, their familiarity with the everyday concerns of the quarriers seems to have stood them in good stead. While there were disputes and strikes at Penrhyn Quarry, relations with their workforce remained cordial, with the same being true at Dinorwic, where William Turner remained.[25] A building depression in the late 1820s caused all the quarries to reduce their output, but the Cassons set about employing their men to build a new road from Conglywal and past a wool mill at Rhyd-y-sarn, thereby bypassing Ffestiniog village for the first time. The other quarries subsequently paid them a toll.

One cause of concern for all quarry owners was that duty was still being levied on seaborne slate. During Thomas' Shrieval year, a Treasury order placed Preston and Ulverston within the port of Lancaster. This gave the Lake District quarries a distinct advantage over those in Wales, as their slate could be shipped free of duty from Ulverston to Preston, and then on to the Midlands by canal.[26] In due course, the Casson brothers would appreciate having the solidarity of other quarry owners in fighting to have the tax removed.

The incomers – Samuel Holland, James Spooner, the young William Oakeley, and Benjamin Smith – settled further into local life. They did not, however, build themselves new houses. Like William Madocks, William Turner and the Cassons before them, they preferred to take over existing properties, integrating themselves into the existing neighbourhood, though making improvements that reflected their standing. Samuel Holland rented Plas Penrhyn from Sir Joseph Huddart, who owned much land in North Wales. It was a low-built house perched on a hill above Penrhyndeudraeth, where Samuel entertained his mother and sisters, and in due course his cousin Elizabeth Stevenson, later to be the novelist, Mrs Gaskell. James Spooner remained at Tan-yr-Allt, in Tremadog, where two more daughters were born. William Oakeley and his wife remained at Glan William, the house they had enlarged at Maentwrog.

The Cassons grew familiar with many of the grander residences in the wider neighbourhood. There was Sir Robert Vaughan, MP, at Hengwrt, a large mansion outside Dolgellau, near Hugh Jones' family house. Near to the Turners (whose family had been completed with the birth of their eleventh child, Llewelyn, in 1823), was Vaynol Hall, a grand house and estate overlooking the Menai Strait; Vaynol Hall was home to Thomas Assheton-Smith, owner of Dinorwic Quarry, in partnership with William Turner and Hugh Jones. No doubt some of these colleagues and friends visited Blaenyddôl in their turn, enjoying its tranquil setting and the company of its growing family. One visitor began to come regularly across the Cob to pay court to Miss Casson, nowadays known as 'Bess' rather than the homelier

'Betty' she was previously called. In May 1829, two months after Thomas completed his Shrieval year, he was in St Michael's Church, giving away his elder daughter, aged twenty-three, in marriage to Mr Benjamin Smith, aged thirty-four, slate engineer and agent at Tal-y-sarn Quarry in the Nantlle valley, close to where Methusalem Jones had lived and worked before he dreamt of the rich slate at Ffestiniog.

Notes

1   Wetmore, Thomas, and Prescott, Edward G., *The Charter and Ordinances of the City of Boston, together with the Acts of the Legislature relating to the city*, 1834, p. 108
2   *Pioneers*, p. 28
3   Evans, *The Old Church Clock*, pp. 207-208
4   *Pioneers*, p. 22
5   'The Memoirs of Samuel Holland One of the Pioneers of the North Wales Slate Industry', *CCHCSF/JMHRS, Extra Publications, Series 1, Number 1*, 1952
6   *Pioneers*, p. 28-29
7   Holland, 'Memoirs', p. 20
8   Lewis, *Sails*, p. 74
9   ibid, p. 73
10 quoted Isherwood, Graham, *The History of the Oakeley Slate Quarries, Blaunau Ffestiniog, Part I, 1800- 1889*, www.aditnow.co.uk p. 12
11 Fereday, R. P., *The Career of Richard Smith 1783-1868*, originally MA Thesis, University of Keele, 1967, printed copy at University of Southampton, p. 12
12 Isherwood, p. 10
13 ibid
14 Gwyn, David, *Gwynedd: Inheriting a Revolution*, 2006, p. 68
15 Gwyn, David, *Welsh Slate: Archaeology and History of an Industry*, 2015, p. 145
16 Smiles, Samuel, *The Life of Thomas Telford, civil engineer with an introductory history of roads and travelling in Great Britain*, 1867, p. 103

17   ibid, p. 109
18   *Pioneers*, p. 11
19   *Sails*, p. 109
20   The late William Oakeley 'Fawr', originally from Staffordshire, had acquired the Tan-y-Bwlch estate by marrying into the Gryfydds, an ancient Meirionydd family. His son, William Gryffydd, the present Mr Oakeley, had married a young woman from Somerset, Louisa Jane Ness, who was to prove a formidable local force.
21   For some reason he was 'excused', perhaps too busy with his banking interests. See Nicholas, Thomas, *Annals and Antiquities of the County Families of Wales*, Vol II, p. 694
22   ibid
23   Account based on 'Court Procedures – Assizes – Victorian Crime and Punishment'. vcp.e2bn.org
24   AM/MRO Z/DCH/4/149
25   Lindsay, *History*, pp. 112-113
26   Pritchard, D Dylan, 'Aspects of the Slate Industry 11: The Expansionist Period 1', *Quarry Managers' Journal*, March 1944, slateroof.co.uk

Chapter 9

Looking to the Future
1830–1839

Bess Casson, the first of the children to marry, had made what looked like a good match. Thomas Smith, father of Benjamin and his older brother Richard, owned much property in Staffordshire; it was said that his mining property was exceeded in value only by that of the Earl of Dudley nearby.[1] Like the Casson brothers, he had stood as High Sheriff for his county. Benjamin was the fifth son, encouraged to make his own career. Bess and he settled in the village of Llanllyfni, just a mile or so from Tal-y-sarn Slate Mine. He was a practical engineer, introducing a 'water balance' and a 'rag and chain' pump, both methods of improving drainage.[2] Bess could look forward to a life not unlike her mother's, and in the country she had known since birth.

The day after Bess's marriage, the Casson family attended the opening of a 'national school' in Ffestiniog, housed in a new gallery in St Michael's Church.[3] Thomas had supported this initiative. In the face of the growing appeal of Nonconformism, there was a movement to create a network of schools in which the children of the poor would be trained in the tenets of the established church. Almost incidentally, they would acquire an elementary education. To this end, the National Society for Promoting Religious Education had been founded eighteen years earlier, with the idea of establishing a school in every parish. The parish priest needed to take the initiative, but the successor to John Gryffyddh as rector of Ffestiniog and Maentwrog had been slow to promote such an enterprise.

Indeed, this gentleman, the Reverend William Lloyd, epitomised the sort of clergyman who contributed to a drift away from the established church. His name was conspicuously absent from parish records. As soon as he was appointed, in 1812, he had been given two years' leave of absence 'on account of the Rectory House being unfit for [his] Residence.'[4] His main preoccupation was to have a new rectory built, but by the time it was achieved, in 1823, on land provided by William Gryffydd Oakeley, he had already resigned and moved to a parish on Anglesey. His successor was the Rev John Jones, who got the benefit of the new rectory, a substantial house near the turnpike road from Ffestiniog to Maentwrog.[5] He was more active. Thomas, when High Sheriff, canvassed support for building an addition to the church, to house both a school, and a larger congregation. Lord Newborough provided the land. With the assistance of the Incorporated Church Building Society (founded in 1818), the building work was accomplished. The school itself would be dependent on voluntary contributions from wealthy members of the community, such as the Cassons and Samuel Holland, as well as the Oakeley family and Lord Newborough.

Religious enthusiasm was on the rise. While the Cassons were loyal members of the established church, they saw no reason to disapprove of those who preferred chapel. Only a few weeks before the national school opened, Thomas granted a lease to the Calvinist Methodist Connexion, the largest of the Welsh Nonconformist sects, on land that he owned in Ffestiniog. He had already allowed them to build a 'Chapel and Dwelling house' and to make a garden on a piece of his land, and he now formalised the arrangement.[6]

There were also matters of more general concern in Wales. In June 1830, the death of King George IV and the accession of King William IV occasioned a general election, as was customary, bringing in a Tory government under the Duke of Wellington. His administration was short-lived, but it brought in a significant change in Wales, by abolishing the Court of Great Sessions, which had been the main criminal court in the principality since 1542, the Cassons' circuit consisting of Ynys Môn, Caernarfonshire and Meirionydd. Now, Wales was fully absorbed into the English legal system. Some felt this to be a step forward, and that Wellington and Lord Lyndhurst, the Lord Chancellor, would be recognized as the 'greatest benefactors Wales has ever known.'[7] But the Casson brothers, having been personally involved in Meirionydd's court when each was High Sheriff, could not but feel regret at the passing of this last bastion of Welsh separateness. At its final session, Chief Justice Jonathan Raine 'took leave of [the grand jury] in a feeling address' and the grand jury, through their foreman, Sir Watkin Williams Wynne, thanked him 'for the attention we have ever received at your hands" and expressed their "personal regret at any change which must remove you from that intercourse with the principality from which we have hitherto derived so much satisfaction.'[8]

Wellington's government fell a few months later, and Lord Grey headed a Whig administration which introduced the first Reform Bill. But there was a matter of more immediate importance to the Cassons than electoral reform – the campaign to have the slate duty lifted. In December 1830, Lord Newborough chaired a meeting in Caernarfon, for 'the Proprietors and Occupiers of Slate Quarries, and others interested in the Slate Trade of North Wales.' The first resolution of the meeting was:

That the duty on Welsh slates, carried coastwise, while slates from Ireland and Ulverston are permitted to enter free of duty, appears to this Meeting partial and unjust, and prevents the due employment of the labouring population of the Principality.

The second resolution was:

That the following Gentlemen be appointed to a Committee, with power to augment their numbers, five of whom be empowered to act, to take the proper measures to apply to Parliament, for a repeal of the coastwise duties on slates.

The twenty-three names that followed included William Turner, William and Thomas Casson, as well as Lord Newborough, William Gryffydd Oakeley, George Homfray from the Welsh Slate Company, and Samuel Holland. Lord Willoughby de Eresby, who, as Baron Gwydyr, owned land around Llanrwst, was to present a petition in the House of Lords, while Charles Griffith-Wynne, MP for Caernarfonshire, would present it in the House of Commons, with William Ormsby-Gore, MP for Caernarfon Boroughs, in support.[9]

A number of meetings and petitions followed. Since the MPs in both counties were Tories, it was helpful that Lord Palmerston, a member of the Whig government, was still part-owner of the Welsh Slate Company and gave his support. In July 1831, Lord Althorp, Chancellor of the Exchequer, moved to repeal the tax on seaborne coal, and as the same revenue office was responsible for collecting the slate tax, this too was lifted, on the grounds of economy. It was a roundabout way of achieving victory, but still a reason for Welsh proprietors to rejoice. The repeal immediately led to a great increase in the use of slate for roofing, especially as tax on tiles remained in place for another two years. Soon, William Oakeley was letting out the ground between Samuel Holland's Rhiwbryfdir and the Welsh Slate Company to a newcomer to the industry, Nathan Mathew, another Englishman, originally from Suffolk.

Now, with the Ffestiniog slate industry on an upward trajectory, the question arose once again of building a railway to transport slate from the quarries down to the coast and across the Cob to Porthmadog. Since the schemes of William Madocks and Nathan Rothschild had failed, there had been no further progress; William Madocks had died a few years earlier, and Rothschild was out of the picture. The man who promoted the railway most energetically was Samuel Holland. The Casson brothers opposed the idea, as did many others. The carters, often local farmers eking out their living, would lose a source of additional income, and the Cassons would lose the toll they raised from the other quarries who used their road. The Ffestiniog Turnpike Trust, on which William Gryffydd Oakeley sat, would also lose revenue. And the Philistines would be redundant.

Samuel Holland found someone to further the railway project. One day when he was returning from his bank in Caernarfon, he stopped to get 'a Cup of Tea or a little Bread and Cheese' at the Stag Inn, Pen-y-groes, in the Nantlle valley, and there he met his man.[10] Not an Englishman this time, but an Irishman, a Dubliner, Henry Archer, who was considering taking over the business of the Nantlle Railway. By that time, the Caernarfonshire quarries all had horse-drawn wagons running along rails down to the quays. The Nantlle Railway was run as a toll, with each user paying for his own wagons and horses. Holland persuaded Archer to come over to see the Ffestiniog quarries and consider putting money into a railway there. He did so, was immediately enthused, and proposed to bring a gentleman with him, an engineer who would look over the land and see how the line could be laid out. This gentleman was none other than Thomas and Esther's son-in-law, Benjamin Smith, who already knew the area well from his time working for Rothschild. Holland objected, because he had James Spooner in mind, the surveyor living in Tremadog.

Fortunately for harmony in the Casson family, Holland prevailed, and it was James Spooner who took on the task of surveying the land and recommending a route, rather than Benjamin Smith. Henry Archer introduced the Railway Bill in Parliament early in 1831, to a storm of protest in and around Ffestiniog. Ffestiniog Vestry held a meeting in March, where it was decided to launch a petition to Parliament, to be signed by everyone adversely affected by the creation of *'y ffordd haiarn'* ('the iron road').[11] The Philistines already held a grudge against Holland, for he had bought three steamers (one of which he cheekily named *'Experiment'*), to carry slate from his storehouse on the Dwyryd wharf, direct to Liverpool, cutting out the boatmen. The Philistines, it was said, 'fought his railway bill with the ferocity of lions.'[12] The petition against the Bill was signed by almost all the inhabitants of Ffestiniog, Maentwrog, and Llandecwyn, a village on the estuary of the river Dwyryd, where many of the Philistines lived. This document has perished, but the gist of it, as noted by Samuel Holland, was that 'the Farmers, the Boatmen and others … thought it would be their ruin.' These 'others' included the Cassons. When the Bill was thrown out on a technicality, Holland was indignant at the jubilation that greeted the news: 'such are the absurd prejudices entertained against the measure, that the intelligence of it having failed was received with joy by the peasantry, and numbers of them made their appearance, last Saturday, at Tremadoc [Tremadog] market, with ribands in their hats, in token of what they foolishly imagined to be an important triumph.'[13] The Cassons may not have sported 'ribands', but they would have breathed a sigh of relief, believing that all would go on in the same way as before.

Just a year later, the redrafted Bill was passed. In February 1833, William Gryffydd Oakeley laid the first ceremonial stone, receiving a large commemorative silver trowel for his pains. He was one of many who accepted the turn of events and joined in the festivities. The Cassons were represented by Thomas and his son George; perhaps William Casson stayed away because he was still unreconciled. William Turner came, with his son Thomas. Mr Oakeley toasted Henry Archer, now director of the new company, as 'The Archer that hit the Bull's Eye.' Mr Archer responded with a flowery speech, in which he described the rail line as 'the lever which resting upon the fulcrum of your industry, will remove those weights which are now pressing like an incubus upon the breast of your country's slumbering wealth, the springs of her energy, and the sinews of her movements.' Mr Oakeley gave a well-turned speech in reply, comparing his county with Caernarfonshire, already benefiting from rail transport: 'But shall the blue veins of Merionethshire not beat in unison with those of the adjoining county?' He referred to the damage done to 'private lands and public ways' by the present system of road transport, and diplomatically resolved 'not to provoke angry discussions, not to foment divisions, but on the contrary, by every means which I may possess, to allay all animosity and irritation.'[14]

According to the *North Wales Chronicle*, a Tory publication, all was jubilation, with bands of quarriers enjoying the roasted ox and '*cwrw da*' ('good beer') that was served in front of the Tan-y-Bwlch Inn. Rounds of rock cannon were fired, a celebratory custom unique to the North Wales quarries. Rock cannons, or *'craig fagnelau'*, were incendiaries, made by boring holes in pieces of rock, filling them with black powder, and setting them off with a fuse made of goose quill, stuffed with powder. The resulting explosions reverberated triumphantly through the hills and 'the acclamations of the surrounding multitudes rent the air.'[15]

The Cassons took Mr Oakeley's hint, and expressed no further public opposition, believing, like him, that social harmony was more important than fighting for vested interests. As if to promote such harmony, at the dinner that Mr Oakeley provided for the gentry that evening, there were toasts to William Turner and Thomas Casson, as late High Sheriffs of their respective counties, as well as to James Spooner, as the engineer who had planned the railway, and to several other dignitaries. There were two toasts to ladies, one being to the widow of William Madocks 'as a lady of high influence and as the generous and liberal promoter of the undertaking.' The other was to Mr Oakeley's wife 'as a lady of active benevolence and unbounded charity ... from whose door the fatherless children and widows, and those that are desolate ... and oppressed never departed unpitied.' (A formidable lady, Mrs Oakeley had already made her mark in the neighbourhood and would continue to do so.) There was no reason why Esther Casson's name should have been similarly honoured on this occasion. Yet this event marked a moment after which the active influence of the older Cassons, William, Thomas and Esther, diminished in and around Ffestiniog.

The building of the rail line got underway, with many dramas and vicissitudes, both technical and financial. Meanwhile, the Cassons carried on running Diffwys in the way they were used to. Another young man arrived in the district, whose career would later impinge on the Casson family. He was John Whitehead Greaves, from Warwickshire, the son of a Quaker banker. As a junior son, he had been told to 'go and seek his fortune in Canada', but he chose to visit Wales first, where he met Samuel Holland and Nathan Mathew and began to take an interest in the slate industry.[16] In 1834, he took over the management of Lord Newborough's quarry.

The following year, William Gryffydd Oakeley died, childless, before the railway was completed. He had intended to leave his estate to the nephew who had been his agent for many years, but he had died some months earlier, leaving a seven-year-old son, William Edward Oakeley. William Gryffydd made the boy his tenant for life, to inherit at the death of his widow, née Louisa Ness, originally from Bath. She was also made tenant for life, and took over the management of the estate.

With an Englishwoman joining William Turner, the Cassons, Samuel Holland and Nathan Mathew as quarry owners, and James Spooner, John W. Greaves and Benjamin Smith also active in and around the industry, we have to wonder why there were so few Welsh entrepreneurs as the slate companies grew. Were these Englishmen exploiting the Welsh or helping them by providing steady employment more lucrative than agricultural labour? Historians have differed in their assessments. In 1856, a local Welsh writer wrote enthusiastically of 'the mighty change wrought by the commercial spirit of English enterprise, which has thus transformed bleak mountain wastes into sources of industrial occupation, private wealth and national prosperity.' He also believed that other interests had profited, since '[t]he development of one branch of industry always tends to the prosperity of other branches.'[17] In 1974,

Jean Lindsay, in *A History of the North Welsh Slate Industry*, stated the simple fact that: 'In Merionethshire ... English capital made a great contribution to the development of the slate industry, and men such as the Hollands, the Cassons, William Turner and the Greaves family played a major part in the industry.'[18] But Jan Morris, writing in the 1980s, maintained that 'Scores of English capitalists made their vast fortunes out of Wales.'[19] She was thinking mainly of the proprietors of coal and iron mines in South Wales, but it was true of the slate industry too, although the enterprises were smaller. The Cassons and William Turner differed from the Englishmen who came later, in that they had built up their business from humbler beginnings. We have seen how, when they bought Diffwys, local resentment was not because they were rich capitalists but because they were considered no better than the local quarrymen who had failed in their own bid.

After many delays, the railway was completed in the spring of 1836. Samuel Holland described the grand opening ceremony: the train of wagons, some carrying slate, some passengers, the fanfare of rock cannon, the descent, the crossing of the Cob, the triumphant entry into Porthmadog, the bands playing there, the dinner provided for the workmen, and the entertainment provided for the 'better company' at Morfa Lodge, originally William Madocks' house above the main part of the town, where James Spooner had now brought his family.[20] Holland omitted to mention that some untested machinery broke down in full public gaze.[21] The slate-filled wagons descended by gravity, with horses travelling in dandy carts at the back, so that they could haul the empty wagons up again. Holland himself was the first to make use of the railway, despite the fact that the line did not reach his quarry. Other quarry owners were slower to follow than he had expected.

Lord Newborough, with John W. Greaves, his manager, had recently built a new quay on the Dwyryd and did not use the railway for a dozen years. Several quarries had no direct access to the railhead. The carters and boatmen, their livelihood threatened, lowered their prices to withstand the competition; ten years later, they would still have almost fifty percent of the business they had held before, including all of the loads from Diffwys, which continued to reach the river via the Cassons' own road.[22]

By the time the railway opened, Thomas and Esther's children were all adults: George was thirty-three, Bess thirty, Ann twenty-seven, young William twenty-two and John just twenty. Their father was nearing seventy, and their uncle well into his eighth decade – not approaching the age of the boys' great-grandfather Walker, but still perhaps ready to step back from day-to-day business affairs. Socially, George began to take over his father's mantle; it was he who represented the family at William Gryffydd Oakeley's funeral. Bess's first child, Thomas Casson Smith, was born in Ffestiniog, the first of the next generation. Ann now lived in Liverpool. Esther's mother had remained there, in the sailors' quarter, until her death in 1830; Ann had met her future husband there and married in 1834.

In February 1839, Thomas Casson died aged seventy-one. Births and deaths now had to be recorded in the General Registry Office for England and Wales, established in 1837. In the final column of Thomas' death certificate appeared the stark word 'Fthisis' ('Pthisis'). It stood for what may have been months or years of debilitating illness from tuberculosis, perhaps exacerbated by silicosis, from years of working in the quarry. That June, his older brother William also died, of 'old age' at seventy-eight. Both men were living at Blaenyddôl. Esther dealt with their last illnesses. Bess was within a few hours' travel, but she was pregnant with her sixth child, who was born just after the older William died. Ann was in Liverpool with one child. But there were other female relatives of the Casson brothers who may have been there to help. Elizabeth Harrison, widowed daughter of their late brother John, and the Dawson sisters, unmarried daughters of one of their deceased sisters were all regular visitors from Seathwaite. Together, perhaps, Esther and one of these nieces, washed and laid out the bodies, and saw each coffin carried up the drive. Workmen and their families lined the road from Blaenyddôl to St Michael's churchyard, paying their respects to the men who had employed them, and their fathers too, for nearly forty years. Thomas was interred near the grave of his firstborn son, and William close to those of his wife and babies.

For nearly forty years, William and Thomas Casson had made their home in Ffestiniog, embedding themselves in Welsh life. Their success had raised them up from the rank of yeomen to that of gentry, known and respected throughout the county, responsible for some of its growing prosperity, and able to pass their heightened status on to the next generation. Neither of these Casson brothers left a memoir, nor did their children write down memories of them. Scraps of information about them have survived by chance. Nothing remains of their own writing except a few signatures on legal documents. No portrait of either of them survives. This account must be their memorial.

Notes

1. Mogridge-Hudson, C. E., *The Manors of Wike Burnell and Wyke Waryn in the County of Worcestershire*, 1901, p. 161
2. Richards, *Gazeteer*, p. 76
3. Holland, p. 25
4. Robinson, p. 71

5   ibid, p. 73

6   LlGC/NLW, No. 28

7   John Frederick, Earl Cawdor, *Letter to the Right Honorourable John, Baron Lyndhurst, Lord High Chancellor ol England on the Administration of Justice in Wales*, 1828, p. 77

8   *NWC* 19 August 1830

9   *NWC*, 30 December 1830

10 Holland, p. 17

11 Williams, *Hanes*, p. 129

12 Hughes, Henry, p. 36

13 Lewis, *Sails*, p. 100

14 *NWC*, 3 May 1833

15 ibid

16 Drage, Dorothy, *Pennies for Friendship*, 1961, p. 9

17 Gwynedd, Madog ap Owain, *Portmadoc and its resources*,1856, ed Walwyn, Richard, 2013, pp. 44-45

18 Lindsay, p. 79

19 Morris, Jan, *The Matter of Wales*, 1984, p. 376

20 Holland, 'Memoirs', p. 19

21 Lewis, M J T, 'Archery and Spoonerisms: the creators of the Festiniog Railway', *CCHCSF/JMHRS*, Vol 13, 1996

22 Richards, Alun John, *The Slate Railways of Wales*, 2001, p. 44

Chapter 10

The Second Generation
1839–1841

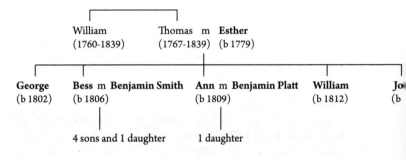

The Casson Family 1839

Esther was now a sixty-year-old widow, the only one left in Ffestiniog of the four Lancastrians who had made their way from Seathwaite. She had seen the transformation of the landscape, new terraces of slate dug out of the hillsides, waste piled up to make new hillocks, and rows of cottages spreading out around the quarries. Horse-drawn wagons now snaked their way up the railway line, through rock and wood, from the Cob and the wharfs and new town of Porthmadog. Where once she had sat at table with her husband and his brother, their places were taken by George and John, while her daughters had homes elsewhere. Her second son, William, had also left Ffestiniog.

George was the executor of his father and uncle's wills. They had agreed the arrangements for their estates and planned for the future of the quarry. The older William left a farm near Maentwrog to George, while his chief heir was his nephew and namesake, the younger William, to whom he left his quarter share in the Gelli land on which Diffwys lay. He also left him his half of Cynfal Fawr. He made provision for all the younger generation, bequeathing legacies to fifteen other nieces and nephews. The first named beneficiary in Thomas' will was 'my dear wife Esther Casson', a hint that their marriage was particularly happy since there is no other such term of affection in his or any other family will. He left her Blaenyddôl and all its contents, and some land he had acquired from the Wern estate, just over the county boundary in Caernarfonshire. The rental would provide her with an annual income; if she were to remarry, the land would go to George. He left his quarter share in Gelli to George, and his half of Cynfal Fawr to his son William, who thus became its sole owner. The rest of Thomas's property went to George. After Esther's death, £6,000 from the estate was to be used to set up a trust paying equal interest to Bess and Ann during their lifetime. They had no control over its management, but Thomas' son-in-law Benjamin Smith kept a beady eye over his wife's inheritance. The cash legacies totalled £22,000, quite apart from the properties. A tidy profit on the share of £1,000 which the brothers originally brought to Wales,

Like their father and uncle, George and young William Casson now each owned a quarter share of the Gelli land, with its farm and quarry. Hugh Jones, the sleeping partner in William Turner & Company, was mainly concerned with his legal practice, and also now ran a bank in Dolgellau; William Turner delegated most of his responsibility in the company to his fourth son, Thomas. George and young William had never been quarriers. For them, Diffwys was a capital investment, rather than a workplace. Their inheritance affected each of them differently; they had started to lead contrasting lives, while their younger brother John had yet to establish a career.

George valued his prosperity and social standing, enjoying the ascent in family fortunes he had himself experienced. Bess and Ann remembered the difficult times that followed the end of the French Revolutionary Wars, and perhaps looked for financial security in their marriages. But for young William and John, those rough beginnings and early struggles were the stuff of stories.

Even before his father's death, George held a high social status in his own right. This was demonstrated when, in March 1836, the High Sheriff for that year appointed him to the grand jury, whose members were drawn exclusively from the landed gentry. They were responsible for instituting the criminal proceedings at the Assizes, now part of the English circuit. George's first experience of the court, and the surrounding events, set a pattern for future appearances. The judge arrived in Bala on Saturday evening and attended Divine Service on Sunday. On Monday, the court opened, and the judge considered the cases which the grand jury put before him. There was considerable delay in impanelling the petty jurors who would try the prisoners. They had only to meet a simple property requirement, but the judge said that he 'would not permit those jurors who did not understand the English language to remain in the jury-box.' According to the press report, 'Other Judges have latterly done the same on the Welsh Circuits.'[1] No-one, it appeared, enquired whether the Judge understood Welsh, yet often the prisoners themselves were not fluent in English.

If George knew about the hazy circumstances surrounding his mother's birth, he may have taken a particular interest in hearing a case about a woman who was charged with having murdered her child. She had escaped from the two constables who had her in custody, and it was they who were being charged at this time. A recent parliamentary Act had established a professional police force in the counties, but it appears from this incident that the Meirionydd constables had not yet improved in efficiency from the days when they had let the murderer, Thomas Edwards, escape over twenty years earlier. Two other cases showed the stern punishment inflicted for theft. One man had stolen a mare, worth £15, another 'some pence, a spoon, knife, seal, combs &c' from a shop near Harlech. Both were sentenced to be transported for life.[2]

George also played a prominent part in Meirionydd politics. In the general election of June 1836, he supported the Conservative candidate. The Great Reform Act had made little difference in the county, beyond enfranchising a few more men. Meirionydd continued to elect one MP. Sir Robert Vaughan, a Tory landowner well known to the Cassons, had stood continuously, unopposed, since 1792. But before this election, now aged sixty-eight, he took the Chiltern Hundreds. He claimed the right to nominate his successor and chose Richard Richards, son of his old friend Sir Richard Richards, Chief Baron of the Exchequer.[3] But the nomination was opposed, making this election a more exciting event than the Cassons had lived through before. The other candidate was Sir William Wynne of Maesnewydd, who appears to have been put up as a nominee of the Whig government, to represent Radical interests. The poll, not yet conducted as a secret ballot, was held over a Friday and Saturday, with voters writing their names in the election books, which were opened the following Monday. One newspaper report referred to 'the braggadaccio [braggadocio] and vaunting' of some who supported the Radical party, but Sir William was resoundingly defeated.[4] Some of his supporters made accusations of cronyism; others claimed that the poll was taken on an outdated register of votes, taking no account of those newly enfranchised by the Reform Act. However, when, a few months later, the death of King William IV and the accession of Queen Victoria in February 1837 occasioned another election, held that August, Richard Richards was elected unopposed. The old order still prevailed in Meirionydd.[5]

On that occasion, both George, and his brother William were present to support Richard Richards' election. He expressed his gratitude that 'the peace of the county has on this occasion been preserved' and he trusted 'that the proceedings of this day will be the means of burying in utter oblivion those feelings of irritation and annoyance, and that temporary vexation of spirit which must necessarily arise at a contested election.[6] He vowed to continue his opposition to Lord Melbourne's Whig administration, which had been re-elected with a reduced majority. The Casson brothers then joined the company which sat down in the Blue Lion Inn, Harlech, to enjoy an election dinner. The wealth that their uncle and father had accumulated from slate had gained them entry into this higher echelon of Welsh society.

There was a lighter side to George's life. A few months after that dinner, he was co-hosting a bachelors' ball in the room above the Market Hall in Tremadog, with nine other gentlemen, including Samuel Holland, James Spooner and John W. Greaves, together with long-established gentry, such as Major Nanney, who was connected with the Wynne family, and John Ralph Ormsby-Gore, MP for Caernarfon Boroughs. One observer wondered if any of the hosts would find a suitable spouse amongst those 'Morwynion Glân Meirionydd' ('Maidens of Meirionydd'), who graced the occasion.[7] Whether or not this was their motive, the gentlemen laid on an elegant affair for over 120 guests. They hired a quadrille band from Liverpool, and there was dancing and dining until six the next morning. The gentlemen were supposed to go hunting the next day, but a hard January frost prevented them, and they made do with a sumptuous dinner at the Madocks Arms Hotel.[8] William Madocks would have been delighted that his created town provided the venue.

This event, like the election dinner, underlined how George, together with Samuel Holland and John W. Greaves, both Ffestiniog quarry owners originally from England, stood socially shoulder to shoulder with members of the older Welsh county families.

Meanwhile, George's brother William began to establish a very different life. Henceforth the name refers to this 'William'. Soon after he attended the election dinner in Harlech, he left Ffestiniog and moved to Liverpool. Over the years, there had been family visits to Liverpool, leading to Ann Casson's marriage to a native of the town, Mr Benjamin Platt. By 1837, William was in residence there, working with Benjamin and his father, John Platt, as a partner in their family business. As a young man in his twenties, he may have wanted to sample the pleasures of urban life. Since there were no major towns in the northern counties of Wales, this thriving port could lay some claim to being considered the real capital of the region. A steamer now plied regularly to and from Bangor. In his native village, William had been in the shadow of his older brother. He may have wanted to carve out a separate career for himself.

Platt father and son ran a tar and turpentine distillery near the docks. They were happy to take a younger man into partnership, perhaps with capital provided by Thomas Casson. William's role was supervisory. He helped to oversee the workers making the tar, burning pinewood slowly in a kiln, creating the odorous black liquid that was coated on ships' rigging. Pitch, made by boiling tar to render a thicker, more concentrated substance, was painted on the sides and bottoms of the wooden ships. These products were essential to the British shipping business. They had other uses too, on the land, and on roads. Turpentine, distilled from the gum secreted by the pine, was also valuable. In the previous century, most tar products had been imported from America, arriving in vats and barrels all ready for use or for further export. But the loss of the Thirteen Colonies had put an end to that source.[9]

The atmosphere of Liverpool, with its constant bustle, the docks always heaving with men and goods, contrasted with the Welsh village of William's childhood. He could watch the ships setting out along the Mersey and imagine what faraway destination they were bound for. Yet, if he dreamed of exotic adventures at this time in his life, the deaths of his father and uncle were a reminder that he had strong ties to Wales, and a position to uphold there. He was more technically-minded than George. If he had become actively involved in the running of Diffwys, he might have been on a par with Benjamin Smith, Samuel Holland and John W. Greaves, advancing mining technology. But Liverpool was too much of a draw, and he stayed there.

As the male head of the family, George soon settled into a life something like that of a country squire, as he rode round his estates, concerning himself with his tenants and with local affairs, while also being the incumbent owner of Diffwys. He may never have lifted a mallet in his life, but he knew how to recognise a likely vein of slate when he saw one, and he made the decisions about the operation of the quarry. Like his father and uncle, he chose never to use the slate railway, nor to acquire a wharf at Porthmadog. He may have felt loyal to the carters and Philistines he had known all his life, or he may have simply preferred sticking to the old ways. The disadvantage in continuing to rely on river transport was that it was limited to the times of the springtides, whereas the quarry managers who used the railway could send out loads of slate more often.

George's relationship with the quarriers and their families was more distant than that of his parents and uncle. There was no repeat of the older William Casson's practical charity, such as when he gave his unwanted clothes to Harri Shôn. Instead, George took a paternalistic interest in his employees' spiritual welfare. He was present when, in August 1840, Mrs Louisa Oakeley, now in charge of her late husband's quarry, laid the foundation stone of St David's Church in Blaenau Ffestiniog. This part of the parish had grown into an identifiable community, known as the 'Slate Horseshoe', drawing together the different hamlets and farms around the quarries.[10] Mrs Oakeley thought it was high time it had its own church, and the other quarry owners, including George, agreed.[11]

George was appointed magistrate. From then on, he sat regularly on the bench at the Quarter Sessions, held in Dolgellau or Bala. When Robert Peel's government introduced the first peacetime income tax in 1842, he was appointed a commissioner. He enjoyed riding with the Harlech hunt, of which he became president, and he joined the Tremadog hunt. Hunt balls were an important date in the social calendar, attracting around 100 guests, serving, on one occasion, 'an ample supply of ices and other refreshments' and an elegant supper which 'displayed the taste of Mr Allen, confectioner from Dublin', whose designs in sugar were particularly admired.[12] George's younger brother John shared in some of these pursuits, enjoying hunting, shooting and fishing, not yet focused on any particular occupation of his own.

In June 1840, Bess Smith gave birth to her seventh child, and she must have been grateful whenever her mother came to visit. Esther travelled to Liverpool, too, to stay with Ann, who had two daughters. The journey, though very different from when she had first made it, was still onerous. A carriage ride down to the Cob and across to Porthmadog, then north, perhaps staying with the Turners *en route*, then boarding *Prince Llewelyn*, the steamer that regularly carried passengers to Liverpool, where the Platt family and William could meet her on the dock.

At the end of 1841 William startled the family by running off to Gretna Green to get married.

The family legend was that William married 'a very wealthy lady from Cheshire.' Searching to find out who she was, where her wealth came from, and why they eloped, I unearthed a tangled genealogical story, made vivid by the discovery of three battered leather cases amongst the family archives, each containing illuminated parchments, heavy with Royal seals, spelling out rights to bear arms, granted to her forebears. William was marrying into a family who were manifestly proud and protective of their pedigree.

His bride was born Frances Galley in 1820, better known as 'Fanny'. She was the fourth of five daughters of John Galley, mercer, in the village of Astbury, just outside the borough of Congleton, Cheshire. Through their paternal grandmother, the girls were connected with the Jacksons, a family of much greater social standing, who had acquired a large estate at Betchton, one of the six townships around the market town of Sandbach. John Galley took pride in this connection, and nurtured expectations of inheriting the estate. He traced the family back to a seventeenth-century great-great-grandfather, Randle Jackson, whose older brother Richard had married into a family with a substantial property outside Sandbach. Three generations later,

Richard Jackson's surviving descendants consisted of three unmarried sisters, the Misses Day Jackson. When the last surviving sister died, in 1821, their name, properties and the right to bear arms went to Randle Jackson's oldest descendant, who was John Galley's older brother, Richard. Already in his fifties, Richard Galley was unmarried, and sixteen years older than John. Fanny and her sisters soon learnt their pedigree and could identify all the family portraits when they visited their uncle at Betchton Hall, including that of Major-General Pudsey of Langley Hall, Sutton Coldfield, who, they were told, was rumoured to be a favourite of King Charles I's wife, Queen Henrietta.[13]

Astbury, Fanny's birthplace, was a quiet village. No mountains, no pounding waterfalls, no nearby harbours and stormy seas, no quarries, nor any major engineering projects. When she was thirteen years old, her mother and older sister died within a month of each other, a sad disruption of her adolescence. Three years later, another older sister, Catharine, brought disgrace upon the family by marrying, underage and without her father's consent, a man with a dubious background. This marriage scandalised the widowed John Galley, who vowed never to let his son-in-law enter his house. He determined to be more vigilant over his remaining three daughters.

Two months after Catharine's marriage, Fanny's uncle, now Richard Galley Day Jackson, died, and John Galley at last came into the property and titles of his spinster cousins. He at once applied for the Royal Licence that would authorise him to add the names 'Day Jackson' to 'Galley', and to bear the arms. Fanny and her two remaining unmarried sisters all added 'Day Jackson' to their names as well, but John Galley Day Jackson had little time to enjoy his property and his new status. He died of 'diseases of the lung' in 1839, two years to the day after he had obtained his Royal

Licence. His youngest daughter had died eight months earlier, at sixteen years of age. Within five years, Fanny had lost her mother, her father, and two sisters, while her sister Catharine was in disgrace. Only her older sister Mary and she were left to carry on their father's line respectably and inherit his estate.

A year later, twenty-year-old Fanny was on the road to Gretna Green. There is no evidence as to when William Casson and she first met. The most likely site of their courtship was Liverpool, where William was already living, and where she may have been studying singing, for it was later reported that she had a trained voice. Her sister Mary and she may have chaperoned each other, glad to leave behind the home they associated with so many deaths, eager to taste the delights of the metropolis. Mary had already earned her father's disapproval by falling in love with the wrong man. Among the provisos in his will, was one stating that if she married John Twiss, the local organist, she would forfeit her entire legacy.[14] But there was no such stipulation about Fanny's future husband. Perhaps John Galley Day Jackson already knew and approved of William Casson, but given his wariness about his prospective sons-in-law, it seems more likely that he did not know she had a suitor. Although Fanny was underage, he did not name a guardian, more evidence that he was unaware of any imminent wedding plan he needed to take into account.

As no guardian was named for Fanny, a court would have to appoint one, and this might have been a lengthy process, severely delaying consent to her marriage. That is the most likely reason why William and she decided to make the trip, to Gretna Green, where they were married on 29 December 1840. There is no record of how Esther Casson and her other children learnt of this turn of events or how they responded. But family pressure was probably behind the couple's decision to have another, more conventional ceremony. In February 1841, two months after the elopement, Fanny and William solemnised their marriage for the second time, at St James' Church, Toxteth Park, where they had taken up residence. It was quite common for couples to feel they had tied the knot more securely if they did it again in England.[15] In fact, their second marriage had no legal standing since their first marriage was valid. The banns were read. Although Fanny was still under the age of consent, no-one protested, and so the ceremony took place.

The drama of the elopement suggests that this was a love-match. But the marriage did bring William a substantial estate. Fanny's sister Mary did not throw away her fortune by marrying the local organist back home. She married, more prudently, a respectable wine merchant, Mr Henry Sandys Salisbury of Low Hill, not far from the centre of Liverpool. Consequently, the Cheshire estate was divided between Mary and Fanny, and passed into their husbands' hands. However, this did not make either man rich. Their late father-in-law, it turned out, had many debts, and his executors had to take out several mortgages to cover them. William had need to call upon his brother George, more versed in legal matters, to help sort out his affairs. George set up a trust, with his brother John and a Liverpool solicitor, to protect Fanny's interests and that of her unborn children.

William and Fanny settled in Lodge Lane, Toxteth Park, then a fashionable part of Liverpool, and William continued as a partner in the distillery. The Jackson connection brought him the Cheshire property and enhanced his social status. While he and his brothers, and his widowed mother, owed their position to the wealth and influence gained by their father and uncle, Fanny's father had been elevated through the chances of genealogy. For both families, their social dominance was largely local; deference was due to the

Jacksons in Cheshire, and to the Cassons in Meirionydd. In Liverpool, the population was less settled, with status linked to commerce rather than to ownership of land, pedigree or inherited wealth.

Notes

1 *NWC*, 22 March, 1836
2 ibid
3 Evans, E D, 'Politics and Parliamentary Representation in Merioneth 1644-1832, Part 2', *CCHCSF/JMHRS*, Vol 15, 2012, p. 433
4 *Westmorland Gazette*, 2 July 1836
5 Evans, E. D, commented, "That Merionethshire should have endured the domination of its county families for so long after the Reform Act is not far to seek. They were the only persons who had the means and leisure to go to Westminster in the days when MPs were unpaid."
6 *NWC*, 8 August 1837
7 *NWC*, 16 January 1838
8 ibid
9 http://www.maritime.org/conf/conf-kaye-tar.htm
10 Tanygrisiau, Rhiwbryfdir, Four Crosses, Conglywal, Bethania and Manod. See Isherwood, p. 1
11 *NWC*, 4 August, 1840
12 *NWC*, 9 November,1841
13 According to a letter written by a later Thomas Casson to his brother, 1893, but I have so far been unable to trace Major Pudsey, even though the family owns a portrait purporting to be him.
14 'Twiss' is a guess, as the name is difficult to read in the copy of the will.
15 Rebecca Probert, author of *Marriage Law for Genealogists*, 2012, confirmed this by email to the author, 6 July 2015.

Chapter 11

Between Liverpool and Ffestiniog
1841–1846

Fanny Casson became pregnant soon after her second wedding ceremony. Esther Casson, who visited Liverpool from time to time, must have felt torn between the needs of her older daughter and her new daughter-in-law, for Bess was expecting her eighth child at the same time. The Benjamin Smith family now lived in a large house, Bron Seiont, on the Menai Strait, just outside Caernarfon. Fanny's baby, a boy, was born in November 1841. Tradition would have dictated this firstborn was called 'Thomas', after William's father, but, as his uncle's chief heir, William wanted that name to be commemorated first, so at the christening in St Peter's, the parish church of Liverpool, the boy was named 'William Galley'. Less than a year later, their second son arrived, and he was named 'Thomas'. Once again, there were two brothers called William and Thomas Casson. The new William was usually known by his middle name, 'Galley', and 'Thomas' was quickly shortened to 'Tom'.

Some letters that the three older Casson brothers exchanged at this time have survived, the earliest substantial primary evidence about the family.[1] They throw light on their different characters, for George's writing was small and neat, and he enjoyed turning a good phrase, while William wrote in a large sprawling hand, dealing mainly with practicalities. John's hand was more like George's. George remained unmarried but took a lively interest in his sisters' families and in William's. Sometimes he asked for items to be sent back from Liverpool to Ffestiniog, by steamer and coach, to enliven the meals at Blaenyddôl. Sometimes the treats came from Cheshire. In one letter, he wrote, 'Among other things, is there any Honey flowing in this Direction? For you have not mentioned this softly soothing matter among your list of edibles' and added 'I am glad to hear of a Cheshire cheese coming, for our lack of this delicacy is getting very low [sic].' In the same letter, he regaled his brother John with a humorous account of a sheep thief who had come up before him in court: 'The Constables ... succeeded in capturing this admirer and patron of the Woolly Tribe.'[2] As a magistrate, a Justice of the Peace, he had been active in appointing such officers two years earlier, when county and district constables were first established, following on from Robert Peel's creation of the metropolitan force.

George kept the rest of the family informed about their mother's health, which was not always good: 'Mother says that she is better today and yesterday, but I have great doubts about it; she intends trying Leeches next week and I hope they will do good.' She had the leeches applied but he reported that 'this has caused more soreness and irritation than usual.'[3] He did not mention the nature of her complaint. Twenty-six-year-old John began acting as an agent for Diffwys Quarry.[4] Often either George or he travelled to Liverpool and dropped in on Bess on the way there or back, keeping everyone up to date with family news. Relations with her husband, Benjamin Smith, were not good. He took issue with the way in which George handled Bess's trust fund, which had already been set up, perhaps at Esther's request, though Thomas's will had specified that it was to come out of the estate after her death.

On one occasion, visiting Liverpool, Benjamin Smith stayed with Benjamin and Ann Platt, William's other brother-in-law and sister. William reported to George that Benjamin Smith had kept the whole family up all night, 'having been very sick with taking two blue pills.' Perhaps these were the mercury-based pills sometimes prescribed for 'melancholy'. William gave no further information about the nature of the sickness or what effect the blue pills were supposed to have, but simply commented 'One really cannot help being amused by him.'[5] However, they could not regard it as a laughing matter when Benjamin Smith threatened legal action over the trust. As the situation deteriorated, he refused to communicate further with George, and the Cassons' solicitor suggested to George that 'the best course to pursue will be for your brother [William] to correspond with him, your brother's letters to be written and revised by myself.'[6] The dispute dragged on for several years, with the Cassons attempting to protect Bess from being affected by the rift. Her husband's curmudgeonly behaviour may have been caused by jealousy of the Casson brothers' substantial estates, and of his brother Richard's prosperity. Richard, having returned from Nova Scotia, had become mine agent for the 1st Earl of Dudley, and moved into 'The Priory', a grand mansion near Dudley Castle in Staffordshire, where he entertained on a much more lavish scale than Benjamin could afford.[7]

One night, a few days before Christmas 1842, the Platt/Casson distillery caught fire. William, aroused from his bed, hurried to the plant. He saw fire engines and men trying to douse an already fearsome blaze. The whole of the warehouse was alight, and flames were spreading to the adjoining buildings. He found Benjamin Platt and his father helplessly watching, as the flames roared on and black smoke billowed around them. Flames a hundred feet high had already burst through the roof, and the warehouses on either side were ablaze too, with clouds of black smoke engulfing them. The air was filled with the sound of crackling flames, loud crashes as parts of the building gave way, and the voices of men shouting instructions and warnings. The fire had already reached the vaults beneath the yard, where tar, turpentine and oil were stored. The heat was so fierce it entirely melted a copper pan in the yard. There was no hope of saving their premises or those of the warehouses on either side. The firemen became concerned with the houses opposite both the back and front of the distillery, which stretched between Parliament Street and Greenland Street. Nearby residents, fearful their own property would catch fire, threw their furniture out of the windows. Streams of burning tar ran down the street, so that the firemen had to douse their own boots as well as the buildings. For the first hour, the fire spread relentlessly outwards, and the spectators had to step further away. A reporter from the local newspaper was moved to eloquence: 'The scene was one of fearful grandeur, and could not fail to impress the spectators with its magnificent yet awful appearance.'[8]

For over three hours, William and the Platts watched as their entire plant was destroyed, policemen keeping back any onlookers as the front wall finally fell inwards. A detachment of foot soldiers arrived to help. Long after the fire had burnt itself out, fortunately without anyone being injured, the scent of turpentine permeated the town air. When daylight came, onlookers remained, watching the smouldering ruins. A local artist later sketched the scene and published a lithograph, which William kept as a vivid reminder of the devastation.

After the fire, the distillery building was nothing but a skeleton. On a quick calculation, the damage would amount

The distillery fire

to £40,000 (equivalent to around £300,000 in 2019). The works were insured against fire, but the insurance company quibbled about exactly how much of the premises was covered, and also tried to bring a conviction against an employee, who had accidentally started the fire by bringing a lighted stick too close to a pan of turpentine. He had worked for the company for over twenty years, and John Platt was relieved when the man was acquitted. Many difficult months lay ahead while the works were rebuilt and the stock was replenished.

No letters survive telling the family in Ffestiniog about the fire. Perhaps William took the opportunity, while business was suspended, to bring his family on a visit. He began to consider moving back to Wales, but the following year, the Corporation of Liverpool took over the distillery premises and gave William and the Platts a lease for seventy-five years. Work began again, and at the beginning of 1844, Fanny's third child, was born, her first daughter. She was christened 'Frances Mary' at St Peter's Church in July, going by the pet name of 'Polly'. Six months later, Fanny was pregnant again.

In the summer of 1845, William did bring his family to Wales, though he did not sell up in Liverpool. He took a lease at Bryn Llewelyn, a house on the southern edge of Ffestiniog, on Lord Newborough's land. His reasons for moving, and his plans, once back in Wales, are a matter of conjecture. Perhaps the prospect of having a fourth child prompted his decision; he may have wanted his children to have the sort of Welsh childhood he himself had enjoyed, with the freedom to explore woods, mountains and rivers. Perhaps Esther's age and poor health was a factor. Perhaps he wanted to be more actively involved with the management of the quarry. Having established his own life and family, he had no need to feel any sense of rivalry with

George. He was certainly enthusiastic about a plan to have a new slate mill built on the river Bowydd, alongside the road that William Turner & Company still used for transport. Completed in 1845, the slate mill had a large waterwheel which drove cutting machines to saw the great slate slabs that were used for flooring.[9] Before his move, William organised the purchase and transport of equipment from Liverpool. He also showed some interest in Cwmorthin Quarry, which his father had worked for a few years, and which was now leased to a London man.[10] He may have set up as an agent for the distillery, once it was back up and running, for Porthmadog was now a thriving shipbuilding centre; a bill survives from Platt, Son & Casson, charging Diffwys Quarry for grease, paint and black lead.[11] Certainly, there was the possibility of a busy and prosperous life based in Ffestiniog.

For Fanny, it was a sad wrench to leave behind the many pleasures to be had in Liverpool. As the town grew in commercial prosperity, its culture rivalled that of London. There was a triennial music festival at St Peter's Church; there were concerts by the Liverpool Philharmonic Society; Italian operas at the Theatre Royal, where international stars such as Giulia Grisi and Marietta Alboni performed; as well as plays by the most popular Victorian dramatists, such as Edward Bulwer Lytton and Douglas Jerrold. Although much of Fanny's married life was taken up with caring for her children, she had enjoyed metropolitan life for at least the last four years, and probably longer. There was also the difficulty of language to consider. She neither spoke nor understood Welsh and until the move had no reason to think she needed to learn.

Esther now had some of her grandchildren living nearby. Galley and Tom were old enough to enjoy the farm and garden at Blaenyddôl, to sit on a horse or hold a fishing-rod, under the tutelage of their Casson uncles. At the beginning of September 1845, Fanny's third son was born. In honour of his older brother, William named the new baby 'George'. The baptism of the boy was a particularly happy occasion because it coincided with the opening of a new church building in Ffestiniog, a project in which the older George, following in his father Thomas's footsteps, had played a major part. Though St Michael's could not vie with the splendour of St Peter's in Liverpool, it nevertheless reflected the growing prosperity of the village, and the important place that the church still played in the community.

In Wales, the growing number of Nonconformist chapels, often more impressive than the parish church, sharpened the need to make improvements. Many churches were no longer fit for purpose. The condition of St Michael's Church, where the Cassons had worshipped for over forty years, was typical. Rector John Jones wrote to the Bishop of Bangor, informing him that:

> the old church having fallen into a state of dilapidation and decay and to be no longer adequate to the increasing population of the village, an offer has been made by the benevolent charitable and well disposed Inhabitants and others to raise a structure more worthy of the place and times by voluntary contribution.

George added that, in his opinion, St Michael's was:

> one small Church … by the ravages of time … fallen into so dilapidated and dangerous a state as to have become altogether unfit for the sacred purpose for which it was designed.[12]

The Bishop approved, architects were appointed, and

George led the supervision of building work and fundraising. Workmen razed the old medieval church to the ground, digging up graves, including those of Esther's baby son, her husband, her brother-in-law, and his wife and children, moving them to a new churchyard. The new church stood to the west of the old one, on land once again provided by Lord Newborough. It was built in fashionable Neo-Gothic style. Open stalls replaced the old box pews, a spacious chancel made room for a proper choir, and the decoration was more elaborate than before. There were hot water pipes to add to the congregation's comfort. The old church could accommodate a congregation of 268, but now there was room for 479. Perhaps some villagers would be lured back from the Calvinist and Wesleyan Methodist chapels. The Cassons, like many of the richer families, paid for their seats, but the majority were free.

The day of consecration, at the end of September, was a triumph for George, though it would be several years before the church was paid for. William slipped easily back into village life. He could take his small sons round the old haunts, where his father had taken him, and regale them with the old tales he remembered from childhood. Up to visit the quarry, down to check on the tenants at Cynfal Fawr, over the field to show them the Pulpit Huw Llwyd, across the Cob to Porthmadog to see the ships, on up to Caernarfon to visit their aunt, their large brood of cousins, and the Turner family. He began to get to know the more recent arrivals, such as the Greaves and Samuel Holland. Ffestiniog was changing, the new church being one example of its development. The Cassons were still at the forefront of local activities. Eager to bring some benefit to the inhabitants, all three brothers joined the committee of the newly-formed 'Festiniog Reading Society', founded by the Rev John Jones. For five shillings a year, or one shilling and sixpence a quarter, people could read newspapers and periodicals, and borrow books for a week at a time. The Library and Reading Room stayed open until ten o'clock at night. While the name of the Society used English spelling, the rules were printed in English and Welsh.

Esther could now see all her sons every day. But for Fanny it was a difficult transition, made harder for her by the language difficulty. While the family spoke English at home, her two sons were soon chattering away in Welsh, quickly picking it up from village children, from servants, and from listening to their father, their uncles and their grandmother. It must have been galling for Fanny when she had to call upon her mother-in-law's help when instructing her own servants. That Christmas, George proposed the traditional toast 'To all old friends round Wallowbarrow Crag'. This no doubt occasioned talk about Seathwaite, and Fanny would have been shown yet another book that celebrated Esther's grandfather. *The Old Church Clock* was a work of fiction built around the character of Robert Walker, and written by Canon Richard Parkinson, Fellow of the Collegiate Church in Manchester. It was first published in two parts in the *Christian Magazine*, then in book form, which proved so popular that it was republished the following year. It had a didactic purpose, depicting a curate who represented the best of the Anglican tradition, now in competition with the large number of Nonconformist sects.

It cannot have been easy for Fanny to have the family of her in-laws celebrated in print, while there existed no such public tribute to the Galley Day Jackson family, despite the prestigious sealed licences to bear arms, stored at Betchton House, and the portraits hanging on its walls. Her later history suggests she found it difficult not to be the chief lady of the house. At Blaenyddôl, her mother-in-law was held in an affection and respect that may have galled her.

The following March, family life was shattered by the death of baby George. Neither William nor Fanny was present when he died, only Lowry Owens, a Welsh servant, who had to break the news to the parents. The fact that he did not sign his name on the death certificate, but made his mark instead, suggests that he had little or no English. He would have explained what happened in words which Fanny could not follow. A doctor later certified that the child died of convulsions. He was not yet seven months old. His grave was one of the first to be dug in the new churchyard.

Within months, William and his family had left Ffestiniog, after less than a year in residence, and returned to Liverpool. Whatever difficulty Fanny had had in settling into her new Welsh life, the baby's death cut it short precipitately. Esther had lost her first son when he too was just a few months old. She had had no choice but to stay, as Ffestiniog was the only home she had, the inn the only source of income, in the early days at the quarry. But it was too much to ask of Fanny to stay on in the house and village where she had lost a child, when another home still awaited, and where Platt, Son & Casson was back in business. By late spring 1846, she was pregnant again. Her next child was born in Liverpool. It would be fifteen years before William and his family took up residence in Wales again.

Notes

1   Casson Collection, Archifau Meirionydd/ Meirionydd Record Office, Dolgellau.
2   George Casson to John Casson, 4 December 1841, Z/DCH/1/1, AM/MRO
3   ibid and George Casson to John Casson, 13 December 1841, Z/DCH/1/2, AM/MRO
4   William Casson to George Casson, 4 March 1844, Z/DCH/4/159, AM/MRO

5 William Casson to George Casson, 4 January 1843, Z/DCH/4/155, AM/MRO

6 Joseph Russell to George Casson, 11 January 1843, Z/DCH/5/223, AM/MRO

7 Fereday, p. 8

8 Account drawn from *Liverpool Mercury*, 23 December 1842

9 Richards, *Gazeteer* p. 186; www.penfmorfa.com:The Slate Industry of North and Mid Wales

10 Amongst his papers was a report of a meeting of its shareholders, of which Sir William Wynne was chairman, held in August 1845.

11 14 May 1846, Z/DCH/4/161, AM/MRO

12 Robinson, p.77

Chapter 12

New Directions
1847–1852

One day, in the spring of 1847, John, the youngest of the three Casson brothers, took an express train from London to Liverpool, completing the journey in six-and-a-half hours. 'I never travelled with so much expedition and comfort,' he recounted in a letter to his brother George.[1] His journey, beginning at Euston Station, had been made possible by the amalgamation of three different railway companies, the previous summer, to form the London and North Western Railway, linking the capital with Birmingham, Manchester and Liverpool. It was the height of the railway boom, transforming British landscapes and townscapes, and changing the way of life for many of the country's inhabitants. Proposals for new lines proliferated. In North Wales, the Chester and Holyhead Railway was under construction, following the route of the Irish Mail. If William Madocks had had his way, Porthdinllaen on the Llŷn peninsula would have replaced Holyhead as the main departure point for Dublin, and a railway running from there through Tremadog and on to Ffestiniog would have been a likely project. Instead, a few months before John Casson was making his way from the south to the north of England, his brothers George and William (visiting from Liverpool) were attending a meeting in Porthmadog. The goal of this meeting was to promote a plan for a line from

Porthdinllaen to join the Chester and Holyhead line at Bangor.[2] While George still did not have his men use the slate railway from Ffestiniog, he was eager, like the other quarry owners, to see Caernarfonshire and Meirionydd connected to the expanding railway network, easing communication with other parts of the country. The North Wales Railway Company had already opened a line between Chester and Wrecsam, and it was hoped this company would take on the project. A line from Chester to Bangor opened in 1848. For the first two years, passengers were ferried across the Menai Strait, and then on to Holyhead. In 1850, Robert Stephenson's Britannia Bridge opened, but the inhabitants of south Caernarfonshire and Meirionydd had to wait several more years for the railway to arrive.

John's visit to London had been to transact financial business. Now in his early thirties, he was taking on a new role, that of a banker. This move showed how his aspirations differed from his father's, and also how the needs of a Victorian community were changing, as industries grew, needing ancillary services to support them. The days when Thomas Casson carried his contribution to the purchase of Diffwys in coins were going. There were banks in Aberystwyth, Treffynnon and Wrecsam by the end of the eighteenth century; but there had been none in Meirionydd until 1803, when the Cassons' partner, Hugh Jones, opened one in Dolgellau, mainly to support the local woollen trade. In 1826, the Country Bankers Act permitted joint-stock banks to be established throughout the land as long as they were sixty-five miles or more from London.[3] More banks opened, to meet the needs of regional businesses. 'What can the Bank of England know of country securities?' a correspondent of a Bangor paper had asked in 1810.[4] The infrastructure of North Wales lagged behind that of prosperous Merseyside, with a dearth of financial houses.

An agent of the Liverpool branch of the Bank of England had reported on the state of affairs before a select committee:

In travelling through Wales [in 1836], I could not help seeing that they were carrying on banking almost farcically, for instead of meeting one's ideas of a respectable establishment, there was a small cottage, more like a huckster's shop than a bank, with 'Bank' written in great characters over it.[5]

In that same year, a group of manufacturers and merchants in Liverpool set up a provisional committee to form a bank 'expressly to meet the growing demands of the principality.[6] It was called the 'North and South Wales Bank', with its Head Office in Liverpool, and a London agent to handle its transactions with the Bank of England. At one of its early meetings, the committee expressed their fear 'that apprehension might arise in the minds of the Welsh people that their branches were mere auxiliaries and cash feeders to Liverpool.' But they concluded that Liverpool was 'the Commercial Metropolis of North Wales', and they sought to reassure the Welsh of their good intentions by selecting trustees from the nobility and gentry of Wales.[7] One was Sir Love Parry Jones Parry, owner of Castell Madryn on the Llŷn peninsula, MP for Caernarfonshire, known affectionately as 'old Sir Love'.

Despite its name, most of the bank branches were in North Wales, including Porthmadog, Ffestiniog and Pwllheli. The 'Wales Bank', as it was usually known, went through some sticky times in its first few years, borrowing from its London agent, when it had overlent. In 1844, the sheer number of banks caused Robert Peel's government to pass the Bank Charter Act, fixing a maximum quantity of banknotes that could be in circulation at any one time, and guaranteeing that there would be sufficient reserves of gold and silver to back up the money in circulation. The following year, Mr George Rae, whom the Cassons were to get to know well, took over as a more competent general manager than his predecessor, and quickly succeeded in wiping out the bank's debts.

The Casson brothers first ventured into the world of banking early in 1846, when the 'Portmadoc and Festiniog [Porthmadog and Ffestiniog] Savings Bank' opened. Sir Love Parry Jones Parry was president, and George Casson was joint vice-president with the Rev Griffith Humphrey Owen, a church minister from near Cricieth. The other trustees included five more ministers, including the Rev John Jones, rector of Ffestiniog and Maentwrog, while the lay members included William Casson, Samuel Holland, and David Williams, a solicitor who lived on the south side of the Cob. This last gentleman was to become a significant figure in Meirionydd; George already knew him as Clerk of the Peace, attending the Quarter Sessions. John Casson was appointed Auditor, alongside Samuel Holland, and the Treasurer was Robert Lloyd, who managed the Wales Bank in Ffestiniog. The purpose of the Savings Bank was to provide 'a place of security' where the 'Labouring classes' could deposit their savings. 'Such a Bank,' read the letter to prospective trustees, 'would not only be of great service to them, in inducing them to save whatever small sum they can spare, and be of infinite benefit to them in times of sickness, want of employment &c, – but would also tend to instil into them, habits of economy, industry and self-dependence, and so make them more useful Members of Society.'[8] A nice mixture of philanthropy and moralising. William Casson's involvement showed his wish to remain in close touch with affairs in Ffestiniog, despite being resident back in Liverpool.

The Cassons might not have taken any further step into the world of banking, had it not been for the panic that hit all the banks in Britain in 1847, as the boom in railway speculation came to an end. The Bank Charter Act was suspended, so that the Bank of England could issue more notes, to restore confidence (anticipating the 'quantitative easing' of modern times). Still, several banks were forced to suspend payment. Under George Rae's prudent management, the Wales Bank should have come through the crisis intact, but in October of that year, a newspaper that circulated in Wales announced, erroneously, that it had stopped payment. Mr Rae issued a statement contradicting the assertion, but it was too late. 'The report,' as Mr Rae put it, 'exploded amongst our branches like a shell, and literally [sic] blew the bank up.'[9] Within weeks he had to close several branches. At that point, George and John Casson stepped in, together with Robert Lloyd, manager of the Ffestiniog branch, and offered to take it over, with the branches at Porthmadog and Pwllheli, and run a private bank. They would operate as 'Messrs Casson, Lloyd & Co, Bankers'. Within a couple of years, the Cassons had bought out Robert Lloyd, and from then on ran the business as 'Messrs Casson & Co, Bankers'.

No accounts survive showing how the two brothers financed the purchase, but since John was not a partner in the quarry and did not stand to inherit property until after his mother's death, it may be assumed that it was George's investment that made the purchase possible. But he remained in the background, while John took over the day-to-day management of the branches. In family lore, John Casson's name came down as 'the founder of the Casson bank.' From Mr Rae in the Head Office in Liverpool, and from those of the branch staff whom he retained, he learnt the nature of the bank's business, and relations with the Wales Bank remained cordial.

The day-to-day work of a country bank was to receive and exchange money in all its various forms: gold sovereigns, which were literally 'worth their weight in gold', so that a 'light' sovereign was not exchangeable for as much as its face value; silver, acceptable in packets of £5 or £10; and notes from other banks. The Wales Bank issued its own banknotes, promising 'to pay the bearer on demand the sum of ... ', but the 1844 Act did not allow new banks to do so. Much of the Casson bank's work and expense lay in turning cheques, drafts on other banks, interest coupons or Post Office orders into legal tender. The bank could make loans against security, such as mortgages on property, and also dealt in bills of exchange, a popular financial instrument of the period, that amounted to a loan. Foreign and investment business had to go through a London bank; the Cassons used the Union Bank in Mansion House as their London agent, lodged their bills of exchange there, and used their account there as reserve funds. Trips to London became a regular feature of John's life. He soon discovered that George and he were not entirely masters of their affairs. Within months of becoming a banker, he had some awkward dealing with the London agent, and wrote to his brother: 'Suffice it to say that we have pacified Mr Scrimgeour for the present, but all must depend upon a strict attention to our London account in the future.'[10]

Messrs Casson & Co was not a large concern; it employed far fewer men than the quarry. Each branch had a manager and an accountant, and an assistant or apprentice. John Casson became a familiar sight, riding between the three branches, encouraging farmers, quarriers, ship-builders and other working men to open an account, overcoming their reluctance and surprise at having to pay someone to look after their own money. He was soon in discussion about opening a sub-branch in Harlech.

The three Casson brothers now led contrasting lives. The quarry continued to occupy George's attention. When the project to build a railway connecting Porthdinllaen with the Chester-Holyhead line at Bangor appeared to be going forward, the Ffestiniog proprietors, including George, pressed for access to it, so as not to lose out to the Caernarfonshire quarries.[11] William's involvement was necessarily less active. But George and he were considering a radical proposal. A gentleman in London, whose identity has not come to light, offered to buy the Gelli land and its quarry. The other partners, William Turner and Hugh Jones, raised no objection and signed a letter authorising the sale.[12] George sent details of the property to the agent: its freehold farm; the quarry itself, yielding more than 4,000 tons of slate and slabs during the previous year; and additional land and houses that brought in rent. It was now providing employment for over 120 men and boys, and shipping mainly to London, Bristol and the east coast of England. He described new machines installed the previous year. Despite having stood out against using the slate railway, he itemised 'a Railway running within a short distance of the quarry, of which advantage might readily be taken.'[13] The one thing he held back on was the price he would be willing to accept. Correspondence continued into 1848, but then petered out. From the start, George had told Hugh Jones, 'I entertain some doubts about the Parties involved.'[14] No sale took place, and there was no further approach, but a seed had been sown in the minds of the second-generation partners.

George had other local responsibilities. Four of the trustees who established the 'Portmadoc and Festiniog Savings Bank' already had experience of working together for the welfare of the community; Samuel Holland, the solicitor David Williams, the Rev Griffith Owen and George were all appointed to the Board of Guardians for the Ffestiniog Union Workhouse. By the Poor Law Amendment Act of 1834, Wales was split into forty-eight unions, each responsible for building a local workhouse. Where once the poor had been helped through the parish Vestry, supplemented by charitable work carried out by women like Esther Casson, and occasional treats laid on by the gentry, there was now a nationwide system, and a new kind of bureaucracy, as the Board, made up of magistrates and elected members, considered the case of each applicant, and reported to the Poor Law Commission in London. The Ffestiniog Union Workhouse, built near Minffordd, opened in 1837, and served fifteen local parishes.[15]

On one occasion, George chaired a dinner at the end of a ploughing match that took place on a field by the inn at Maentwrog. In proposing his health, the vice-chairman 'dwelt upon his coming forward at all times in aid of anything that tends in any way to benefit his country and neighbourhood.' George returned thanks 'in an eloquent and clever speech, saying that he was glad, and ever should be so, to support such institutions.'[16] He sat regularly at the Meirionydd Quarter Sessions in Dolgellau and was appointed to the grand jury on a number of occasions. He also expanded his property portfolio. In 1849, he bought an estate north of Ffestiniog, 'Hafod Ysbyty and Gamallt'. In the sixteenth century, it had been owned by Robert Dudley, Earl of Leicester, who conveyed it to his brother, after which it came into Welsh hands. George's main interest was less in its history than in its mineral rights, as deposits of lead and copper had been detected there.

He remained active in St Michael's Church, and in its national school. In 1846, the Government set up an enquiry into the state of education in Wales. Three commissioners were appointed, who submitted their report, published in three blue volumes, in April 1847. Their account of the school in Ffestiniog was positive. Of nearly ninety children enrolled, over three-quarters of them were in attendance on the day the commissioner visited (since the visit was in December, few of the boys would have been absent through work in the quarries). The children were considered to be 'decidedly superior in Scriptural knowledge', and many could understand simple questions in English and answer in English. Other subjects were reading, writing, arithmetic, geography and music, the last of these being an unusual addition, to which George, who was a great music-lover, may have given special encouragement.[17] But overall, the report was damning; the commissioners did not speak Welsh, and they exaggerated the weaknesses and defects they found in many communities. The report was especially critical of the Welsh language, stating that is was 'a vast drawback to Wales, and a manifold barrier to the moral progress and commercial prosperity of the people.'[18] Some views, gleaned from clergymen opposed to Nonconformism, suggested that the meetings and Bible study classes of the Calvinist Methodists, the dominant sect in North Wales, were 'nurseries of licentiousness.'[19] The result was a rise in Welsh patriotism in reaction. The publication of the report came to be known as 'Brad y Llyfrau Gleision', the 'Treachery of the Blue Books', an echo of the Treachery of the Long Knives, when the Saxons had begun their conquest of native Britons. The Calvinist Methodists, who had previously had little interest in politics, began to consider the need to have a greater voice in Parliament and to question the union between church and state.[20]

In the ensuing debates, George, firmly supporting the church, had an ecumenical outlook. Politically, he was a staunch Tory, and enjoyed a close relationship, both socially and politically with Richard Richards, MP for Meirionydd. In the general election of August 1847, he seconded Richard Richards' nomination, and referred to his support eleven years earlier. Richard Richards, elected unopposed, spoke warmly of George's endorsement, explained how firmly he supported the established church, and how he would not support any kind of endowment to the Roman Catholic church, nor the admission of Jews into Parliament (this was the election when Lionel Rothschild, son of Nathan Meyer Rothschild, won in the City of London, but would not swear the usual oath and so could not take his seat).

Both William and John were present at Richard Richards' election dinner, but in Liverpool, William was coming under another influence. Benjamin Platt's father, John Platt, was a local Liberal councillor for South Toxteth and had long been a supporter of electoral reform. William began to shift his loyalty away from the Conservative Party. Although distanced from Welsh politics, he had enough concerns in Wales to bring him back from time to time, remaining an adopted Welshman at heart. He supported the Welsh charity schools, which catered for the children of the numerous Welsh families in Liverpool; he joined the Liverpool Cambrian Society, and participated in the local celebrations of St David's Day. He also threw himself into the wider cultural life of the town. In the summer of 1849, he and his brother-in-law, Benjamin Platt, were on the organising committee of a 'Grand Fancy Floral and Musical Festival', in aid of the charity hospitals.

The explicit purpose of the festival was to include 'the industrious classes', as well as the better off. There were regimental bands, and a grand marquee housing the 'fancy fair', consisting of needlework and other craftwork. There were works of art and a specimen of a land tortoise from the Galapagos Islands, supposed to have been 200 years old, but unfortunately dead before it reached England. The refreshment tent served champagne, sherry and wine, ale and porter at; it offered a monster cheese weighing 625 pounds, a loaf three yards in length, and plenty of roast beef.

William instilled in his boys a love of things scientific and mechanical. They enjoyed the exhibits that showed off new technological wonders: a model of the new Corporation Baths about to be erected in the town; a mechanism whereby a squirrel, revolving on a drum wheel between two glass cases, started two jets of water to play inside the cases. The Telegraph Company set up sheds where they explained and demonstrated the principles of the telegraph, sending short-distance messages. They watched a galvanic battery blowing up a ship. They admired the ingenuity of electric mechanisms, including a device designed to catch a burglar; by stepping on a certain spot, he would set off a spring that completed the current to a pistol, which then fired. There was a theatre, there were boat races. A boy who fell into the water was saved by a man wearing a newly patented American life preserver. There were balloon ascents and a 'Monster Concert' in the Theatre Royal.[21]

The contrast with George Casson's social life was marked. In the same month that William Casson was introducing his family to these public splendours, his older brother was attending the coming-of-age of William Edward Oakeley, heir of Tan-y-Bwlch, proposing his health and regaling the whole company with a song.[22] He was a well-known, well-liked, prominent member of the small group of landed gentry (including quarry owners) around Ffestiniog – a big fish in a small pond – while William was one among thousands enjoying the wider world of industrial development. Members of the family kept in touch through letters and visits.

Esther continued to head the household at Blaenyddôl. She collected more grandchildren, with Bess completing her brood of six sons and three daughters, while Fanny produced two more daughters, another Ann and another

Esther, and then a third son, Randal, the name coming from her father's family. George's correspondence contained references to cousins from Seathwaite, who spent time at Blaenyddôl. When they were old enough, William's two older sons, Galley and Tom, visited Ffestiniog independently of their parents, continuing to join in country sports with their uncles and growing more fluent in Welsh. (Tom would later remember a Seathwaite relation who arrived for a fortnight's visit and stayed for 'a year or so'[23].) Relations with Benjamin Smith remained cool, though John was able to write to his mother to assure her that he had stayed with Bess and that: 'My reception has been very pleasant in every respect and no allusion has been made in the slightest to past differences.'[24] The other Benjamin was popular with the Cassons. On one occasion John changed his plans to make sure he would be at Blaenyddôl to coincide with his favoured brother-in-law's fishing trip there: 'By so doing I can with better grace devote more time to our brother piscator Benjamin Platt.'[25]

The Census taken in the spring of 1851 offers a glimpse into the household of each branch of the family. Esther was at home at Blaenyddôl, with John. She kept two men, William and Robert Lloyd, to look after the farm work, while another man and one maid, worked in the house. Her children had more numerous households. Benjamin and Bess Smith, at Bron Seiont with their nine children, had three servants: a cook, a general servant and another maid, who combined the duties of waitress and nursemaid. Their oldest son, Thomas Casson Smith, was training for the church, while the other children attended day school in Caernarfon. In Liverpool, Benjamin and Ann Platt lived with their two daughters, two maidservants, one Irish and one Welsh, and a governess. William and Fanny were entertaining their brother George as a houseguest. Their household included one Welsh maid and one from the Isle of Man, an Irish nursemaid to look after Randal, and a governess from Cornwall, evidence of the high level of immigration to the town.

Barely a month after this poll-count of the four households was recorded, the family was in mourning, for Esther's younger daughter Ann died of peritonitis, at the age of forty-three, after suffering three days of agonising pain. The cause – a burst appendix, a perforated ulcer, or diverticulitis – was not recorded. Four months later, John Casson was still writing on black-edged notepaper. Towards the end of that year, William made some changes. In September, John Platt died. The financial state of his company was parlous; it had never prospered since the fire. In January, his son Benjamin and William Casson dissolved their partnership by mutual consent.[26] By March, Benjamin narrowly escaped bankruptcy.[27] William took over the distillery, and in order to fund it, he asked George to take out a mortgage on his Cynfal property. Then, he sold his share in Diffwys to George. This decision, like the earlier negotiations on selling, disrupted the continuity that his father and uncle had planned for.

The Casson brothers' outlook contrasted with that of John W. Greaves, who saw his future in acquiring, working and improving a quarry of his own. After running the Oakeley quarry for twelve years, he had bought land on the northern side of Blaenau, at Llechwedd. For years, according to the story that came down through his family, he failed to strike the rich vein he hoped lay beneath it and was on the verge of ruin. At last, at the time William was selling his share of Diffwys, Greaves was advised to try in a slightly different place, and so he made contact with the Old Vein that stretched into the Casson land and his fortunes changed. He became the prosperous owner of what was to become the longest surviving quarry in Ffestiniog.[28] The hint leading to his find came from a Diffwys man. Forty years later, Tom Casson would write to one of his brothers that '[the Greaves family] owe us everything.'[29]

While Esther must have regretted William cutting off his connection with the quarry, and endured the sorrow of Ann's death, she could rejoice at the succession of George to the office held by her late brother-in-law and by her late husband, for he too was appointed 'High Sheriff of Merionethshire', for the year 1852/3. At the end of June, he sent a formal summons to his brother William, as a member of the landed gentry, to serve on the grand jury for the Assizes the following month. Like his uncle, George presided over a general election, this one caused by the collapse of Lord John Russell's Whig government. His friend Richard Richards had retired, and the Conservative candidate, again elected unopposed in July of that year, was William Watkin Edward Wynne of Peniarth, son of the William Wynne who had sold the quarry land to the Cassons. There was the usual victory dinner at the Blue Lion Inn, Harlech, where the High Sheriff's health was drunk. George responded, saying that in performing his official duties earlier in the day, he had sworn not to show 'partiality, favour, or affection.' But now, he was about to show partiality by proposing the health of the newly elected member, which he then did. [30]

Later in the proceedings, a local clergyman, the Rev Evan Owen, proposed the health of Mrs Casson, of Blaenyddôl, the mother of the High Sheriff, 'a lady,' he said, 'whose worth was little known from her unobtrusive life.' He could speak of her worth, he went on, 'from having professionally witnessed her many charitable acts and kindnesses to the poor in her neighbourhood.'[31] According to the newspaper account, 'the High Sheriff returned thanks in feeling terms.'

After several more toasts, the new MP proposed the usual tribute to '*Morwynion Glân Meirionydd*', and one gentleman, considered something of a local wag, was invited to sing a song in their honour. Rather than sing, he made a speech in which he contended 'that some of his friends around him – the High Sheriff at their head – acted very inconsistently in drinking the health of *Morwynion Glân Meirionydd*, when they were doing all in their power to injure their health by refusing to take them as the partners of their joys, and the soothers of their sorrows.' George made no response to this teasing about his single status, but he had another reason to feel the effect of what was said on that occasion. As he acknowledged the words in praise of his mother, his thoughts must have turned to her frail state of health. A week after he attended the election dinner, she became seriously ill, and died three weeks later, from 'disease of the liver and stomach', probably cancer, while attended by her old servant, William Lloyd.

Esther was buried beside her husband in St Michael's churchyard. No-one left any account of what she contributed to public life. The Rev Evan Owen's words of praise, reported so near the end of her life, were the only recorded acknowledgment of her worth that was made in her adopted homeland. Yet there was one other published tribute to her. In the year of her death, there was a new edition of *The Old Church Clock*, to which Canon Parkinson added a more extensive introduction. He included a statement from an (unnamed) friend of the family, praising Esther's late mother and aunts, loyal members of St Thomas' Church in Liverpool, then comparing Esther and her family with them:

Mrs Casson, daughter of Mrs. Wilson, residing at Festiniog, Merionethshire [is] ... equally amiable, and admirable for every Christian virtue, and in no way degenerate from the parent stock. She had three sons and two daughters, all arrived at maturity, and all giving abundant promise of handing down the practical example of love and obedience in which they had been trained from their infancy.[32]

As well as these words of conventional praise for her charitable acts and virtue, Esther's reputation has been passed down each generation of her family, as a woman to be admired for what she contributed to her family and neighbourhood. One reason we remember her is that we have her portrait. Ever since it was finished, her gaze has been directed out towards those who look on it. It has hung on the walls of a succession of family houses. She has sat, as if overseeing the lives of her descendants, a motherly figure, to whom you might turn for encouragement, but whose expression – purposeful, yet serene – might make you hesitate before you undertook some rash or selfish action.

Esther Casson

Esther Casson was not the heroine who single-handedly pioneered a slate industry and saved the family fortunes. But she did enough, above and beyond her role as a wife and mother, to be praised, and remembered with pride by her family. The values she came to represent could be said to bind her descendants together: the importance of appreciating the women's achievements alongside the men's; a work ethic inescapably bound up with a sense of social responsibility; pride in being, if only by adoption, Welsh. Hers was indeed an unobtrusive life, which might best be understood through the words of the novelist George Eliot, describing Dorothea in *Middlemarch*:

> the effect of her being on those around her was incalculably diffusive: for the growing good of the world is partly dependent on unhistoric acts; and that things are not so ill with you and me as they might have been, is half owing to the number who lived faithfully a hidden life ... [33]

Notes

1 John Casson to George Casson, 13 May 1847, Z/DCH/1/3, AM/MRO
2 *NWC*, 2 February 1847
3 Orbell, John and Turton, Alison, *British Banking: A Guide to Historical Records*, 2001, p. 3
4 Dodd, p. 319
5 Orbell and Turton p. 180
6 *The North and South Wales Bank, 1836-1908*, p 4, HSBC London archives
7 ibid, p. 6
8 Holland, Appendix II, p32
9 Orbell and Turton, p. 183
10 John Casson to George Casson, 30 July 1848, Z/DCH/1/6, AM/MRO
11 It did not materialise. A line from Bangor to Caernarfon opened in 1851, at which time John Casson immediately proposed an extension to Porthmadog, *NWC*, 9 Oct 1851
12 Letter of Authority signed by William Turner and Hugh Jones, 11 February 1847, Z/DCH/3/80, AM/MRO
13 George Casson to Mr Lewis Lloyd, Finsbury Square, London, 31 January 1848, Z/DCH/3/84, AM/MRO

14 Draft of letter from George Casson to Hugh Jones, on the back of Hugh Jones to George Casson, 16 June, 1847, Z/DCH/3/81, AM/MRO

15 Minute Books of Ffestiniog Union Workhouse, AM/MRO

16 *NWC*, 23 March, 1847.

17 *Reports of the Commissioners of Enqury into the State of Education in Wales* Appendix A, p. 120

18 *Reports*, p. 66

19 Davies, John, *A History of Wales*, New Edition, 2007, p. 381

20 ibid, p. 382, quoting Lewis Edwards of Bala, editor of *Y Traethodydd*, 'The Essayist'

21 Account taken from *Liverpool Echo*, 14 August 1849

22 *NWC*, 7 August 1849

23 Tom Casson to Randal Casson, 14 August, 1903, family papers

24 John Casson to Esther Casson, Sep 3 1851, Z/DCH/1/9, AM/MRO

25 John Casson to George Casson, 11 June 1848, Z/DCH/1/4, AM/MRO

26 Notice in *Liverpool Mercury*, 9 January 1852

27 William Casson to George Casson, 13 March 1852, Z/DCH/3/90, AM/MRO

28 Drage, p. 10

29 Tom Casson to Randal Casson, 5 January 1891, family papers

30 *NWC*, 23 July, 1852

31 ibid

32 Parkinson, ed Evans, p. 43

33 Eliot, George, *Middlemarch*, The Folio Society, 1999, p. 759

Chapter 13

Victorian Gentlemen
1853–1859

In the period following their mother's death in 1852, the three Casson brothers, George, William and John, enjoyed what the historian G. M. Trevelyan called 'the fat years of mid-Victorian prosperity.'[1] The Ffestiniog slate quarries, including Diffwys, were thriving. The town of Porthmadog was an important shipbuilding centre, and Liverpool vied with London as the first port in the kingdom, handling larger ships and carrying greater tonnage.[2] In England, a network of canals enabled transport by water, while railway lines ran through much of the country. But communication in Meirionydd and Caernarfonshire still lagged behind England, the mountainous terrain making engineering schemes daunting. George and John Casson were amongst those eager to promote improvements. In May 1853, John attended a meeting to pursue a scheme to build a railway line from Caernarfon to Pwllheli and Porthmadog, but it was not advanced enough to put before Parliament that session.[3] In December, both brothers attended a meeting in Porthmadog, to discuss a resolution to build a road bridge across Traeth Bach, at the estuary of the river Dwyryd, facilitating the journey between the two counties. At this time, travellers had either to cross the sands at low tide, just as they had across Traeth Mawr before the Cob was built, or take a seven-mile detour on the Maentwrog turnpike.

Objections came from some residents at Tan-y-Bwlch and Maentwrog, since the turnpike brought them valuable trade which might be lost. Those who supported the new bridge argued that summer tourists, who now made up much of this trade, would not be deterred from visiting the well-known beauty spots in the vale of Ffestiniog.

There were familiar faces at the meeting: W. W. E. Wynne, the Meirionydd MP; James Spooner of Morfa Lodge; John W. Greaves, now living at Tan-yr-Allt, Madocks' Tremadog house; Samuel Holland, married and living at Plas Penrhyn, a hilltop property overlooking both Traeths; and David Williams, the solicitor who had joined the Cassons as trustee of the Savings Bank, and had sat with George on the Board of Trustees of the Ffestiniog Union Workhouse. He had built a fine house, which he called 'Castell Deudraeth', in honour of the ancient castle ruins that stood nearby. He had some of the nearby swampy land drained, and began to develop a planned town, Penrhyndeudraeth, partly modelled on Tremadog. Also present was someone new to the neighbourhood, who was to become closely linked with the Casson family. Lewis Holland Thomas, a retired master mariner, had recently bought a property at Talsarnau, on the south side of Traeth Bach, north of Harlech (where there was now a sub-branch of the Messrs Casson & Co). The scheme for the bridge did not receive parliamentary approval and was dropped.[4] It would be over ten years before it was revived.

In earlier times, William Turner would have been at that meeting, but he had died a month before, aged eighty-seven. For some years, he had taken little part in public life, but he was still honoured as a major figure in the local area. He had been High Sheriff of Caernarfonshire in 1823 and of Meirionydd in 1832, played a leading part in the development of the Dinorwic Quarry, and had an interest in others. The quarry at Diffwys still operated as 'William Turner & Company', even though it was more familiarly known as 'Mr Casson's quarry'. On the day of Turner's funeral, all the shops in Caernarfon closed as a mark of respect.[5]

George Casson and Thomas Turner, who had taken over his father's interests in Ffestiniog, now began to think seriously about selling Gelli. Although William Casson had sold his share, he involved himself closely in their plans. There was another potential purchaser, but again, no record of their identity. This time, the three men were considering the possibility that they might join in with any new company that bought the land and worked the quarry. 'I coincide with William's and I believe your views,' wrote Thomas Turner to George, three weeks after his father's death, 'that if by taking an interest we could increase the price in a larger proportion than without it, I should have no objection to take a limited amount in the new concern.'[6]

There was much concern about the Crimean War at this time. In November 1854, John Casson was at a meeting in Bala to consider the setting up of a Patriotic Fund 'for the relief and succour of those whose husbands and parents may fall in the present war with Russia.' Britain had entered the war eight months earlier, to stop Russia gaining too much power over the waning Ottoman Empire. In September, the year-long Siege of Sevastopol had begun. John Casson shared the sentiments of Lord Mostyn, Lord Lieutenant of Merionethshire, who spoke eloquently at the Bala meeting, of 'England's cause and England's glory.' For them, the cause and glory of Wales was identical with that of England: 'The Principality would not be backward in following the example set us by our more affluent countrymen [in England], but that every man, woman, and child, would contribute, according to their means, in mitigating the sufferings of the soldier's widow and the soldier's orphan.'[7]

A month later, Alfred Tennyson's poem, 'The Charge of the Light Brigade', was published, increasing patriotic fervour. John Casson became Treasurer of the Fund in Ffestiniog, receiving contributions amounting to over £100 from all the quarries.

When the war ended, early in 1856, much was made of the returning officers. William and John, their brother-in-law Benjamin Smith and his oldest son all subscribed to a collection, of which Thomas Turner was Treasurer, honouring a local hero, Major Hugh Rowland[8] (later Sir Hugh) for his gallantry at the Battle of Inkerman in 1854. He was one of nineteen men, and the first Welshman, to be awarded the Victoria Cross, a medal newly created by Queen Victoria early in 1856, and backdated to that battle. The Cassons' support for the military and patriotic cause did not die down with the end of the war. They became closely involved in the volunteer movement, which now gathered force.

Despite the fact that the British and French had fought beside one another in Crimea, fear of French aggression was the chief motivation of those who wanted to re-establish volunteer companies in Britain. In 1858, Felice Orsini, an Italian revolutionary, attempted to assassinate the French Emperor Napoleon III (nephew of Napoleon Bonaparte) and Empress Eugenie, throwing bombs at their carriage. The fact that the bombs had been manufactured and tested in England led to fierce anti-British feelings amongst many of the French. Neither regular Army and Navy officers, nor the governments (alternating between that of Viscount Palmerston, Liberal; and the Earl of Derby, Conservative) were enthusiastic about raising Volunteer Corps. But pressure came from the general public, encouraged by newspapers, influencing such men as the Cassons to 'arm for peace', a popular slogan. Queen Victoria and Prince

Albert added to the pressure, bringing back their impression of the extent of French fortifications, when they visited Cherbourg in August 1858.[9] Lord Tennyson expressed the popular view in a four-verse poem 'The War', published in *The Times* in 1859, where he privileged military readiness over political reform:

Let your reforms for a moment go!
Look to your butts and take good aims!
Better a rotten borough or so,
Than a rotten flesh and a city in flames!
Storm, Storm, Riflemen form!
Ready, be ready, against the storm!
Riflemen, riflemen, riflemen form!

The politicians capitulated to popular opinion. Derby's government authorised Lords Lieutenant in the counties to raise a corps under the provisions of the Volunteer Act 1804. At first, the terms of employment were vague, and Prince Albert drafted more specific instructions: the Volunteer Corps were to operate in closed country, using their skill with the rifle, reliance on their comrades, and their knowledge of local topography 'to hang with the most telling effect upon the flanks and communications of a hostile army.'[10] Palmerston, returning to power, became convinced of the French Emperor's aggressive intentions; and Sidney Herbert, as his Secretary for War, established the Volunteer Corps more firmly. The Casson brothers were quick to support the movement. In April 1860, George chaired a meeting in Penrhyndeudraeth to discuss the proposed creation of a Volunteer Rifle Corps in the area. John W. Greaves, High Sheriff of Caernarfonshire that year, was in favour, as were Nathan Mathew, Deputy Lieutenant of the county; Samuel Holland and Lewis Holland Thomas also attended. The following week, George chaired a second meeting at the Oakeley Arms (the name by which the Tan-y-Bwlch Inn was sometimes known). 'We firmly believe,' the press report stated, 'that such a movement expresses the true feeling and spirit of our young Welshmen and with proper and enlightened guidance and encouragement, there would be found no lack of men ready, nay anxious to serve their Queen and country.'[11]

Within months, there were three 'Merionethshire Rifle Volunteer Corps', the 3rd being captained by John Casson, with divisions at Ffestiniog, Blaenau Ffestiniog, Maentwrog, Trawsfynydd and Harlech. Each one had to exercise on a site with a safe range of 200 yards; it had to have a 'place of custody' for arms, and a uniform for the men, approved by the Lord Mostyn. The government supplied twenty-five Enfield rifles per 100 volunteers.[12] Two drill sergeants set about training the men, engaging every night with one or another of the divisions. There was much discussion about the uniform the men would wear, but by March 1861, nothing had been decided, as 'there is a dispute as to the colour.'[13] However, by Easter Monday, the first open-air drill took place at Maentwrog. Like the Cader Idris Volunteers, active during the Napoleonic Wars, in which Thomas Casson may well have served, the Merionethshire Volunteer Corps resembled *Dad's Army* in their early efforts. The press report of that Easter Monday drill damned with faint praise:

> As this was the first time … it could not be expected to come off very satisfactorily. It must also be remembered that all the divisions had not been joined together in one company before … Making due allowances we may safely say, that the different evolutions were gone through with great credit.

A military officer who was present further testified 'that he never saw a body of men before acquitting themselves so creditably ... considering the short time they had been under instruction.' The best part of the day was no doubt the 'jolly refreshment prepared for them by the order of Captain Casson at the Tanybwlch [Tan-y-Bwlch] and Grape's Inns.' The men, it was reported, 'behaved themselves very becomingly, and the day was passed in a very pleasant manner.'[14] Clearly, reasons for signing up as a volunteer were social as much as patriotic. A few months later, Captain John Casson put the men through their drill himself. Again, allowances had to be made. 'We sincerely hope,' ran the press report, 'that he will continue, being confident that, with a little practice, he will become an efficient master of the duties which he has undertaken to perform, as commander of the above corps.'[15] However, two months after that, Captain Casson tendered his resignation. The men were too widely dispersed; although there were 125 members, only eight or nine turned up for drill in one place at the same time. The officers were disappointed at the lukewarm attitude of the men, while the men were offended that Captain Casson appeared only at the drill in Maentwrog, leaving the other divisions entirely to the drill sergeants. At the end of the following year, George invited all who subscribed to the funds of the Corps to attend a meeting at the Grapes Inn, Maentwrog, to discuss 'the expedience of dissolving the corps, or making further efforts to promote its efficiency.'[16] The 2nd and 3rd Merionethshire were then combined with the 1st.[17] Despite the scattered population, there was still enthusiasm for this patriotic endeavour.

Captain John Casson's resignation was not the end of the family's active participation in the Volunteer Corps. In Liverpool, where there was a more cohesive population, the movement thrived. While William Casson did not take any part himself, his two older sons, now in their teens, were enthusiastic members. Thirteen battalions of the Lancashire Rifle Volunteer Corps had formed by the end of 1859.[18] In February 1860, the Welsh Literary Society formed the 39th Battalion, which was known as the 'Liverpool Welsh'. Tom Casson joined immediately. He proved to be such a good shot that in November, when he had just turned eighteen years of age, he won a cup in a competition of the County of Lancaster Rifle Association. When the Liverpool Welsh had its first annual meeting in December, he was seated in a place of honour in front of the chairman 'and attracted much attention.'[19] His older brother, Galley, did not make his mark in the Liverpool Welsh. By 1861, aged nineteen, he had moved to Wales, where he began working in the Casson bank in Pwllheli. He joined the 5th Battalion of the 'Caernarvonshire Rifle Volunteers' based in that town and was soon appointed Ensign. From then on, their activities as volunteers became an important part of both the young men's lives.

George continued to pursue the sale of Diffwys and appointed a local agent to handle the matter. Tom Casson soon joined his older brother, to work in the Porthmadog branch of the Casson bank. If either of the two young men had expressed interest in slate, the future of Diffwys might have looked different, but neither of them had known the first William or Thomas; the continuity was broken. While banking offered both young men secure employment, it by no means offered a high-flying career, or entailed sophisticated fund management. A year or so before Tom Casson joined, there was a theft of money from the Porthmadog branch. The perpetrator was caught; John Casson was an important witness at the trial, which was held at the Chester Assizes, rather than Caernarfon, to avoid jury prejudice.[20] The account of the trial reveals the casual, not to say ramshackle, methods of operation.

There was a discrepancy of over £1,000 in the accounts, arising, John Casson said, 'from small payments made by the firm during several years, which had not been written off.' The accused, a Mr Maurice, had been employed by the bank for six months, and promoted to manager, despite having no previous experience. He had left the bank and opened his own account there. The theft of a bag containing £600 in gold occurred because the apprentice placed it in a safe which was kept unlocked throughout the day. Mr Maurice had come into the bank and asked about a cheque, which the accountant went to fetch, leaving Mr Maurice near the unlocked safe. There was further circumstantial evidence against him, and the jury found him guilty. At the end of the trial, the Counsel for the Defence 'made strong observations on the loose manner in which the business of the bank was conducted.'[21]

George Casson, sitting on the bench for the Petty Sessions, now held in Penrhyndeudraeth, had more minor matters to deal with. On one occasion, his own servant, Robert Lloyd, was charged with 'riding without reins' on the public highway. He was fined 5 shillings for that offence, and as he was drunk at the time, an extra 5 shillings, as well as costs of 8s 6d.[22] On another occasion, the three presiding magistrates dealt with a deserter, remanding him in custody while awaiting a decision from the Secretary of War.[23] Cases showing the plight of mothers without financial support were still frequent. One day, George attended the examination of a young woman from Maentwrog who was accused of concealing the birth of a child; the examination lasted for four-and-a-half hours, and the woman was committed for trial at the Assizes.

Notwithstanding the casual accounting methods

adopted at the bank, George Casson saw a more orderly society than in his youth. When W. W. E. Wynne, MP, presided at one of the Petty Sessions, he congratulated the local police force on the low rate of crime in the county. Her Majesty's Inspectorate of Constabulary had been established a few years before, with a clear staffing structure of constables and inspectors.[24] One of its reports referred to the police of Meirionydd being 'though a small force, in the highest degree efficient.'[25]

St Michael's Church continued to be the focus for much of George's social life. By 1853, the cost of the new building had been paid off, thanks to the efforts of the Treasurer, Mr George Chessell, agent in the Welsh Slate Company, and a good friend of the Cassons. George Casson was eager to promote harmony between church and chapel in Ffestiniog and Blaenau. He organised a concert, the profits to be divided between the national school in Ffestiniog, run by the church; and the British school, run by the chapels. The Rev Edward Stephens, minister of Horeb Congregational Church in Dwygyfylchi, a village near Conwy, conducted his own composition. It was sung by the hundred voices of the Ffestiniog choir, of which George was an enthusiastic supporter. He also instigated the Fishing Society as well as the 'Festiniog Reading Society', and joined the committee of the Royal Welsh Yacht Club, the first in Wales, founded by Llewelyn Turner, youngest son of William Turner, now Mayor of Caernarfon. Though not involved in Porthmadog's *eisteddfod* in 1852, George was president of the one held in Ffestiniog in 1854.[26] The revival of this tradition had gathered pace in reaction to the publication of the Blue Books, so critical of Welsh language, culture and education. One of Her Majesty's Inspectors of Schools was Matthew Arnold (already a published poet).[27] He had received the Blue Books and stated, as part of his response:

It must always be the desire of a Government to render its dominions, as far as possible, homogeneous ... Sooner or later, the difference of language between Wales and England will probably be effaced ... an event which is socially and politically so desirable.[28]

Welsh indignation did not yet take organised political form but led to greater promotion of the language and culture. George and his brothers were all comfortable in the Welsh language and encouraged the use of it. On one occasion, he accompanied William and Fanny to the examinations of the children at the Welsh schools in Liverpool, where one boy delivered an entire chapter from the Book of Proverbs in Welsh.[29]

Although he visited Liverpool from time to time, George was firmly based at Blaenyddôl, enjoying the high status he shared with other quarry owners. John was more peripatetic. His letters to George were full of family news and outings he had been on: a concert with two of Bess's children in Caernarfon, where he was delighted to hear 'some of our own glees very creditably performed'; and another in Liverpool, 'better singing I never heard I think.'[30] He went on a visit with William's family to the Lees at Ashton-under-Lyne. Samuel Lees and his wife had been wealthy manufacturers who created some impressive ironworks at Park Bridge, building rollers and spindles for the cotton industry.[31] Now their sons, friends of the William Cassons, ran it, living in nearby Dean House, described by one visitor as 'a little lofty Palace' surrounded by meadows and woodland.

Liverpool itself offered a wealth of leisure activities to the William Casson and Platt families. As well as supporting the Welsh charity schools and helping to organise a ball to raise funds for it, William continued to attend meetings of the

William Casson

Liverpool Cambrian Society, which met to dine and celebrate Welsh culture. Toxteth Park, where he and his family lived, was then a pleasant area of southern Liverpool, near Princes Park, an elegant civic park designed by Joseph Paxton, some years before he created the Crystal Palace for the Great Exhibition. William and Fanny could promenade there, dressed in the fashionable outfits of the day. William top-hatted, wearing a morning coat or frock coat, depending on the time of day (a well-dressed man was expected to have four kinds of coats). He had his likeness taken in a photograph, showing his fashionable curled hair and side-whiskers.

No surviving portrait or photograph can be clearly identified as Fanny. She had black hair, which would have been parted in the middle and coiled around her ears. She would have worn numerous layers of petticoats over her chemise and drawers, suffered the restrictions of a whalebone corset, and worn a crinoline cage to support her full skirts. New dyes meant she displayed a dazzling array of colours in her bonnets, shawls and dresses.

Theatres and concerts continued to offer them entertainment and some opportunities for participation. One of William's nieces, Benjamin Platt's daughter, wrote and performed a prologue for the Sheridan Amateur Theatrical Society's production of Bulwer Lytton's *Money* in

October 1855. Tom Casson, a proficient keyboard player, was delighted when that same year saw the installation of a superb organ in the newly opened St George's Hall. This was an impressive edifice built by Liverpool Corporation to house the Assize Courts and provide the town with a great hall for entertainments, as well as a smaller, elegant concert hall. Members of the Liverpool Corporation had travelled to the Great Exhibition in London to choose an organ-builder. There, they heard William Thomas Best, already the organist of the Liverpool Philharmonic Society, playing an organ designed by one of the greatest of English organ-builders, Henry Willis. They immediately contracted him to design the instrument for St George's Hall. Before moving to Wales, Tom Casson struck up an acquaintance with W. T. Best, and developed an interest in organ design that would shape his future career.

For some years, William kept a scrapbook, into which he glued miscellaneous items that took his fancy. It holds the dance card for a charity ball and the menu for a grand ball at the Town Hall. These items conjure up images of Fanny and William stepping into a carriage which took them through the gas-lit streets to the grand Town Hall, and entering its brightly illuminated ballroom, Fanny decked in a wide, double-skirted gown of silk, her neck and lower arms bare, flowers in her hair, jewels on her wrist, while William would have worn black trousers and a black tail coat, with white waistcoat and cravat.

Other civic splendours followed. In 1858, William attended a public breakfast at St George's Hall, in honour of William Brown, Liberal MP for South Lancashire, to commemorate the laying of the foundation stone of the grand building which was to house a free public library, much of which Mr Brown was financing. It opened two years later, named after its benefactor. Its grandeur contrasted with the one-room Library and Reading Room in Ffestiniog. Yet both demonstrate how Victorian gentlemen like George and William encouraged opportunities for general education, as well as the Bible-based curriculum offered by the national school in Ffestiniog and the Welsh charity school in Liverpool. William's own boys attended the Royal Institute School, while a distant cousin of his, Mrs Forster (a great-granddaughter of Robert Walker), was matron of the Bluecoat Hospital School for poor children.

If Fanny perused her husband's scrapbook, she would have noted that, as well as souvenirs of events in Liverpool, there were many items commemorating events and activities in Wales. This might have given her warning that, as the 1850s ended, he was contemplating a return there.

Notes

1 Trevelyan, G. M. *A Shortened History of England,* reprint 1970, p. 482
2 Aughton, Peter, *Liverpool, A People's History,* 1990, p. 219
3 *NWC,* 27 May 1853
4 Dodd, p. 319
5 *Carnarvon and Denbigh Herald,* 12 November, 1853
6 Thomas Turner to George Casson, 28 November 1853, Z/DCH/3/93, AM/MRO
7 *NWC* 18 November,1854
8 *NWC* 19 July, 2 August 1856
9 Beckett, Ian F W, *Riflemen Form: A Study of the Rifle Volunteer Movement, 1859-1908,* 1982, p. 17
10 ibid p. 22
11 *NWC* 14 April,1860
12 Beckett p. 24
13 *NWC* 30 March, 1861
14 *NWC* 6 April 1861
15 *NWC* 7 September 1861
16 *NWC* 5 December 1862
17 Beckett p. 298

18 ibid pp. 293-295

19 *Liverpool Daily Post*, 1 November and 8 December, 1860.

20 In 1856, Palmer's Act had been passed, allowing a criminal case to be tried on neutral territory, rather than locally, to avoid jury prejudice. (Wikipedia: Central Criminal Court Act, 1856)

21 *NWC* 15 August 1859. There were witnesses to Mr Maurice having paid several debts later that day, and then left Porthmadog; when the police apprehended him, he had only 4s 11d on him.

22 *NWC*,7 April 1860

23 *NWC*, 9 January 1858

24 *The History of the Her Majesty's Inspectorate of Constabulary: the first 150 years*, justiceinspectorates.gov.uk, 2006, p 7

25 *NWC*, 13 April 1861

26 *North Wales Observer and Express*, 22 July 1898

27 Two inspectors had been appointed since 1837, to report on the national and British schools.

28 quoted by Saunders Lewis, BBC Radio 4, February 1962.

29 *Liverpool Daily Post*, 4 March 1857

30 John Casson to George Casson, 20 November 1856, Z/DCH/1/12 and 27 November 1856, Z/DCH/3/96, AR/MRO

31 Ashmore, Owen, *The Industrial Archaeology of North West England*, 1982, p. 77

Chapter 14

Family Affairs
1859–1865

Neither William's scrapbook nor the surviving letters to his brother George provide clear evidence of his thoughts and plans. Both his older sons had joined the bank, Messrs Casson & Co. That may have been behind his decision to bring the rest of his family back to his homeland, and was also, perhaps, sufficient incentive to make Fanny content to move there, despite her unhappy memories. Whatever William's motive, it took him more than eighteen months to tie up his affairs in Liverpool. In March 1860, an advertisement in the *Liverpool Mercury* announced the sale by auction of 'substantial HOUSEHOLD FURNITURE and other effects, the property of Mr William Casson, who is leaving Liverpool, having disposed of his business.'[1] But the distillery was still in his hands that November. Six months later, in June 1861, the lease of the entire premises was to be auctioned, 'unless previously disposed of by Private Treaty', together with all the 'Fixtures and Utensils' and the various pieces of machinery.[2] William wrote to his brother George that there were 'several parties nibbling' and that he was hopeful of finding a tenant to take over 84 Lodge Lane, 'houses being very scarce and much wanted.'[3]

William was closely involved with the negotiations over Diffwys Quarry, perhaps still intending to take a financial interest in its future. He wrote to George about a German gentleman he had met while visiting Caernarfon, who wanted to order a large load of slate for roofing a railway station, to be supplied the following spring.[4] Exports of Welsh slate to Germany had been brisk ever since a great fire had devastated Hamburg in 1842. In Ffestiniog, Nathan Mathew, owner of Middle Quarry, took advantage of this market, but the German gentleman reported that he was unable to supply on this occasion. William hinted that George would do well to follow up the sales opportunity.

The Casson brothers and Thomas Turner were actively pursuing ways of putting the Diffwys company into an advantageous position for attracting new investors. William recommended some pumping engines he had seen in Liverpool. He listed shipments of quarry materials he was sending to George, and was in contact with Charles Easton Spooner, one of James Spooner's sons, who had worked on building the 'Festiniog Railway' as it was officially called, and now, his father having died in 1856, was managing it. Knowing the terrain well, he helped the Cassons to establish the precise boundaries of the property and to obtain a valuation.[5] For several years, when Diffwys was the only active quarry in Ffestiniog, the first Casson brothers had been casual about where they dumped the slate waste. There was now a quantity of rubbish lying on land that might not have been strictly theirs. Meanwhile, George was negotiating through David Williams, the solicitor, to lease some land by Porthmadog's harbour on which a wharf could be built. Whatever the reason he had been reluctant to acquire a wharf for his own use, he knew it would be a useful bargaining point with a prospective purchaser.

By October 1861, William had handed over his house keys to a new tenant, and was lodging with Benjamin Platt, while he completed his Liverpool affairs. His daughters Polly and Annie were farmed out with the Lees family at

Park Bridge. His youngest son Randal remained in Liverpool, to finish his schooling. Fanny and their youngest daughter, Esther, made the move to Ffestiniog, but William was not permanently back in Wales until the following year.

However disruptive Fanny found it to give up her life in Liverpool and set up house in North Wales, she had made a better marriage than her sister-in-law Bess Smith, whose husband Benjamin continued to be on bad terms with George Casson. On one occasion, Benjamin's brother Richard, still the prosperous agent for Lord Dudley's ironworks in Staffordshire, wrote to George: 'too much misunderstanding has too long [existed] between you and my Brother, possibly altogether his fault.'[6] Both George and he were concerned about their Smith nephews, who habitually preyed on their uncles for financial support. The oldest, Thomas Casson Smith, graduated from Jesus College, Oxford, where many Welsh students destined for the church were educated. After he was ordained, he accepted a curacy in Leicestershire. He was soon complaining to George that his stipend of £70 was 'utterly impossible.'[7] Richard Smith sent the second son, Ben, to study mathematics and mechanics in London, with the intent of employing him in his own business, which now included the Round Oak Iron Works, a substantial operation a few miles south of Dudley. Both uncles tried to sort out the third son, George, who had emigrated to Australia but was then 'exported' back to England, a term which seems to imply some disgraceful circumstance. Bess wrote humbly but distractedly to her brother George, asking him not to let 'Mr Smith' (as she referred to her husband) know that young George had not repaid a loan from his uncle.[8] The best solution seemed to be for young George to go to sea, which he did. By the autumn of 1861, one of the sons (it is not clear which) was trying to access Bess's trust funds. William wrote to George

'The conduct of the Father has tended no doubt to drive the lad to act in this way and to anticipate his mother's death.' He and Fanny prepared to go to Caernarfon to try and resolve the situation. 'I don't think that much good would be done only that Bess would be glad to see us.'[9] It was a good thing they went. Bess was already very ill, and that December, she died of 'General Paralysis', presumably a stroke. She was fifty-five. Neither of Esther Casson's daughters had lived into old age.

William and Fanny began their new life in Wales. They were quickly absorbed into the social scene in Ffestiniog and its neighbourhood, finding that much of it now centred around the volunteer movement. At the beginning of 1862, on one of his frequent trips to North Wales before his final move, William attended a dinner for the Merionethshire Volunteer Rifles held in Ffestiniog Town Hall. This was an opportunity for William to get to know David Williams, the solicitor already well known to his brothers. Mr Williams was High Sheriff that year and presided at the dinner. Other guests included Samuel Holland, who together with John Casson, was vice-president of the Volunteer Corps, and Captain Mathew, son of slate proprietor Nathan Mathew, who commanded the 'Portmadoc Volunteer Corps', of which Tom Casson was by now an enthusiastic member.

Proposing the loyal toast, Mr Williams pointed out that, as it was within a month of the Prince Consort's death, the usual 'rapturous applause' would not be appropriate on this occasion. The leader of the Ffestiniog choir led the assembled company in singing 'God Save the Queen', in a version specially written for 'the present mourning circumstances of the Royal family.' Mr Williams then proposed a toast to the Prince of Wales, and as he prided himself on his knowledge of Welsh history, he expatiated on the whole history of that title, and hoped that the Prince might one day visit Ffestiniog, perhaps in the presence of Lord Palmerston (who still had an interest in the Welsh Slate Company). There were many other toasts, including one to George Casson, his absence through ill health regretted. The Ffestiniog choir performed a concert following the dinner.[10] Later in the year, there was a ball for the Portmadoc Volunteer Corps in the Town Hall at Tremadog. This was 'a very rare occurrence in this part of Wales', no ball having taken place for the last twelve years. This time George was well enough to attend, with Fanny and her eldest daughter. It was as grand an affair as any of the balls Fanny had attended in Liverpool, the hall splendidly decorated in patriotic military style, and lit by both gas-lamps and candles.

Both Fanny and her son Tom were soon joining in the musical life of the neighbourhood. There was nothing in or around Porthmadog to rival the professional performances on offer in Liverpool, but the amateur scene was flourishing. Early in 1863, they took prominent parts in a charity concert of sacred music given by the 'Portmadoc [Porthmadog] Harmonic Society', Tom sharing the harmonium accompaniment with Captain Mathew's wife. He opened the concert with the 'War March' from Mendelssohn's *Athalie*, a piece that was to be a mainstay of his repertoire for many years to come. Fanny sang an aria from Mendelssohn's *St Paul*, a popular oratorio at the time. A press report praised her performance:

> Mrs Casson possesses a splendid voice, which evidently has been highly cultivated ... and nothing could be finer than the style in which she rendered the following touching and most melancholy plaint, 'Jerusalem! Jerusalem! ... how often would I have gathered unto me thy children, and ye would not.' This splendid and

beautiful piece was followed by protracted and hearty cheering.

Tom was cheered for his rendering of a recitative and solo from *Elijah*. They both sang in a Rossini piece, and Fanny sang a solo from Handel's *Solomon* and was 'loudly cheered' at the end. The concert ended with the 'Hallelujah' chorus.[11] George continued to encourage the musical life of Ffestiniog, providing dinner for the choir after one of its concerts. The guests on that occasion included the Misses Thomas, of Caerffynnon Hall, the elder daughters of Lewis Holland Thomas. George's friendship with the retired sea captain had flourished; the two young ladies had already attended a party at Ffestiniog's national school, two years earlier. That occasion was the first Christmas tree festival ever seen at Ffestiniog, when a curtain was drawn back to reveal the tree in all its splendour, 'loaded with a variety of presents ... to the great astonishment and delight of the children.'[12]

No event showed more clearly the prominence of the Casson family in Meirionydd and Caernarfonshire than the marriage of the Prince of Wales to Princess Alexandra of Denmark in March 1863. Every town and many of the villages mounted events honouring their Prince and his bride. There were street decorations, illuminations, peals of bells, choir-singing, processions, the firing of rock cannon and *feu de joie*, fireworks, rural sports (including pig races), tea and *bara brith* for the children, joints of beef for the poor, and dinners for the selected few. Messrs Casson & Co provided a tea party at Diffwys Quarry for the poor and widowed inhabitants of Blaenau; John Casson presided at a dinner in Ffestiniog, in place of his older brother, who, as seemed frequently to happen at this time, was indisposed. George had, however, sat on the committee planning the events in Porthmadog, together with William and Fanny. In Pwllheli, Ensign (Galley) Casson honoured the schoolchildren with his presence at their tea party, attended the dinner, and had his health drunk as 'deserving of special recognition' for his volunteer activities. Sergeant (Tom) Casson marched in the procession in Porthmadog, and, with his father, attended the dinner in Tremadog, where David Williams, presiding, took the opportunity to itemise all sixteen of the Princes of Wales who preceded this one, to praise the Queen, to aver that this event was 'calculated to disperse that cloud which has lately darkened her path', and to hope that 'increased happiness and long life are reserved for her.'[13]

Neither these jollifications nor his state of health distracted George from his main preoccupation, the sale of the Gelli land. An agreement had been drafted as early as March 1862, but it was another year before it was finalised. Perhaps the intervening time was spent negotiating the price, for the quarriers were working a new rich rock of slate.[14] At last, in April 1863, George Casson, Thomas Turner and the assignees of Hugh Jones' daughters signed an agreement to sell the land, for the sum of £120,000 (over £10 million in 2019).[15] David Lloyd, a local hotelier (1/4 share), and Thomas Savin, a railway engineer involved in the building of several Welsh lines (3/8 share), signed on behalf of two others: Thomas Barnes, Liberal MP for Bolton, a successful businessman with interests in cotton, banking and railway (1/4 share); and Hugh Owen (1/8 share), a local man who was best known for his work promoting Welsh education. In the end, neither the Casson brothers nor Thomas Turner invested in the new company, perhaps satisfied with the price they had obtained. The original investment of £1,000, so difficult for their fathers and uncle to raise in 1800, had increased 120-fold. 'Plant,

Machinery, Goods, Chattels and effects' went for £1,209. George's foresight in arranging to lease land for a wharf on Porthmadog's harbour meant that they sold that lease for an extra £30,000. The first payment was for £20,000 plus the extra £1,209, and was duly split between George, (£10,000), Thomas Turner (£5,000) and assignees of Hugh Jones' two daughters (£2,500 each). The balance was to be paid over twelve equal quarterly instalments, divided in the same way.

In July, the new company was registered as the 'Diphwys Casson Slate Company' (using the anglicised name for Diffwys). All the years the Cassons had been running the quarry, they had continued to trade as William Turner & Company, yet now, as they relinquished their interest, their name was to be perpetuated. The family's long involvement clearly carried enough good will for the new owners to wish to take advantage of it. Sentimentally, William Casson kept a copy of the last price list issued by William Turner & Company at the end of 1861. In January 1864, the new company held its first general meeting, in Westminster. The directors and shareholders had need of those who had practical knowledge of quarrying. A hotelier, David Lloyd, was to be managing director, and he had none; they appointed a sub-manager, Mr Evan P. Jones, recommended by Hugh Owen. This young man had started his working life at William Turner's Dinorwic Quarry at the age of twelve. He had later studied at the Government School of Mines in London.[16] The directors were also in consultation with a 'Mr Spooner' about the possibility of building an incline in the quarry, to save on horse labour.[17] This was Charles Easton Spooner, who, as a railwayman himself, and familiar with the terrain, had perhaps played some part in finding the purchasers.

George Casson, with his failing health, must have felt relieved at shedding the responsibility of managing the quarry. John, who had at one time acted as quarry agent, was now fully occupied with the banks, employing his two nephews, Galley in the Pwllheli branch and Tom in Porthmadog. William, just fifty years old when the quarry was sold, now sought some new business enterprise. Although he had not worked at Diffwys himself, he had always taken an interest in industrial processes and development, whether it was distilling, slate-working or advances in electricity. In one letter to George, Thomas Turner described how William and he had done a bit of quarrying near his home, just for enjoyment.[18] If his life had taken a different turn, he might have taken over the quarry and actively managed it. Instead, he began to explore an ancillary business, manufacturing and selling explosives for the quarries in a small factory in Penrhyndeudraeth. In particular, he began marketing gun cotton.

Gun cotton was a volatile explosive made by treating cotton with concentrated sulphuric acid and nitric to produce cellulose trinitrate. Early experiments had led to dangerous explosions, but it could now be manufactured with less risk; Samuel Holland was one quarry proprietor who found it effective for blasting. William Casson became the agent for Thomas Prentice, a Suffolk manufacturer, and advertised its benefits in the local newspaper:

THOMAS PRENTICE & CO

Begs to intimate to Quarry Proprietors, Miners and Contractors that they are prepared to execute orders for GUN COTTON, suitable to every description of Work.

THOMAS PRENTICE AND CO would call special attention to the great advantage offered by this material, as Gun Cotton produces no smoke, so that the work can be proceeded with much more rapidly, and with less injury to the health of the miners.

Gun cotton was much cheaper than gunpowder and was soon in general use, both for mining and for weaponry.

Having found a new business, William needed a new home. Samuel Holland was relinquishing his lease on Plas Penrhyn, where he had lived for over thirty years, and moving to Glan William on the Oakeley estate. He had extended Plas Penrhyn into a comfortable two-storey villa, similar in style to William Madocks' Tan-yr-Allt in Tremadog, and he had worked the surrounding farmland. Now William took over the lease from the son of Sir Joseph Huddart, the original owner. The house stood on a hill above Boston Lodge, where the Festiniog Railway had its workshops, its north-facing veranda looking out across Traeth Bach to the flatland, ringed with mountains, created out of what had once been Traeth Mawr. From the top of the hill above the house, there was a panoramic view across Bae Ceredigion. All William's family, except Galley in Pwllheli and Randal during his school terms, settled there, developing a close friendship with the David Williams family at nearby Castell Deudraeth.

Towards the end of 1863, John Casson, now forty-seven years old, got married. His bride was Emily Gibson, from Great Baddow, in Essex. She was twenty-four, little more than a year older than John's oldest nephew, Galley. Little is known about her, and there is no record of how the couple met. The wedding was at her Essex home, but George provided hospitality to the servants and workmen at Blaenyddôl on the day. Full celebrations of the occasion awaited the couple's arrival in Ffestiniog on Christmas Eve. The schoolchildren sang in honour of the occasion, receiving buns and oranges as their reward, while the poorest residents received half a pound of tea. When the carriage carrying the couple approached the village, a crowd of people went to meet them, and 'amid high glee and unbounded enthusiasm', pulled the carriage into the square in front of the Pengwern Arms, and then, 'with deafening cheers and hurrahs', on towards Blaenyddôl, where they entered the drive through a triumphal arch of evergreen. John made a speech in Welsh, assuring them that Mrs Casson had promised him she would try to learn the language. George also returned thanks 'for the good feeling which had been manifested towards his brother and his wife.' It was a fine evening; a bonfire burnt brightly, rockets were fired, a volley of cannon was discharged, and all the houses were illuminated with candles. 'A merrier Christmas Eve,' it was said, 'was never seen at Festiniog [Ffestiniog].'[19] But this happy occasion did not lead to a fruitful marriage. Within a few months of her wedding, Emily Casson grew ill with consumption. With George's health also precarious, the next year or so was a gloomy time at Blaenyddôl. The family there was glad when Galley moved to the Ffestiniog branch of Messrs Casson & Co and took lodgings in the village. Emily died just eighteen months after those Christmas Eve celebrations.

The third generation of Cassons in Wales was now coming into its own. Tom Casson had already set eyes on a young lady he would like to marry. According to his own account, he was riding through the village of Talsarnau one day, when he set eyes on a beautiful dark-haired girl on the other side of a garden wall. He made an excuse to stop and chat. The garden belonged to Caerffynnon Hall. The young lady was the oldest daughter of Mr Lewis Holland Thomas, the retired sea captain.

The two young people may actually have met some years before, for they were both present at the party in Ffestiniog where the first Christmas tree was displayed. Soon after the meeting over the wall, Tom was sufficiently well known to the Thomas family that he played at a concert in Talsarnau, in aid of the local school which Mr Thomas himself had helped to establish. The two Misses Thomas played an instrumental duet: 'The enthusiasm consequent on the very able manner in which those young ladies played was very great; and they kindly acceded to the wishes of the company for an encore.'[20] At the time of the concert, Mr Thomas had four daughters and a baby son. As Tom Casson's interest in his oldest daughter grew, he soon learnt more about her father and her childhood. It was quite a story.

Notes

[1] *Liverpool Daily Post,* 23 March, 1860
[2] ibid, 5 June 1861
[3] William Casson to George Casson, 18 June 1861, Z/DCH/3/102 AM/MRO
[4] William Casson to George Casson, 6 Feb 1861 Z/DCH/3/101 AM/MRO
[5] ibid
[6] Richard Smith to George Casson, 8 December 1855, Z/DCH/1/11 AM/MRO
[7] Thomas Casson Smith to George Casson, 2 January 1860, Z/DCH/1/16 AM/MRO
[8] Bess Smith to George Casson, undated, probably 1854, Z/DCH/1/8 AM/MRO
[9] William Casson to George Casson, 17 October 1861, Z/DCH/A/21/73 AM/MRO
[10] *NWC,* 18 January 1863
[11] *NWC,* 14 February 1863
[12] *NWC,* 2 February 1861
[13] *NWC,* 14 March 1863
[14] Thomas Turner to George Casson, 8 March 1862, Z/DCH/2/64 AM/MRO
[15] according to moneysorter.co.uk
[16] Letter from local historian Steffan ap Owen to Neil & Moira Richards, 11 April 2000.
[17] *NWC,* 23 January 1864,

18 Thomas Turner to George Casson, 8 March 1862, Z/DCH/2/64
    AM/MRO
19 *NWC*, 2 January 1864
20 *NWC*, 18 June 1864

Chapter 15

Interlude: The Master Mariner's Tale

In 1812, the year before William Casson was born to an already prosperous English quarry owner in Ffestiniog, another boy was born, not many miles away, whose circumstances were very different. This boy's grandfather, Thomas Lewis, was a mariner who married a farmer's daughter in Llanfair, a village just south of Harlech, and then acquired the tenancy of a local inn. They had eleven children, one of whom was known as Lewis Thomas (an example of identifying a son through his father's given name). Lewis Thomas, born about 1779, spent his childhood in Llanfair.[1] He then moved away, marrying a young woman from Llanrwst, Conwy. Lewis Thomas and his wife had two sons and two daughters, but they died destitute, and their children were put upon the parish. The local rector, Howell Holland Edwards, treated them kindly, and that may have been the reason that the oldest of the siblings, another Lewis Thomas, later added 'Holland' to his name.[2] He was rescued from penury by going to live with his father's sister, Jane Lewis, who had stayed in Llanfair and married a local farmer. Lewis lived with them until he was twelve years old. Then he decided to follow in his grandfather's footsteps and went to sea, setting out from nearby Aber-maw (Barmouth).[3]

Young Lewis Holland Thomas started out as an apprentice, indentured with the consent of his uncle for four years, to learn the arts of seamanship, probably on a collier schooner, often used for training. The conditions were rough. One shipmaster described the merchant seamen as 'ungovernable beasts', and many of the master mariners were cruel, overbearing and often intoxicated.[4] There was no formal training; he would have learnt how to navigate by rule of thumb, relying on information from superior officers and on his own experience to steer his way to his destination.

Some ships were well managed, with reasonable provisions, fair discipline, thorough training, and encouragement for the boys to read the Bible. Lewis Thomas must have been one of the lucky boys in that respect, for he became a devout churchgoer, and was soon fluent in English. He rose swiftly through the ranks. By 1835, when he was twenty-two, he was master of a schooner, *Enfield*. As the major trading nation at this time, Britain imported goods from its colonies to the ports of London, Liverpool and Bristol, exporting colonial goods such as coffee, timber and palm oil, and home products such as Manchester cotton, to the rest of the world. Captain Thomas sailed the *Enfield* along the coasts of Chile and western Mexico, both recently freed from Spanish rule, their governments eager to encourage trade. He sold what he had brought from England, and took on other goods, either on commission or that he had purchased himself. He once crossed the Isthmus of Panama by putting his ship on a roller-track. He might have witnessed the great earthquake of February 1835 at Concepcion, Chile, which Charles Darwin observed from HMS *Beagle*.

In 1839, Captain Thomas returned to Wales. He had stayed in close touch with his aunt's family, especially with one of her daughters, Ellen. He had made enough profit to buy a house in Porthmadog for Ellen. There, he met the young woman who would become his wife. Two years younger than him, she was Mary Winifred Williams, known as 'Winny'. She was staying with her widowed grandmother, on a farm near Porthmadog. This grandmother was a sister of Captain Thomas' own maternal grandmother, so the couple were second cousins.[5] Like Lewis, Winny had lost her father at an early age. Her mother remarried, taking Winny's two brothers to Middlesex, but she farmed out Winny to her brother-in-law, the Rev Ellis Williams and his wife, in Pinxton, Derbyshire. This uncle and aunt became as parents to her.

The couple were attracted to each other. They met once again, when Winny was staying with cousin Ellen, but there was little time for them to develop their relationship, as Lewis was about to set off across the seas again. He left for Liverpool in December that year, where he went into joint ownership of a brig, *Laura Ann*, first registered in 1833, then undergoing a major refit. The other main owner was a friend of his, another master mariner, Richard Roberts. At 145 tons, the *Laura Ann* was a little bigger than the *Enfield* but still small, sailing with a crew of eight.

By the end of March 1840, just about the time William Casson was wooing Fanny Galley Day Jackson, Captain Thomas was ready to set sail again. This time it was a two-year voyage, initially to Peru, and then to the other western ports of South America. Winny and he exchanged letters; they fell in love by correspondence. On his return in February 1842, he pursued the relationship, and in late June her uncle married them at Pinxton. They set off for Liverpool, where the *Laura Ann* was being prepared for her next voyage. Winny was to start her married life on board the ship with him. Captain Thomas loaded the *Laura Ann*, of which he now owned a 5/8 share, with a mixture of commissioned cargo and items he knew he could sell. His plan was to return to the west coast of South America, where he had done well before. In July, two weeks after their wedding, they set sail.

They were away for three and a half years, sailing to Valparaiso, up along the coasts of Chile and Peru to Nicaragua, and back to Valparaiso, where Winny stayed, to give birth to her first child, who was named 'Laura Ann' after the ship. She soon re-embarked, with the baby, and their next voyage was to French Polynesia and the Sandwich Islands (now 'Hawaii'). Eighteen months later, Captain Thomas left his wife in Valparaiso again, to give birth to their second daughter, Mary Ellen. At last, when he returned, they made plans to sail back to England; Winny wanted her uncle to christen the new baby. In January 1846, they docked in London. They then settled in Liverpool. But Winny was already unwell, growing worse through the winter. In April, she died, from 'dilation and atrophy of all the cavities of the heart with complications.' She was thirty-one years old and had spent virtually her whole married life at sea.

Fifteen months later, Captain Thomas began to write an account of his marriage and the voyage, for his daughters, 'thankful to my merciful Father for the home he has provided for their infant years, as well as to the Dear Friends who have undertaken such a charge.'[6] The home that was offered to the children was with their great-uncle and great-aunt in Derbyshire. After the funeral, the sea captain returned to the life he had led before his marriage, to make enough money to support his daughters. He had the *Laura Ann* refitted for her third voyage and set sail for Valparaiso. There, early in 1847, surrounded by memories and sympathetic friends, he began his account, which his older daughter, Laura Ann, treasured and passed down through her family. By September 1848, he had reached San Francisco, where a new phase of his life began.

The gold mines had recently been opened and the town

The Laura Ann, *photograph of a painting owned by the Mathews family.*

was drawing thousands of eager prospectors. Several of the crew deserted to join them. Early in 1849, he decided to end his sailing days and sold the *Laura Ann* to his chief mate, Robert Mathews, a native of Harlech who had sailed with him on the earlier voyages. He used his share of the money to invest in several plots of land on the shoreline, where he built wooden houses for the many prospectors seeking accommodation on their return from the mines. His properties were known as 'Thomas's Lots'. But disaster struck, as a fierce fire broke out and the entire investment disappeared in smoke. He stood on a hill above the town watching the conflagration. A stranger standing beside him spoke:

'A fine sight, isn't it?'
'Yes,' agreed the Captain.
'But a sad one for the owner,' the stranger continued.

'I am the owner,' said the Captain.

'And you can stand there so calm and watch your property go up in smoke?'

'I've learnt in my life,' the Captain explained, 'that God never takes anything from me without giving me something else in its place.'[7]

He stayed and bought more lots, and whether by God's favour or by his own business acumen, the land swiftly gained in value. It was time to sell up and go home to Wales. He had happy memories of his childhood near Llanfair, Ardudwy, and soon heard of an available nearby property, at Caerffynnon, near Harlech, where he could build a house fit for a gentleman. In January 1851, an agreement was signed. The sea captain completed his affairs in San Francisco, then took ship for England, and then Wales. On his arrival, the building of Caerffynnon Hall took up much of his time. He visited his daughters, but there was no question of their living with him yet, so they stayed in Pinxton, while he lodged in Liverpool, and resumed his friendship with Richard Roberts and his family. The life of a widower did not suit him. Before long, his friendship with the Roberts' daughter, Elizabeth, whom he had known since she was a child, blossomed into romance. Remarriage had the added attraction that he could offer his daughters a real home back in Wales. They were married at St Bride's Church, Liverpool, in September 1855. He signed himself 'L H Thomas, Gentleman'; his seafaring days were over.

Notes

1 see Lloyd, Lewis, 'Captain Lewis Holland Thomas (1812-1888) as a Pacific Trader, 1835-1848/9', *Cymru a'r Môr/Maritime Wales*, No 14,1991, p. 25

2   Thanks to Veronica Millington for this suggestion, as he had no traceable forebears called 'Holland'.

3   Lloyd, pp. 26-27

4   Course, AG, *The Merchant Navy: A Social History*, 1963, p. 196

5   More thanks to Veronica Millington, for tracking down a possible genealogy to explain this connection.

6   Captain Holland Thomas's memoir, ms, family papers

7   Isambard Owen, Heulwen and Hedydd, *The Caerffynnon Story*, private publication, 1973, p9 (Other versions of the story circulate within the family.)

Chapter 16

Pillars of the Community
1865–1869

Although no Cassons now worked the 'blue veins of Merionethshire' (as William Gryffydd Oakeley had described them), the family profile was never higher than in the 1860s. The name 'Messrs Casson & Co' stood above the entrance of each branch of the bank: at Ffestiniog and Harlech in Meirionydd, at Pwllheli and Porthmadog in Caernarfonshire. Business grew so fast that by the end of 1864, there were plans for new bank premises in Porthmadog, including a manager's residence. Few tales have come down through the family from these years and since they all lived close to one another, they had no need to write letters. But hardly a week went by without the Casson name appearing in the local press. When, in December 1869, a new branch of the bank opened in Blaenau, serving the quarries and their accompanying trades, the *North Wales Chronicle* paid tribute: "The vast improvements and changes that have taken place here since Messrs Cassons came to reside at Festiniog [Ffestiniog] to commence working and opening out the slate trade about the year 1799, is [sic] truly wonderful."[1]

William Casson developed his explosives business in Penrhyndeudraeth. The area around it had developed greatly during the years he had been in Liverpool. When he walked down from his home at Plas Penrhyn, through the farm, towards the station at Minffordd, he could hear the hooting of the Blaenau-Porthmadog train as it trundled across the Cob. Now powered by steam, instead of horses, it carried passengers as well as slate. In the summer, tourists waved from the carriages. Porthmadog was a busy harbour that must have reminded William of the Liverpool docks: the swaying masts of the ships jostling by the wharfs, the familiar smell of tar, timber and paint, the shouts of men loading and unloading cargo. At night, the streets were lit by gas, illuminating the way home for weary workers or carousing sailors. The number of shipbuilding workshops grew, expanding westwards round the coast to Borth-y-gest, the small harbour just east of Ynys Cyngar, the outcrop where his father and uncle had had their ships loaded. George Casson was a major investor in a steam packet, *Wave of Life*, that now towed vessels over the treacherous bar out into the open sea. Messrs Casson & Co advanced a large sum towards its purchase. Soon after that, Porthmadog's first steamship, *Rebecca*, was launched, to carry slate to Liverpool and bring back provisions and household goods. In 1863, the *George Casson* brigantine was built, registered by a local merchant and named as a mark of respect to George. She was a phosphate ship, sailing across the Atlantic to the West Indies, bringing cargo back to Europe, to be used as fertiliser.[2]

By 1866, the long-awaited toll bridge across Traeth Bach was completed, Pont Briwet. It shortened journeys between Harlech and Minffordd but proved to be the final blow to the trade of the remaining Philistines, whose boats had continued to serve at least one of the Ffestiniog quarries until the new bridge obstructed navigation along the Dwyryd.[3] A railway now carried goods and passengers from one of the stations on the Blaenau-Porthmadog line to the village of Ffestiniog – a distance of less than four miles.

George Casson was the first director of the small company promoting this line, which eased the life of its inhabitants, who, until it was built, had to bring everything into the village by cart.

George acted as chairman of the Petty Sessions in Penrhyndeudraeth. His brothers William and John were also appointed JPs, as was his nephew Galley, a few years later, all of them sitting regularly at the Petty Sessions and the Quarterly Assizes. The family continued to support the volunteer movement. In 1865, George presided over the dissolution of the Merionethshire Rifle Corps, but the Caernarfonshire Rifle Volunteers were active, all three older Cassons being regular patrons, while Tom Casson moved swiftly up the ranks to become Captain. Galley was a keen angler. The Royal Welsh Yacht Club's regattas attracted several of the gentry families, including the Cassons, the Mathews and the Turners.

The Cassons supported the national schools in Ffestiniog and Porthmadog and were present at the Christmas parties for the schoolchildren, where a tree laden with presents was by this time a regular feature. At one such party for the Sunday school in Ffestiniog, the children were given the usual tea, *bara brith* and entertainment, and also heard a stern word from John Casson, who 'spoke very forcibly on the importance of instructing the young in God's Word.'[4] William and Fanny Casson and their daughters attended Holy Trinity in Penrhyndeudraeth, but Tom Casson rarely went with them, as his services were in great demand at the harmonium or the organ. He also stole the limelight at a bazaar his uncle, John Casson, organised in Ffestiniog, in aid of the national school. Dressed up as a country-fair showman, Tom occupied a whole room in the village hall, where he operated an automaton monkey to play a drum and was 'rewarded with bursts of hearty acclamation.'[5] It was not the only occasion when Tom played the clown. At one of the light entertainment evenings known as 'penny readings', he gave a rendering of 'Villikins and his Dinah', a burlesque version of a sentimental ballad recounting a tale reminiscent of *Romeo and Juliet*, with a popular 'tóo ra la, lóo ra la, lóo ra la lay' chorus. It ended with the death of the hero and heroine, and a moral, which he delivered in a suitably lugubrious manner:

> Now all you young maidens take a warning by her.
> Never not by no means disobey your governor.
> And all you young fellows mind who you clap eyes on,
> Think of Villikins and Dinah, and the cup of cold pison.[6]

In Porthmadog, concerts were held in the schoolroom. Tom accompanied on the harmonium and sang. Sometimes his mother sang; sometimes one of his sisters played or sang. Secular programmes combined comic and serious, classical and Welsh. On one occasion, his mother and his sister Polly moved the audience with the 'Vesper Hymn', while Percival Spooner, one of Charles Easton Spooner's sons, performed 'comical tricks with a hat.'[7] At another, young Esther Casson and her Platt cousin played a piano duet which was 'much admired' and Mrs Casson led the singing of a Mendelssohn quartet.[8] Tom also played at concerts in Caernarfon and Harlech. In Ffestiniog, George Casson supported a quarrymen's choir, Côr y Teilia Mawr, and a brass band. The curate at St Michael's Church praised its choir as one of the best in North Wales, and its leader, William Davies of Cae'r Blaidd, one of the first musicians in the principality.

While the Casson men were kept busy with their businesses, their civic duties and their social activities, there were also political developments that affected them. While George continued to support the Conservative Party, a more progressive movement was growing in influence. Two of the men at the forefront were David Williams and Samuel Holland, both Liberals.

During the first half of the century, the working people of Meirionydd had taken little active interest in parliamentary politics, few of them having the vote. But in the second half of the century, activists began to emerge from other social ranks than the landed gentry. Bala, where the Calvinist Methodists thrived, was a centre of intellectual development. Gradually, interest in progressive politics grew. There were efforts to encourage more men who were entitled to the franchise to register. By 1859, the number had reached over 1,000. In that year, Bala became an incorporated borough, partly through the offices of the solicitor David Williams, who, with his interest in Welsh history, had unearthed the original charters for the town.

In May 1859, David Williams had stood as a Liberal candidate in Meirionydd, his nomination seconded by Samuel Holland. W. W. E. Wynne stood again as Conservative and won, but by only thirty-nine votes (389 votes to 350, out of a registered electorate of 1091), George and John Casson accounting for two of the Conservative votes, and Lewis Holland Thomas for another. The local Liberal paper claimed this close result as 'a thrilling augury and sure precursor of a future victory.'[9] The near win led to the formation of the Reform Society, the origin of the 'Merioneth Liberal Association'. Nationally, the 1859 election brought Lord Palmerston back into power for the second time, leading a party that united Whigs, Radicals and Peelites, including William Gladstone. This administration lasted for six years, until Palmerston's death in October 1865. In the subsequent election, David Williams stood again. W. W. E. Wynne had resigned, and his son William Robert Maurice Wynne stood in his place. By this time,

William Casson was firmly in residence in Meirionydd, a close neighbour of David Williams and a Liberal himself. His support for the party had developed in Liverpool, under the influence of Benjamin Platt's father. It had continued when William Brown stood successfully as Liberal candidate for Liverpool in 1846, a seat which he held until retiring in 1859.

By 1865, the registered electorate in Meirionydd had risen to over 1,500, and hopes were high for a Liberal victory, but again the Conservative candidate won, this time by only thirty-one votes. There were allegations of pressure being put on tenants by some of the Tory landlords, including threats of eviction. Liberal hopes in Meirionydd now lay in the prospect of the Second Reform Act that would enfranchise more of the working population. This finally passed in August 1867, under Lord Derby's next Conservative government rather than Lord Russell's last Liberal government.

The political opposition between the two families at Blaenyddôl and Plas Penrhyn created no rift. A more immediate concern that autumn was George's declining health; he died from heart failure before the year was out. Many in the village turned out to pay a last tribute, as the funeral procession wended its way up the drive from Blaenyddôl. The Rev David Edwards led the service in St Michael's Church, rebuilt twenty years before, largely through George's efforts. He was buried in the churchyard, which now held many Casson graves.

George's death was timely, in that the values of the community in which he had played a major role were shifting from those he had grown up to cherish. It was later said of him, as of the Hollands and the Greaves, that 'these were men who, by virtue of their controlling influence on the industrial life of the parish, occupied a status comparable with that of the [Welsh] rural gentry.'[10] They were 'gentlemen capitalists', but George was the least progressive of them. He cherished the hard-earned prosperity and social respect his father and uncle had gained him, rather than empathising with members of the local community who might have had their own aspirations towards upward mobility. He was described in his obituary in the *North Wales Chronicle* as 'a good type of our old country gentleman.' He had thrown open the doors of Blaenyddôl to offer hospitality to tenants and workers. He had been a fair landlord and had supported many charities and societies that helped the quarriers' families. But he saw his duty as encouraging moral, rather than social improvement amongst his own workers.

Given his high profile in Ffestiniog, and the fact that he was the male head of the Casson family in Wales for nearly twenty years, it is surprising that George played no part in any family story that has come down the generations. He was close to his siblings, and to his numerous nieces and nephews, and had much influence over them, but he was not commemorated by their descendants. He bore no known children; there is no surviving portrait of him; none of his books or papers survived amongst family possessions. Yet from the sequence of letters between his brothers and him that found their way to the Archifau Gwynedd in Dolgellau, there emerges the character of a wise, caring and sometimes humorous man.[11]

By the time of his death, George owned a considerable amount of land in and around Ffestiniog, as well as half the sale value of the quarry. He specified in his will that his brother William should receive back the worth of the quarter share of the quarry he had sold. This would be paid out of the instalments made by the Diphwys Casson Slate Company in purchasing William Turner & Company, less a debt to the bank for a loan William had taken when setting up his explosives business. George thus restored to his brother that stake in the quarry he had relinquished sixteen years earlier. Like his childless uncle William, George left money to each of his nieces and nephews. His residual heir was his widower brother John.

John continued in residence at Blaenyddôl, William and his family at Plas Penrhyn, where his household was augmented by one. Randal, his youngest son, was now seventeen years old and was offered a bright future through the David Williams family. Soon after David Williams married, he had taken responsibility for a fatherless nephew, then seven years old. When the boy, Edward Breese, was old enough, he was articled to his uncle David in his Porthmadog office. Edward qualified as a solicitor, ten years before Randal Casson came to live in Wales. When David Williams first stood for Parliament, he had handed over some of his responsibilities to Edward Breese, including his position as Clerk of the Peace, and his management of William Madocks' estate (henceforth referred to as the 'Tremadog estate'). The heir to the estate was William Roche, not yet of age, the son of William Madocks' daughter, Eliza, by her second husband, John Webb Roche, an Irishman connected to the 2nd Baron Fermoy's family. Like his uncle, Edward Breese was a Liberal and a churchman. Also, like his uncle, he developed a strong interest in local antiquities. In 1867, Edward Breese offered to take Randal Casson into his Porthmadog law office and train him in law. The professional relationship brought the Williams and Casson families closer together.

A bare two months after George Casson's death, Lord Derby, Conservative Prime Minister, resigned through ill health, and his ambitious Chancellor, Benjamin Disraeli, succeeded him, calling a general election a few months later, in November 1868. Having played a prominent role in the passing of the Second Reform Act, he hoped a grateful electorate would return him to office, but he had miscalculated. The MP for Meirionydd, W. R. M. Wynne, was more aware of the political climate, at least locally. The electorate had doubled to 3,185 (out of a population of about 40,000), mainly around Ffestiniog.[12] Many of the local gentry were now Liberal, though not John Casson or Lewis Holland Thomas, both of whom promoted Mr Wynne's candidacy. When David Williams addressed a meeting in Blaenau, 3,000 people turned out to hear him. Mr Wynne, seeing the likelihood that he would lose the seat, stood down. At the third time of standing, David Williams was at last elected, unopposed, the first Liberal MP for the county. Caernarfon Boroughs, Caernarfonshire and Anglesey also returned Liberal candidates, the latter two for the first time. David Williams entered Parliament as William Gladstone became Prime Minister, but his triumph was short-lived, as his health had broken down, and he was rarely able to attend.[13]

The friendship between David William's family at Castell Deudraeth and William Casson's at nearby Plas Penrhyn flourished and was much in evidence when William Casson hosted the marriage of his oldest daughter in the spring of 1869. Frances Mary, formerly known as 'Polly', now dignified as 'Mary', married an English clergyman, the Rev William Ranken. 'Great interest,' wrote the local society journalist, 'was felt in the happy event throughout the districts … [The Casson families] are large slate quarry proprietors.' The name 'Diphwys Casson', used long after the family interest in the quarry had ceased, was clearly misleading.

Flags on the hill at Plas Penrhyn could be seen across the whole vale, while the Williams family mounted one on the top of Castell Deudraeth. More flags festooned arches on the turnpike road, across the front of the workhouse and at the entrance to the village. The customary rock cannon were fired and also 'a curious combustible', perhaps a particular device contrived by William Casson, or by his workers at the factory. At night, there were illuminations in many of the shops and houses, in front of the workhouse and in Porthmadog. Rain poured down throughout most of the day, which 'damped curiosity and enthusiasm alike' amongst the villagers. But they still stood to watch the arrival of the carriages. After the church service, there was a 'sumptuous luncheon' for the bridal party at Plas Penrhyn, after which the couple set off for Paris and the Continent. William hosted a dinner in the farmyard for all the tenants and workmen, while Fanny provided a dinner of roast beef and plum pudding for the inmates of the workhouse.[14]

The wedding festivities manifested William's high standing in the community, just as George's funeral had led to a demonstration of respect and loyalty from his tenants and workmen. Meirionydd was still remote from any metropolis; events in the life of the gentry provided the best opportunities for public celebration. Another social event of 1869 showed the pride that the Cassons and Turners took in their social position. At the end of June, John Casson attended a dinner in Beddgelert. This Caernarfonshire village lay to the south of Snowdon, at the confluence of two rivers, flowing into the river Glaslyn. Early in the century, the innkeeper had begun popularising, or perhaps perpetrating, a legend that the village was named after Llywelyn the Great's dog, Gelert, supposedly a gift from King John of England. According to the legend, Prince Llywelyn returned from hunting one day to find his baby missing, its cradle overturned and Gelert's mouth smeared with blood. Believing the dog had attacked his son, he took his sword and killed it, only to discover that the baby lay unharmed beneath the cradle, beside a dead wolf, which Gelert had killed, saving the baby's life. The innkeeper claimed to have identified the very spot where the remorseful Prince buried Gelert, and he maintained that it was the origin of the village name, which means 'Gelert's grave'. The story (now thought to have little or no basis in fact) was widely interpreted in word and image and helped to make the village a famous tourist spot, no doubt fulfilling the innkeeper's intentions. The inn, previously 'The Goat', was renamed the 'Royal and Goat Hotel', in honour of a recent visit by the Prince of Wales and was being reopened under new management. It was the occasion of a grand house-warming, to include many of the local gentry, helping to put the hotel firmly on the map for the many visitors.[15]

Llewelyn Turner, youngest son of William Turner, and Mayor of Caernarfon, chaired the dinner, with John Casson as his vice-chairman, both of them being co-trustees of the hotel. The bill of fare was lavish, beginning with a choice of three soups and four fish dishes. Next came sixteen joints of meat; and then the entremets, offering sixteen sweets and five savouries. The puddings were cabinet, Snowdon (created especially for the occasion), macaroni cheese and soufflé. Finally, a dazzling array of fruits for dessert. After the loyal toasts, Llewelyn Turner gave fulsome praise to the church, and then to the Army and the Navy, expressing some regret that the Armed Forces were not always as highly regarded as he thought they should be. His speech harked back to the glory days of Nelson and Wellington. Next, he turned his attention to the Lord Lieutenant of the county, Edward Douglas-Pennant, recently ennobled as Baron Penrhyn, proprietor of the great Penrhyn Quarry; he had been Conservative MP for Caernarfonshire until 1866, when he was succeeded by his son, who then lost his seat to the Liberal Thomas Love D. Jones-Parry. Llewelyn praised the Baron's 'boundless generosity' to his workmen – either unaware, or choosing to ignore the fact that industrial unrest was beginning to simmer amongst the Penrhyn quarriers.

John Casson rose to propose the next toasts, to Mr Jones-Parry and Mr Bulkeley-Hughes, Liberal MPs for Caernarfonshire and Caernarfon Boroughs, respectively. He declared that they were 'two gentlemen who had the interests of the county and borough sincerely at heart.' He was sure 'they were anxious to perform with interest and energy what they had undertaken.' Just as Llewelyn used this occasion to emphasise patriotic continuity, John used it to persuade himself that solidarity amongst gentlemen would overcome any political opposition between them. He proposed a toast to Llewelyn Turner, as chairman of the dinner. The effects of wine were beginning to be felt, for he told the company that that gentleman had held 'the high post of Mayor of Caernarfon for a great part of a century', forgetting that his old friend was not born until 1823 and had been Mayor for just ten years. He referred to the benefits Llewelyn had brought to his fellow townsmen and his fellow countrymen. (Llewelyn had indeed overseen many improvements, clearing slum dwellings and working hard to contain a cholera epidemic two years before.)

By this point in the evening, the close relationship between the two families led to tributes that were more informal. John declared that the Mayor was 'a jolly good fellow'; Llewelyn responded and toasted his old friend, pointing out that 'had his [the Mayor's] father lived until now, he would be 105 years of age, and it was a very long time since he and the father and uncle of Mr Casson came to this part of the country.' He went on to say that 'nothing could be said of Mr Casson and his family but what was honest, and just, and true.' This statement was greeted with cheers. He referred to the death of George Casson as a 'common loss to the country.' After Welsh toasts had been drunk to the proprietress of the hotel and to the new managers, the recital of *englynion* (celebratory poems) in praise of the establishment, and a song, John stood up to propose one more toast, declaring that Thomas Turner, who was seated on his left, was 'without exception, the most kind-hearted, generous man he had ever met', to which that gentleman responded appropriately. The party broke up in a mood of pride in the prosperity families like the Cassons (English by blood) and Turners (Anglo-Irish) had helped to bring to Wales. They warmly identified with the country, the interests of which they saw as being identical to those of the rest of Britain, and they had confidence that its future was safe in the hands of gentlemen like them, whatever their political persuasion.

Notes

[1] *NWC*, 18 December 1869

[2] Hughes, Henry, pp. 112, 173

[3] Richards, Alun John, *The Rails and Slates of Welsh Slate*, 2011, p. 83

[4] *NWC*, 25 December 1869

[5] *NWC*, 28 August 1869

[6] See Wikipedia

[7] *NWC*, 6 November, 1869

[8] *NWC*, 7 September 1867

[9] *Caernarvonshire and Denbigh Herald*, 14 May 1859, quoted by Jones, Iewan Gwynedd, 'Merioneth Politics in the mid-nineteenth century', *CCHCSF/JMHRS*, Vol 5:4 1968, p. 275

[10] Jones, Iewan Gwynedd, op. cit. p. 315

[11] How these letters reached the archives is something of a mystery. They were deposited by a Casson living at Hen Stablau, Pen y Mount, Ffestiniog, who cannot be directly traced to the Blaenyddôl Cassons.

[12] 34,500 in 1831, 46,849 in 1911 Wikipedia – Merioneth (UK Parliament Constituency)

13 Jones, Iewan Gwynedd, op. cit.

14 *NWC*, 17 April, 1869

15 See *NWC*, 3 July, 1869, for an account of the dinner.

Chapter 17

The Line Continues
1870–1876

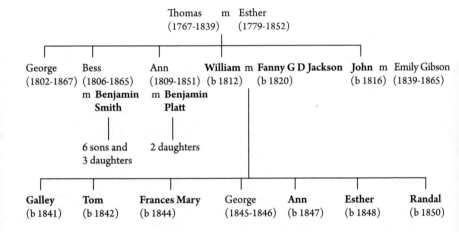

The Casson Family 1869

By the time John Casson became the principal resident at Blaenyddôl, it was no longer a one-storey farmhouse but a three-storey Victorian mansion boasting nine bedrooms. Perhaps George and he had the house extended at the time of his marriage, in the hope that some of the rooms would be needed as nurseries. Instead, the death of his young wife and his older brother had left his Platt nieces as the only family members living with him, while his nephew Galley lodged elsewhere in the village. Life in William and Fanny's house at Plas Penrhyn was jollier, with four young adults and their friends enjoying the social life of the two counties.

Now in his fifties, John decided to take a second wife. In the summer of 1870, he married Mary Chessell, the daughter of George and Eliza Chessell, his long-time neighbours at Pen-y-Mount, just outside Ffestiniog. Mr Chessell was agent of the Welsh Slate Company, and brother-in-law of the Rev Richard Killin, now rector of St Michael's. Again, John's wife was much younger than himself, for she was just about to celebrate her twenty-third birthday. Again, the villagers turned out to celebrate the occasion, for the Chessell family was as well-known as the Cassons. There were the usual decorative arches, flags and banners. The Rev Killin conducted the ceremony, with John's nephew, Thomas Casson Smith, assisting. Llewelyn Turner was his groomsman. As the bride and groom left the church, twelve little girls strewed flowers along the church path. After luncheon at Pen-y-Mount, the couple set off for their honeymoon, passing through Blaenau, where the inhabitants were equally enthusiastic, on their way to Betws-y-coed, where they were to catch a train and travel up to the Lake District.[1]

John was eager to show his new bride where his English family had sprung from. It must have been on this occasion that he unearthed a coat-of-arms that had originally been granted to a branch of the Casson family based in Millom, a few miles north of Barrow-in-Furness. It had three red chevrons, each with a star-shaped spur on it, and a red square in the right-hand corner; its heraldic description was: 'Ar.three chev. and a canton gu. on each chev. a mullet of the field.' The crest was an azure dove rising from a tower, and the motto was 'Prosequor alis', meaning 'Pursue on wings'. From then on, he began to use the shield and the crest, claiming

Coat of arms

that this branch of the Cassons was 'subsequently of Frith Hall', from where he could certainly trace his ancestry. It was not unusual for 'new' gentry to hunt around for appropriate insignia, unauthorised by the College of Heraldry. The Turners had done the same. John started his new married life with a heightened social status, which he hoped to bestow on a son in due course. His brother William soon adopted the same arms.

The question of ancestry and inheritance was not only a matter of family prestige. At the time of his brother John's marriage, William was involved in a legal case relating to the Jackson properties in Cheshire. Fanny's father had intended that her sister (Mary Salisbury) and Fanny herself should inherit equal shares in his estate, but his executors had mortgaged or sold chunks of the property, in order to pay off his debts, leaving the Salisburys with a larger share. Since Mr Salisbury was unwilling to rectify the situation, William and Fanny took the matter to the Court of Chancery; their share of the property was adjusted, and now included Betchton House, the main residence on the estate, an elegant eighteenth-century country house.

John Casson's was not the only family wedding that year. At the time of his second marriage, he made both his nephews Galley and Tom partners in Messrs Casson & Co. This step made Tom financially secure enough to propose to Laura Ann Thomas, whom he had been courting for

Caerffynnon Hall, Talsarnau

some months, walking across the sands of Traeth Bach at low tide, to visit her at Caerffynnon Hall.

While the Casson residences at Blaenyddôl and Plas Penrhyn were substantial family houses, they were humble compared with the splendour of Lewis Holland Thomas' home. A drive led up from the village of Talsarnau, opening out to a site that offered panoramic views of Bae Ceredigion and the Snowdon range. The house was designed by a Liverpool architect, to Mr Thomas' instructions. It was built of Welsh stone, faced with sandstone, with a slate roof. A gabled porch led into a hall with mosaic tiles on the floor. On the right was a large drawing-room with a carved marble fireplace, and decorative plasterwork made by craftsmen especially brought from Spain. Here, he displayed souvenirs of his travels. Tall bay windows looked out on the mountains, the Dwyryd estuary and the sea beyond. The doors were made of Canadian birdseye maple with gold traceries. On the other side of the hall was a large slate-floored kitchen and dining-room. Out of the hall rose a double stairway leading up to the first-floor bedrooms. Behind it was a huge window with heraldic shields on the panes. At the back of the house were outhouses for horses, cows, pigs and poultry, as well as a coalhouse and washhouse. Water for the household came from a spring-fed well. The grounds sloped up to an old fort, which Mr Thomas had established as his look-out, from which he liked to watch the ships setting out, reminding him of his own seafaring days. At the front was a flower garden, beyond it the kitchen garden and a paddock.

The alliance with the Thomas family embedded the Cassons further into the Meirionydd community. Laura's father held a prominent position in the village of Talsarnau. He had raised himself to the level of gentry through his prosperous voyages and purchases of property. He never referred to himself as 'Captain', always as 'L H Thomas, Gentleman.' His family now consisted of his wife Winny's daughters, Laura and Ellen; his second wife Elizabeth; and five daughters of this marriage – Anna, Lily, Mabel, Fanny and Ethel. Their first boy, named after his father, had lived for only sixteen months, but now there was a new baby boy, Richard, called 'Dickie'. A series of nursemaids took charge of the children. Mrs Thomas was regarded as 'Lady Bountiful' of the village, providing baskets of comforts and visiting the sick. Villagers looked out for the sight of the waggonette carrying the family to church on Sundays, the children's sailor hats bobbing around their mother.

Tom and Laura's wedding in November 1870 was an occasion for more local celebration. Again, it poured with rain, but that did not stop the festivities. Somehow, bonfires were lit, and rounds of rock cannon were fired around the village, the house and at Plas Penrhyn. Both families hung out large flags, visible from miles around. Villagers who could not afford flags hung coloured handkerchiefs out, determined to honour the occasion. The bride's carriage wended its way through arches carrying mottos of good wishes, some in Welsh, such as *'Llwyddiant i Mr a Mrs Casson'* (Success to Mrs and Mrs Casson), some in English, such as 'Long life to the bride and bridegroom.' Laura was attended by her sister Ellen, Tom's sister Annie, and the older three of her half-sisters, Anna, Lily and Mabel, dressed in white alpaca, with blue tunics and white bonnets. Fanny, four years old, and Ethel, two years old, did not go to the wedding, but joined in the reception, dressed in white frocks with blue sashes for the occasion. Even baby Dickie was decked out in a blue tunic. Tom's best man was Ernest Greaves, son of John W. Greaves, the proprietor of the quarry known as 'Llechwedd'.[2] They were married by the Rev David Edwards at the same Penrhyndeudraeth church as Mary Casson. There was a good family turn-out, including Laura's cousin, Theodore Williams, son of the great-uncle and great-aunt who had brought up her mother, and looked after Ellen and herself. After the main reception was over, and the couple had departed for Yorkshire from Talsarnau Station, the bride's father treated nearly 200 children to a tea party and laid on a grand supper for all his workers and families. The day ended with fireworks.

But the festivities were not over. Talsarnau villagers felt that greater honours were due to the Thomas family, and to Tom Casson, who had already contributed to the musical life of the neighbourhood. Rowland Roberts, principal of the British school in the village, which Mr Thomas had helped to establish, was appointed secretary of a planning committee. They collected subscriptions for a handsome Bible to be presented to the new Mrs Casson, together with a special celebratory address, engrossed on vellum. When Tom and Laura returned from their honeymoon, there was a presentation evening at the school, and 160 residents of

Talsarnau and its neighbourhood had contributed. The largest subscription was ten shillings, from the vicar of nearby Llanfihangel Church, and the smallest, tuppence. The total raised was just over £10 (worth over £800 in 2019). The programme for the evening included nine different speeches to the couple, as well as a celebratory address. The groom and the bride's father replied. The choir performed glees and a Mendessohn hunting song. There was a comic duet, and solo songs specially composed for the event, best of all being a version of 'The March of the Men of Harlech', with words specially written for the couple by David Evans. The opening words read:

Nawr neu byth, o byddwch barod –
I roi clod o doed pob tafod,
I ein Casson gydai Briod, –
Ein dewsol rai.

(Now or never be you ready –
May each tongue be here to praise
Our Casson with his Bride
Our chosen ones.)

The verse went on to wish the family every success, to hope that they would live in Wales, and have a long and happy journey, and it urged the company to praise them in Welsh. Afterwards, Rowland Roberts penned a report of the event in beautiful copperplate script and presented it to Laura. His eloquent account survives, long after the Bible and vellum have disappeared:

The meeting passed off in every respect most successfully. The feeling throughout was admirable.

Indeed everything went to prove that the whole neighbourhood had its heart – and that deeply and truly – in the undertaking; and it was a matter of great satisfaction to all that the Committee succeeded so well in giving expression to the general feeling, and in a form acceptable and pleasing to those whom the people wished so earnestly to honour.

Tom and Laura moved into his parents' house, Plas Penrhyn, as William and Fanny had decided to take up residence in Betchton House, on their Cheshire property. Since the death of John Galley Day Jackson, Fanny's father, a series of long-term tenants had occupied the house, but at the time of the settlement which assigned it to William and Fanny, it was uninhabited. For the next few years, Betchton was their official residence, although William's civic duties brought him regularly back to Wales. He was a magistrate, and now 'Deputy Lieutenant of Merionethshire', a largely honorary position, like that of High Sheriff. He used the Casson coat-of-arms, not having the right to carry the Jackson arms of Fanny's family. His friend David Williams, who had also held the office of Deputy Lieutenant, was not alive to congratulate him on his position. He had died after serving only one year as MP, and was succeeded by Samuel Holland, who consolidated the Liberal victory, decisively breaking the dominance of Tory landowners in Meirionydd.

All three of William's sons continued to be active volunteers, while Tom and Randal were initiated into the newly established Madoc Lodge of Freemasons, No. 1509. Galley had succeeded his uncle on the Ffestiniog Board of Guardians, and he spoke at the opening of the first board school, established in response to the Elementary Education Act of 1870, which introduced universal education for children between nine and thirteen years old. Tom, now married to a Welsh woman, was particularly keen to encourage Welsh initiatives. He chaired a meeting to promote Welsh education, where his father made a short speech in Welsh.[3] He was also vocal in condemning the appointment of a judge who could not speak Welsh; he proposed sending a deputation to Parliament in protest.[4]

The question of the Welsh language had become a matter of debate beyond the borders of Wales. A few years earlier, Matthew Arnold had published a letter in *The Times* stating his belief that 'to preserve and honour the Welsh language and literature is quite compatible with not thwarting or delaying for a single hour the introduction, so undeniably useful, of a knowledge of English among all classes in Wales', but his moderate approach had aroused a fierce, unsigned response condemning the Welsh language as 'the curse of Wales', excluding the Welsh people from 'the civilisation of their English neighbours', terming the *eisteddfod* 'one of the most mischievous and selfish pieces of sentimentalism which could possibly be perpetrated', and concluding that 'the sooner all Welsh specialities disappear from the face of the Earth, the better.'[5] Later, Arnold developed his thoughts further, maintaining that 'the sooner the Welsh language disappears as an instrument of the practical, political and social life of Wales, the better for Wales itself', and he criticised the *eisteddfodau* for encouraging 'a fantastic and mischief-working delusion', while advocating the idea of 'hammering [English] into the elementary schools.'[6] Neither Galley nor Tom supported such opinions. They were happy to speak Welsh in their day-to-day business at the bank and were staunch in their support of the *eisteddfodau*, Galley acting as president of the *eisteddfod* held in Blaenau Ffestiniog on Whit Monday in 1872, while Tom and his father-in-law were both involved in the *eisteddfod* held at Harlech around the same time.[7]

Randal, too, could speak Welsh when his legal work required it.

The family was now spread throughout the neighbourhood. After their wedding, Tom and Laura were resident at Plas Penrhyn for only a matter of months, joined there by Randal and one servant girl. Once their father had given up the lease, Tom and Laura moved into Porthmadog and lived at Bank House, attached to Tom's place of work, while Randal took lodgings within easy reach of the law office. In due course, there were three new daughters in the family. Mrs John Casson gave birth to Mary Ethel in Ffestiniog and Laura bore her first child, Frances Winifred. Laura's stepmother, Elizabeth Thomas, gave birth to her sixth and last daughter, also called 'Winifred'. Mary Ranken (née Casson) in Gloucestershire had not produced, but Mrs John was soon pregnant again, and hoping for a son. However, life at Blaenyddôl was about to be brutally disrupted. John Casson was suffering from rheumatic gout. Early in 1873, he was taken to a nursing home in Llandudno, where he died suddenly of a heart attack, in March. He was fifty-seven.

'The greatest gloom pervaded all classes in this [Ffestiniog] neighbourhood,' read the press account of his death and burial. 'The funeral ... was attended by a large concourse of people from all parts.' He was described as 'a kind and peaceful man ... highly respected by all.' He had 'filled many important offices in connection with this neighbourhood, being a justice of the peace, a banker ... guardian of the parish ... a generous and genuine Churchman, and a firm supporter of religious education.' He would be mourned by 'a wide circle of relations and friends.'[8]

A month later, his widow gave birth to a boy who was christened 'John Walker George', the only Casson child to carry on the name of Wonderful Walker. The mixed emotion aroused by this birth, following so close upon the death, threatened to overshadow two happier occasions that summer in William's family, when his daughter Annie was married, from Betchton House, to Robert Griffith, a solicitor from a well-established family in Dolgellau, and his daughter-in-law Laura gave birth to his first grandson, the next William Casson, to be known as 'Will'. Mr and Mrs Robert Griffith settled in Rock Cottage, on the outskirts of Dolgellau, in the foothills of Cader Idris, where they kept open house for her parents and her sister Esther.

Amongst some extant family letters, one survives from about this time written from Cheshire by twenty-six-year-old Esther Casson, youngest daughter of William and Fanny. It throws a sad light on her limited prospects, hardly different from those of a gentlewoman in Jane Austen's time. She began: 'My dearest Bundle [pet name for her youngest brother, Randal], Mary says she wrote to you telling you of the melancholy and hopeless state of my engagement and I want your advice concerning it.' She explained that she had had a letter from 'Franco' and that she had answered it, 'telling him that I thought it would be better for both of us if it was broken off unless he had some prospect of being able to marry within a reasonable time.'

Who Franco was, is unknown; perhaps she was engaged to marry Francis Wynne Turner, a son of Thomas Turner. Whoever he was, he had some determination, for he had not taken her at her word, but had written back, in a letter which she had forwarded to her sister Mary in Gloucestershire, to get her opinion of it. She recounted the bare facts to Randal: that Franco was negotiating for a piece of land, but his chances of getting it were not very good; that he might become a slate merchant, but if he did 'it will be perhaps years before he is able to marry.' She then spelt out her true difficulty: 'I really don't think I could exist at home for so long a time as it would undoubtedly be before we could marry.' The departure of her sister Annie had left her the only child at home. 'I don't want to give him up if I can possibly help it, but it would be better than waiting for years, and perhaps at the end he would not be able to marry. I am in a state of bewilderment but I hope you can make sense of this.' A more cheerful passage followed, in which she described a ball she had attended, which she had 'enjoyed immensely, for I got lots of nice partners and ladies being scarce nice men were plentiful.' Perhaps a wish to be free to entertain a new marriage prospect underlay her bewilderment. Whatever advice her brother Randal and her sister Mary gave her, it did not lead to her marriage to Franco or to anyone else. For the time being, she looked forward to 'the melancholy pleasure of spending Christmas alone', her parents – William and Fanny – being the sole members of the family she would be sharing it with.[9] It was not perhaps the festive occasion William remembered from his own youth, as he raised his glass for the annual toast 'To all old friends round Wallowbarrow Crag.'

In Wales, Tom became involved in a scheme to build a church in Porthmadog. While the planned town of Tremadog had boasted a church and chapel from its beginning, and Penrhyndeudraeth had had a church since 1858, Porthmadog had grown haphazardly and had none. For over twenty years, services had been held in the schoolroom of the national school. The initiative was typical of the response to the spread of Nonconformism in Wales. Tom had been promoting the idea of the church for several years, together with his uncle John. He was appointed secretary of a committee working towards its construction. He had imbibed his uncle George's ecumenical principles and combined them with an attitude of political tolerance.

He therefore responded briskly to a correspondent to the *North Wales Chronicle*, who noted that the name of the Liberal MP for Caernarfonshire, Thomas Love Jones-Parry, was not on the subscribers' list, implying that the building of the church was purely a Conservative initiative. Tom, always strident in expressing his opinions, pointed out that in fact the MP *had* subscribed, and he went on: 'The funds have hitherto been contributed most liberally by all parties; Conservatives and Liberals, Churchmen and Dissenters, so that I may as well inform your correspondent that the good cause is not likely to be much helped by remarks directed against anyone in his political or religious capacity.'[10] The chosen site for the church was above the High Street, on land that was part of the Tremadog estate. In October 1873, William Roche, young heir to the estate, laid the foundation stone. The weather was 'boisterous and wet, the rain falling in torrents during the performance of the ceremony.'[11]

The third generation of Casson brothers seemed settled in their Welsh life. By 1875, Randal was a partner in the legal firm to which he had been articled, henceforth known as 'Breese, Jones and Casson', with its office in Porthmadog High Street. But his brothers' careers were about to be turned upside down. John Casson's will, drafted and signed a few months after his second marriage, was proved in September 1874. He had already settled a part of his estate in trust for the benefit of his wife. He left Blaenyddôl to his brother William. The rest of his estate, including all the property that George had bequeathed him, was to go to his wife during her widowhood, then to his children. She was executrix, together with Galley and Randal as executors, and they would be guardians of his children in the event of her death or remarriage. These arrangements seemed straightforward, but John Casson's financial affairs were not. His personal estate was insufficient to pay his debts and was under 'very heavy liabilities' in respect of the bank. The accounts of Messrs Casson & Co have not survived, but clearly John and/or his nephews had authorised loans and investments which the bank did not have the capital to support. It did, however, have funds left by George Casson, some of which should have been distributed as legacies. Galley and Tom admitted that these funds had remained in the bank 'to prop up its position.'

It may be remembered that, as early as 1848, John Casson had had to pacify the London agent about the precarious position of the bank. At the time of the bank theft in 1859, he had been criticised about his casual arrangements for security. He may have been a 'kind and peaceful man', as described at his death, but perhaps his handling of business affairs had always been cavalier, and his nephews had colluded in allowing a situation that was untenable. Galley and Randal, as executors, were faced with an impenetrable tangle to unravel, with their sister-in-law anxious to safeguard her interests and those of her two children. Two men were particularly helpful at this time: Edward Breese, Randal's senior partner; and George Rae, who was still the general manager of the North and South Wales Bank, long recovered from its setback in the 1840s. Mr Rae arranged not only to purchase Messrs Casson & Co, but also to provide employment for Galley and Tom. The sum agreed was £12,000.

John's widow requested, on behalf of her children and herself, that her late husband's estate be administered by the Court of Chancery. The large estate which John had inherited from his older brother, including Blaenyddôl, disappeared into the fog of Chancery. If matters had been straightforward, William would have taken ownership of his childhood home, and perhaps brought Fanny back to live there. As it was, his sister-in-law, Mrs Mary Casson, remained in residence there for the next few years, protecting her children's interests. In February 1875, the clients of Messrs Casson & Co received a circular letter alerting them to the change of ownership and asking them 'as a personal favour … [to] continue with the North and South Wales [Bank] the business connection which we have so much valued.' The letter ended with 'our most sincere thanks to you and all our old friends and customers who have so kindly supported our Bank during a period of nearly thirty years.' Thus, Messrs Casson & Co came to an ignominious end. In practice, Galley did not find the change too difficult. He was courting Maggie Evans, the daughter of a Welsh farmer from Llannor, near Pwllheli. He was soon confirmed as the manager of what was now the North and South Wales Bank in that town, where he had worked before and had friends. He proposed marriage and was accepted. But for Tom, the change was more drastic.

Soon after the agreement with the North and South Wales Bank was signed, Laura became pregnant with their third child. Mr Rae brought Tom to Liverpool for a few months of further training in the Head Office. Perhaps he wanted to prepare him to manage the Porthmadog branch, the most important in the North Wales region. Laura accompanied him, and they took up lodgings in Birkenhead. But their path was not smooth. Tom had a row with other officers in the bank and threatened to resign. Galley wrote to Randal expressing concern that his brother was about to do something 'so preposterous and foolish' as to sacrifice his salary and his position. In Galley's view, he was making unreasonable demands, not taking into account the odd position the two of them were in, which might well have aroused some jealousy. 'He ought to remember,' he wrote, 'the number of years Mr Breese and Mr Rae have shown themselves our friend [sic].'[12] Since Tom was not an executor of his uncle's will (perhaps John Casson had been wary of his fiery temperament), he had played no part in the negotiations. He was resentful at his lack of influence and loss of status, he and his brother being employees now, where they had previously been partners. Also, his enthusiasm for music, and especially for church organs, about which he was something of an expert, was a distraction from the career in which he found himself. Somehow, with the help of Randal and of their father, he was persuaded not to resign. A few days after Galley's letter, Laura's third child was born in Birkenhead. He was christened Lewis Thomas, after his maternal grandfather. They returned to Wales. Perhaps Tom had blotted his copybook, as Galley feared. He was appointed manager, but not in Porthmadog.

He was to move fifty miles east to the Wales Bank in Denbigh [Dinbych].

Thus, when, in May 1876, St John's Church opened in Porthmadog, Tom had officially left town. His standing in Porthmadog that day was high. The night before, he attended a dinner party given by Major Mathew, the chairman of the church committee, where the Bishop of

St John's Church, Porthmadog

237

Bangor was the chief guest. The next morning was fine, and he made his way to the national school, where all the dignitaries were assembling, together with the choir and clerics.

The original design for the church was by John Roberts, an architect working from Dolgellau, an admirer of the Arts and Crafts movement, but he had died two years before, and the work had progressed slowly after that, with new drawings prepared by Axmann and Perrott, a London company of ecclesiastical architects. It was in the fashionable Gothic Revival style, influenced by the great Victorian architect, Augustus Pugin. The tower which would crown the church had not yet been erected. The procession made its way up the hill and entered the west door through an arched porch, its slate shafts forming the door jambs. There was a long nave, with aisles on either side, clerestory above, and chancel beyond, laid with encaustic tiles, in the style of William De Morgan, another leader in the Arts and Crafts movement. The church was lit by gas fittings suspended from the roof. On its east wall were enamelled slate tablets, inscribed with the Ten Commandments, the Creed and the Lord's Prayer, alternating with designs of wheat and vine. The organ chamber and vestry were on the south side, with a heating room below. The furnishings were of carved oak, and there was ornamental ironwork on the doors.

A Matins service was held in English, and a Welsh service in the afternoon. The singing was led by combined choirs from Porthmadog, Penrhyndeudraeth, Tremadog and Cricieth, and three singers from Beddgelert. The Bishop preached. Tom Casson accompanied all the singing and showed off the power of the organ with a postlude. The grandeur of the sound matched the grandeur of the architecture. After the service, the Cassons scattered to their various homes: William and Fanny back to Betchton, but with frequent visits to Dolgellau, where Annie helped to nurse Esther, who was seriously ill with consumption; Galley to Pwllheli, with his wife Maggie, whom he had married a month before; and Tom and Laura to Denbigh, to set up their new home. Randal remained in Porthmadog. Of the descendants of the first Thomas and Esther Casson, only John Casson's two fatherless children now lived in Ffestiniog.

Only a few months later, the family gathered once more for the saddest of occasions. William wrote to Randal from the Griffiths' home at Rock Cottage to tell him, 'Esther is gradually sinking, her pulse is much weaker. She is free from all pain except the distressing fits of coughing, which occasionally come on'[13] She died of consumption three days later, a few weeks short of her twenty-eighth birthday, and was buried in the churchyard in Dolgellau. The cortège consisted of the men of the family, as was customary, but not her father. Already suffering from a heart condition, he was unable to muster the strength to accompany his daughter's coffin. Fanny and he retreated to Denbigh, seeking the comfort of the presence of their three small grandchildren.

Notes

1   *NWC*, 13 August 1870. There was now a branch line from Betws to Conwy, joining the main Holyhead-London line; they could change at Chester for lines north, to Kendal.
2   *NWC*, 3 December 1870
3   *NWC*, 28 January 1871
4   *NWC*, 9 March 1872
5   The correspondence appeared in September 1866, and was quoted in Arnold, Matthew, *On the Study of Celtic Literature*, 1867, based on lectures he gave as Professor of Poetry at Oxford University.
6   ibid

7   *NWC*, 25 May 1872
8   *NWC*, 12 April 1873
9   Esther Casson to Randal Casson, 15 December 1874, family papers
10 *NWC* 3 February 1872
11 *NWC* 25 October 1873
12 William Galley Casson to Randal Casson, 11 October 1875, family papers
13 William Casson to Randal Casson, 2 August 1876, family papers

Chapter 18

A Sense of Place
1876–1883

While William Casson's family was gathered in Dolgellau for Esther's funeral, he took the opportunity to explain how he intended to leave his estate, wanting to make better arrangements for the future than his brother John had done. The quarry had gone, and the Casson banks; it was not clear if Blaenyddôl could be saved. He still owned Cynfal Fawr, as well as Betchton House and the surrounding estates. The gathering quickly turned fretful. Disappointment was inevitable as the prosperity represented by their uncle George had not been passed on to them. His children all had different needs and wants. Galley, now married, wanted the best for his wife and himself; Tom was responsible for a wife and three children. As boys, these two had enjoyed a friendly rivalry but their relationship became prickly in adulthood. Their sister Mary's husband, the Rev William Ranken, had a good living in Gloucestershire, but she was sensitive about money, often suspicious that she was not being given her just deserts. Annie and her solicitor husband lived comfortably and were the most relaxed about any arrangements her father wanted to make, but she was already frail in health, and would soon be diagnosed with consumption, perhaps contracted while nursing her sister. Bachelor Randal, though sanguine about his own future, felt qualified to give firm opinions about all matters relating to law and property.

William made a Deed of Appointment, dividing his Cheshire property between Galley and Tom, while giving Fanny a lifetime interest.[1] Each of them gained property valued at £19,000 (£1.5 million in 2019), with rental income from tenants, though some of the estate was mortgaged. They would share whatever was left from the Blaenyddôl estate, but that remained frozen in Chancery. William was negotiating with William Davies of Cae'r Blaidd in Ffestiniog, to sell Cynfal Fawr, left to him by his father and uncle, and still tenanted.[2] He made a will, naming Galley and Tom as his executors, instructing them to set up a trust providing Fanny with additional income, and making monetary bequests to the other children.

Esther's death had shaken William. Over the next few months, his health deteriorated. Early in 1877, Fanny and he were again staying with Annie and Robert Griffith in Dolgellau. (Betchton House was a melancholy place with just the two of them.) Already suffering from degeneration of the heart, he contracted bronchitis and died there after a few days' illness. He was sixty-three. Barely five months after Esther's death, another cortège made its way to St Mary the Virgin Church in Dolgellau. His three sons and his son-in-law, Robert, accompanied the coffin. They were joined by his old friend Samuel Holland, MP, now resident at Caerdeon, near Aber-maw; and also by Lewis Holland Thomas, William Davies, and David Homfray, a friend from Porthmadog. It would have pleased William that he was buried near his daughter, and in Wales, since the periods he had spent away, in Liverpool and Cheshire, had sharpened his affection for the land of his birth.

The last child of the Cassons who had come to Wales from Seathwaite was gone. Within months, William's two brothers-in-law also died, Henry Sandys Salisbury, husband of Fanny's sister, and Benjamin Smith, husband of his sister

Bess. With Fanny and her sister Mary both being widows, the question arose where they were to live. It was arranged that 'Aunt Salisbury', as she was known in the Casson family, should join Fanny at Betchton House. This was not entirely an act of charity, as she would pay rent and share the cost of servants. However, it turned out not to be a very happy arrangement, and Fanny spent much of her time staying with one or another of her children. Once again, there were three Casson brothers living in Wales, the third generation, carving out their different niches in the communities they lived amongst.

Galley and his wife lived just outside Pwllheli, near Maggie's parents' farm. This historic borough was busy with fishing and shipbuilding, its ancient market serving the whole Llŷn peninsula. It was the last station on the railway that ran north from Aberystwyth, and then west from Porthmadog. They lived comfortably, with a groom, a cook and a housemaid. They had no children, but Galley still managed to run up considerable debts and he tried to pay off a loan from the bank by taking cash from mortgages on the Cheshire properties, and looking to his father-in-law, John Evans, for additional help. Family lore attaches some unspecified disapproval of Galley. Perhaps he drank or gambled. Whatever his faults, he continued to sit on the bench, supported his local church in Llannor and was often to be seen at local events. He was comfortable in the Welsh language, at home, at work and in the community.

Tom and Laura settled in Denbigh. Like Pwllheli, this thriving market town had been well established by medieval times. It sat in the Vale of Clwyd, surrounded by low Welsh hills, a much gentler terrain than Snowdonia. A railway connected it to Rhyl on the north coast and Corwen to the south, from where there was a direct line to London. The Wales Bank was near the top of Vale Street, a main thoroughfare just below the ruins of the castle that commanded the Vale of Clwyd. For the first few years Tom, Laura and their children lived in the Bank House, just as they had in Porthmadog. Before long Tom was made a magistrate. He was adjutant for the 'Flintshire Volunteer Corps' and was known as 'Major Casson' throughout his years in the town. Near the railway station was Denbigh Infirmary, built at the beginning of the century. Just as his parents had sent provisions to the Ffestiniog Union Workhouse, considering it part of their charitable duty, he offered his services to the infirmary and was soon appointed to its committee. A few miles outside the town stood the magnificent Gothic Revival edifice that was Denbigh Asylum, completed in 1848, and housing up to 200 patients with mental illness. In time, his whole family would pay visits there.

That family was growing. Nine months after Esther Casson's death, Laura gave birth to her second daughter. She was named after the aunt she would never meet, the third 'Esther Casson' in the family, known in her childhood as 'Etty'. The Bank House was overcrowded, with four children, a nursemaid and a general servant. Fortunately, their living arrangements were about to change. Tom was given a raise at the bank and was advised by the Head Office – Mr Rae's influence again – that he should use the ground floor for business purposes and rent out the top floor. Tom suggested to his mother that he might build a house that would be large enough for her to come and live with them. Her financial contribution would allow him more generous accommodation than he could manage on his income alone, and she would have her own base in Wales, where all her children lived. He began to draw up plans for a house at the lower end of the town, near the infirmary, along a road that led to the nearby town of Rhuthun. Before the new house

Cae Derw, Denbigh

was finished, their third son was born, in January 1879, and named Randal, after his uncle, who stood as his godfather. A year later, the house was ready to move into. They called it 'Cae Derw', 'field of oaks', and Tom planted two oak trees by the gate. It was a substantial, modern, red-brick building, with double gables, a spacious garden to the rear, and a farm next door which could provide some fresh supplies. The ground floor included a bedroom and boudoir for Fanny; there was a coach-house and stable, with accommodation for her coachman above it. There was a nursery where the children and servants ate, while the dining-room doubled as a schoolroom. A sturdy oak staircase rose up from near the front door, turning before it reached a landing, from where all the upstairs bedrooms led off. There was no separate staircase for the servants, an unusually democratic arrangement. There was room for a cook/general servant, a governess, a nursemaid, and a maid to wait upon Fanny. They installed some unsold furniture from Plas Penrhyn. Tom was a keen handyman and liked setting up his house with modern conveniences. His greatest innovation was a water turbine to power Laura's treadle sewing-machine, by that time an indispensable household item.

In a business-like way, anxious to anticipate any difficulties, Tom detailed the future arrangement of bringing his mother Fanny into his household.[3] She had made a financial contribution and would be paying a rent for her keep and that of her coachman; and he laid down what would be the reduction in rent when she was absent. While the house was still in construction, she raised the question of where her maid, Miss Evans, was to sleep. Tom had not expected her maid to have a separate bedroom from the other servants. 'I have no bedroom to spare,' he explained, and suggested something he knew she would not like, 'but I can partition off a part of yours without difficulty. Shall I do this at once?' He pointed out that if Miss Evans had a room of her own, she would expect to be waited on herself. 'And there is all the additional cleaning up, as well as the grates.' The sharp exchange of letters that ensued between mother and son did not augur well for the arrangement, each thinking they were doing the other a favour.

Fanny did not take well to widowhood. She had been used to having her own way in all matters of the household. And perhaps William had indulged her. Contemplating her future without him, she had fallen in with Tom's plan, enjoying the idea of having young people about her. But really, it was tiresome to be tripping over Etty whenever she emerged from her room, or to be woken in the morning by young Randal crying. And the house itself, though comfortable, lacked the elegance of Betchton House. On the other hand, although she had been glad of the extra money to run the household there, she did not like being the younger sister, Mary and she always on the edge of a squabble. For the next few years, therefore, she lived a peripatetic life. As well as occupying her room at Cae Derw, she spent time at Rock Cottage in Dolgellau, although Annie's health was deteriorating there; or at the Rankens' home in Maisey Hampton, which was full of rowdy boy boarders, as her son-in-law ran a school as well as the church; or in Llannor with Galley and Maggie, who were self-sufficient in their village life; or with Randal, who was out all day, and often all evening. She was becoming a selfish and interfering old woman.

The senior Randal lived a comfortable bachelor life in Porthmadog. He lodged on the High Street, in the same premises as the offices of Breese, Jones and Casson, and was cared for by a housekeeper from Dolgellau. Next door was Bank House, once occupied by his brother Tom, while on the other side lived his friend, David Homfray, another solicitor, with his wife and family. Edward Breese, the senior partner of the firm, lived with his family at nearby Morfa Lodge, the generously proportioned house that stood on the slope above the High Street, formerly the residence of James Spooner and his family. Mr Breese played an important part in the development of Porthmadog. He was Clerk of the Peace, an antiquarian, and agent for the Tremadog estate, now owned by William Roche, William Madocks' grandson, who had come of age in 1875. The other partner, Robert Jones, had an agricultural background. He was described by one of the clerks as 'racy of the soil' and was most at his ease dealing with local farmers.[4] Amongst Randal's close friends were Percival and Edwin Spooner. They were grandsons of James Spooner and sons of Charles Easton Spooner, manager of the Festiniog Railway, who had helped Randal's father and uncle over the sale of the quarry. The Spooners lived at Bron y Garth, a handsome grey stone house perched on a hill that overlooked Porthmadog's harbour. There, visitors could enjoy the novelty of the miniature steam locomotive, 'Topsy', which Mr Charles Spooner had had built, at one-seventh the size of those used on the line itself.

In 1879, the same year that Randal's namesake nephew was born, Mr Breese took on a young clerk from nearby Cricieth. His name was Dafydd, or David, Lloyd George; he lived with his widowed mother, a sister, a younger brother and his mother's brother, Richard Lloyd. Mr Lloyd was a formidable character, a cobbler, and a dedicated Disciple of Christ, a strict Baptist sect. He saw potential in the older of his two nephews and was determined to further his career. He encouraged him to study for the preliminary law examination, the first hurdle to becoming a solicitor for any young man who had not reached matriculation standard in school.[5] Young David Lloyd George was brought to Mr Breese's attention through another antiquarian, Merfydd Fardd, a friend of Mr Lloyd. It was decided he would be articled to Randal, who immediately took him under his wing. Twice the age of his pupil, Randal enjoyed training him in law, and educating him in other ways as well. They drank beer together, and the young clerk worked in his garden. He soon had him signed up with the 'Caernarvon Volunteers', a commitment which the boy had to keep secret from his uncle, who would not have approved. He kept his uniform at Porthmadog, rather than Cricieth, and when he spent a fortnight camping at Conwy, he explained it away to Uncle Lloyd as a holiday.[6]

The year after David Lloyd George began his articles, there was a general election. Gladstone, after being defeated six years earlier, and handing over his leadership of the Liberal Party, had been re-enthused by his successful Midlothian campaign. He had made a series of passionate speeches against Benjamin Disraeli, now Lord Beaconsfield, for his handling of both domestic and foreign policy.

Beaconsfield dissolved Parliament, hopeful that he would be returned on a wave of imperialism. Lloyd George was already beginning to take an interest in politics, and joined Mr Breese and Mr Casson, canvassing for the Liberal Party in Caernarfonshire. In March 1880, the Conservatives were soundly defeated in all parts of Britain except Ireland. In Wales, there remained only four Conservative members out of thirty-three. Gladstone became Prime Minister again, the 'Grand Old Man' of British politics. Lloyd George's priority at this time was his legal training, a gateway to a successful career.

A few months after the election, Mr Breese was badly injured in a shooting accident, from which he did not recover. He died in March 1881, leaving Lloyd George to the sole management of his principal, Mr Casson, a sterner master, who now became senior partner. On one occasion, Lloyd George made a stupid error, sending out notices of an important meeting without stamping them. He described in his diary how he had waited in some trepidation for Mr Casson to return to the office, when he had to admit his mistake. He kept the diary in English, taking the opportunity to practise writing in that language, while family life was conducted in Welsh. Mr Casson dealt with the misdemeanour like a stern but kindly schoolmaster:

> He did not foam as I expected, but told me in a very solemn and indeed agreeable manner that I must not read so much; that I am muddling my head with law reports etc., not that he did not like to see me do it, as it was proof that I intended getting on, but it would not do instead of office work.[7]

When it was time for Lloyd George to take his intermediate law examination, he made his first trip to London. He saw electric light for the first time, dined with a previous clerk of the firm, in a restaurant in Chancery Lane, and visited Madame Tussaud's waxworks. Messrs Jones and Casson encouraged him to stay a week or longer, sending him extra money for the purpose. 'There is plenty to do in one's first visit to London,' wrote Mr Casson, enclosing the order, 'and I hope you will enjoy yourself thoroughly.'[8]

Around this time, Randal Casson made the acquaintance of a young Englishwoman who soon became important to him. Lucy Jane Nisbet was staying with her mother and stepfather, then living at Tan-yr-Allt, William Madocks' old home in Tremadog. Her background was impressive, her father being the late Sir Alexander Cockburn Nisbet, an eminent Scottish surgeon, and her mother Lady Lucy Susanna (née Davenport), member of a well-to-do aristocratic family whose seat was Davenport House in Worfield, Shropshire. Lucy Jane, was born in 1858. After her father died, in 1874, her mother remarried, but kept her name and title. Lady Nisbet's second husband, Rev Walton Kitching, was a director of Hafod y Llan, a quarry on the south side of Snowdon; this interest brought them to Tremadog.

Lucy Jane Nisbet was an independent, well-educated young woman. She was sent to France, to learn the language; she studied art in London, and subsequently went to live in Oxford. Her relationship with Randal Casson developed slowly. It would later be said by his brothers that he waited ten years before proposing marriage, wanting to establish her in a suitably grand house. An alliance with the Nisbet/Davenport family would raise his social status higher than that of his older brother Galley, and of Tom.

Visits between the three Casson brothers were infrequent. Despite the large network of lines across Britain by this time, the mountainous terrain still necessitated complicated journeys, but Tom and Laura took their children on frequent visits to her family in Talsarnau. The children enjoyed the company of their younger 'aunts', the youngest, Winnie, being the same age as Frances Casson, while Winnie's next sisters, Fanny and Ethel, were not much older. Some diaries that these three sisters kept during their childhood survive, giving a lively account of outings to Rhaeadr Cynfal, Harlech or to the beach at Llandudno; lessons, games, church attendance, errands and calls on friends, neighbours and family. Randal Casson was a welcome visitor. There were visits to Laura's sister Ellen in the hills at Ysbyty Ifan, where she lived with her clergyman husband. There were occasional return visits to Cae Derw in Denbigh.

Laura's stepmother, Elizabeth Thomas, was a firm believer in education for girls. She had sent her three older girls to boarding school in Liverpool, followed by finishing school in Switzerland and Paris. Her husband did not entirely approve when they returned with elaborate dresses and coiffures, out of place in the village of Talsarnau. Although he was proud of his brood of daughters, the older ones were conscious of the fact that they could never, in their father's eyes, replace his firstborn son, who had died as a baby. His third daughter, Mabel, remembered how she and her sisters were brought up to believe that 'little Lewis ... was a being of superior essence to ourselves, of whom the world is not worthy.'[9] When his second son, Dickie, also died, at only nine years old, their father suffered a grief from which he never fully recovered. Family life at Caerffynnon was further disrupted when their oldest daughter, Anna, died the following year. They must have been somewhat cheered when, in April 1881, Tom and Laura had another daughter, who was named Elizabeth, after Mrs Thomas, and known as 'Elsie'.

A few months later, an event took place which affected all

the Casson family; John Casson's widow remarried. Since her husband's death she had continued to live at Blaenyddôl, holding a respected position, and living on what she inherited that lay outside Chancery. Like her late mother-in-law, Esther, whom she had known in her childhood, she had carried out charitable works. On one occasion she was reported as superintending the distribution of soup at a penny per quart in Blaenau, 'in consequence of the dullness of the slate trade ... and the recent severe weather.' It was she, ran the report, 'who in conjunction with Samuel Holland, MP, had originated the practice.'[10] Late Victorian society proclaimed its philanthropy more vocally than in the time of Esther Casson's 'unobtrusive' good works.

Mary's new husband was James Douglas Spooner, nephew of Charles Easton Spooner of Bron y Garth, and a cousin of Randal Casson's friends, Percival and Edwin Spooner. James Douglas's father was another railway engineer but James Douglas himself had gone to sea.[11] Like Lewis Holland Thomas, he made a success of his maritime career, and was Commander of the Royal Mail Service at the time of the marriage. The couple married in London and he settled his bride in Winchester with her two children. There was now no-one left carrying the Casson name in Ffestiniog. When the first history of the parish was written, G J Williams' *Hanes Plwyf Ffestiniog* in 1882, there were no Cassons to tell their part of its story; they appear only fleetingly in its pages. On just one occasion the following year, the local newspaper reported 'Master Casson, Blaenddol' as being present when a curate of the Rev Killin left the village. This 'Master Casson' was ten-year-old John Walker George, posthumous son of John Casson. Galley and Randal had relinquished the guardianship of John Walker George and of his older sister Ethel, and more or less lost touch with them, while Mr and Mrs Spooner soon started a family of their own.

However, another Casson was about to return to the Ffestiniog area, for Galley was moved from Pwllheli to Blaenau, to manage the bank there. This town was by now considerably bigger than the original Ffestiniog. Quarriers' houses stretched along its streets. Grey hillsides, terraced and scarred with slate works loomed up around it, dominating the landscape. Maggie must have felt some regret at leaving Pwllheli, and the softness of the Llŷn peninsula, for this harsh terrain, but it was familiar ground for Galley, and the move was particularly advantageous as he had recently acquired 'Hafod Ysbyty and Gamallt', the nearby property his uncle George had bought thirty years earlier, then being disposed of under the direction of the Chancery judge. Galley paid the ten percent deposit of £175, but he must have raised the rest of the money from his mother-in-law, Mrs Evans, for he immediately mortgaged it to her. He obtained a Crown lease for the mineral rights in case that should turn out to be a source of useful income. Meanwhile, he enjoyed the excellent fishing on Llyn Gamallt.

In September 1883, a notice appeared in the *North Wales Chronicle*, advertising the sale of:

The MANSION HOUSE known as
BLAENYDDÔL
in the parish of Festiniog, with the Tenants, Fixtures,
Gardens, Ornamental Grounds, Plantations, with about 24
ACRES OF LAND and the remaining portions of the
Farm and Lands of Blaenyddôl aforesaid (in 15 convenient
Lots), comprising the Dwelling-house known as GLASDO,
the Chapel kown as PENIEL, and many excellent pieces of
PASTURE, WOODLAND, AND BUILDING LAND,
situate close to the village of Festiniog.

Forty-seven lots from the estate were to be auctioned at the Oakeley Arms on 18 September. Particulars, plans and conditions of the sale could be obtained from 'Messrs Spooners and Co, Surveyors' and 'Messrs Breese, Jones and Casson, Solicitors', a circumstance that must have caused Randal some chagrin. However, this sale was the beginning, rather than the end of the affair, for notices of sales were repeated the following year, and the Chancery case ground on. Galley acquired another piece of Casson property. Not real estate, but an item from Blaenyddôl that he clearly felt should stay within the family. He became the owner of the Walker clock, which he must have removed from the house at an opportune moment. By that time, its purported history had been recorded. Tom Casson had subscribed to the fifth edition of *The Old Church Clock*, the book that commemorated Wonderful Walker. He provided information to its new editor about all the descendants of his grandmother Esther and supplemented the account of Robert Walker's life. 'Rebellion, treason, and bloodshed frequently surrounded him', were the words Robert Bamford had written in his 1819 narrative. The new editor added a footnote: 'Thomas Casson says "When there was a rumour of the Pretender being near Seathwaite ... Robert Walker shouldered his clock, and hid it in the mountains somewhere until the danger was past".'[12]

Secure in their position in Wales, the three Casson brothers still cherished their English roots. For them, and for those whose lives touched them, their identity was forged by their sense of place, in terms of location, family history, social position and stage of life. The oldest members of the extended family, Lewis Holland Thomas and Fanny Galley Day Casson, looked back on contrasting lives, the former proud at having built up his fortune single-handedly, the latter anxious to protect a gentility she had inherited.

The Casson brothers made the most of a situation that was less prosperous than what they had expected, Galley living somewhat beyond his means, Tom managing his finances carefully, to support his growing family, Randal building a successful career, and harbouring an aspiration to acquire a valuable property in due course and set up a prosperous establishment. Of the women, Elizabeth Thomas provided her daughters with opportunities that had not been open to girls when she was young, opportunities from which Randal's friend, Lucy Nisbet, as yet a visitor to Wales, had already benefited. Mrs Thomas encouraged her stepdaughter Laura Casson to give her children an upbringing rich in culture and education, if not in money. Outside the family circle, Richard Lloyd nursed an ambition equal to that of Mrs Thomas, determined that his nephew Dafydd/David should fulfil his potential, and achieve a success that would carry him far beyond Cricieth. For each of the younger generation, their home country, Wales, meant something different, and would change in what it represented to them as they grew up.

Notes

1   Schedule of Deeds and Writings relating to estates in Betchton, Smallwood, Testo, Newton, Alsager and Bradwall, 1877, family papers

2   William Davies' wife was a cousin of William Casson, being a granddaughter of his uncle John Casson of Seathwaite..

3   Letters between Fanny G D Casson and Tom Casson, 18 May 1878- 2 Dec 1879, family papers

4   George, William, *My Brother and I*, 1958, p. 121

5   Abel, Richard L, *The Making of the English Legal Profession*, 1998, p. 142

6   George, p. 119

7   ibid p. 114

8   George, pp. 16-17, quoting Randal Casson to David Lloyd George, 11 November 1881

9   Holland Grave, Mabel, *Some Welsh Children*, published anonymously, 1898, p. 81

10 *NWC*, 25 February 1871

11 Wilson, D H, 'The Spooners up to Date', *Festiniog Railway Magazine*, No 77, Summer 1977

12 Parkinson, ed Evans, p. 38

Chapter 19

Separate Paths
1882–1889

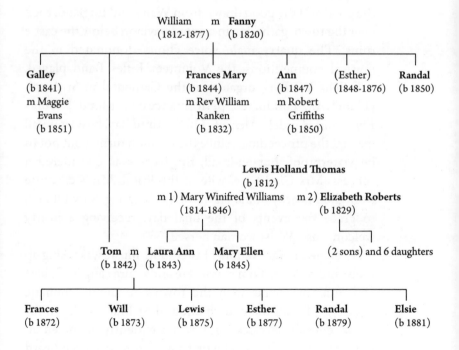

The Casson Family 1882

In the summer of 1882, Denbigh hosted the National Eisteddfod, 'the great annual event of the Principality', and

Tom Casson served on the Music Committee.[1] The town had hosted two provincial *eisteddfodau* in the 1820s, the second attended by the Duke of Suffolk, brother of King George IV. In 1858, there had been a Grand Eisteddfod in Llangollen, leading to the idea of an annual National Eisteddfod, the first one held in Aberdare in 1861, and continuing annually, despite, or perhaps because of, the contempt for the Welsh language felt by some.

For five days in August, after months of preparation, competitors, speakers, performers, spectators and many of the great and the good drawn from Wales and England, took over the town, gathering in a grand pavilion below the castle ruins. The quarry male voice choirs dominated in the musical competitions, the Volunteer Rifles Band played, and Felix Watkins, organist at the Cathedral in St Asaph [Llanelwy], conducted performances of Mendelssohn's *Elijah* and Handel's *Messiah*. On the third day, heavy rainfall marred the proceedings, since the pavilion turned out not to be waterproof, but all-in-all, the week was considered a success. Mrs Gladstone, wife of the Prime Minister, came from their nearby home Hawarden ('Penarlâg, Sîr y Fflint'), to grace the events of the final day, receiving a hearty welcome as a Welshwoman herself.

Even before the National Eisteddfod, music was taking up more and more of Tom's time. He and Laura sang in Gilbert and Sullivan operas with the town's Amateur Dramatic Society.[2] He ran the church choir at St Mary's, played for many church services, and was frequently involved in musical performances. The first time Tom's children heard a full orchestra was when he gathered instrumentalists together for a rendering of the 'War March' from Mendelssohn's *Athalie*.[3] He was equally happy to lighten a local event with a comic song. One called 'Paddy Blake's Echo' proved popular at a concert in aid of the infirmary.[4]

When the Denbigh Philharmonic Society held its first concert after the National Eisteddfod, Tom suggested that the town should mount a music festival and perform oratorios on a regular basis. However, the press report was discouraging, pointing out that the hall was only half full that night, and that there was insufficient local support:

We agree entirely with the remarks made at the Denbigh concert by Dr Turnour, that the music-loving public owe many thanks to Mr Watkins, Major T. Casson and others for their efforts to promote the performance of oratorios in Denbigh; but it is at the same time lamentable to see what little interest the general public appear to take in the matter. The great majority seem to prefer a string of popular ballads, sprinkled pretty thickly with comic songs. Those are the kind of programmes to 'fetch 'em'. We should hail with much satisfaction the musical festival on a grand scale; and if Mr Watkins and men of his stamp undertook the movement, it would be a musical success. But what about the finances?[5]

This would not be the only time that Tom's enthusiasm and ambition led him towards ventures that were financially precarious. His chief interest outside the home, as it had been ever since his Liverpool boyhood, was the design of church organs. He considered the organ 'the king of instruments', had acquired several patents for improvements in design, and was an occasional contributor to *Musical Opinion*, a periodical established five years earlier. In June 1883, he published a booklet, entitled:

THE MODERN ORGAN:
A CONSIDERATION OF THE PREVALENT
THEORETICAL AND PRACTICAL DEFECTS
IN ITS CONSTRUCTION
WITH
PLANS AND SUGGESTIONS FOR THEIR REMOVAL
Fully illustrated
BY
THOMAS CASSON

This was his first major venture into print, and was dedicated to his mentor, W. T. Best. Organ design was a topic of passionate interest to a dedicated number of specialists, who vied with each other to supply suitable instruments for both ecclesiastical and secular venues. The organ had become an essential part of church services, where there was a greater emphasis on music than in earlier periods, influenced by the popularity of the Methodists' congregational singing, and by the return to pre-Reformation practices in some Anglican churches, encouraged by the Oxford Movement from the 1830s onwards. Hymns became an integral part of the services, the standard collection being *Hymns Ancient and Modern*, first published in 1861. Carols were now a regular part of Christmas. No longer was it sufficient to have a couple of bassoons accompanying a metrical Psalm; the organ was increasingly to be heard resounding through the church. The previous forty years had seen a revival of the established church, as it competed with the growth of Nonconformism, and nowhere more so than in Wales. Many churches were repaired, like St Michael's in Ffestiniog, or newly built, like St John the Divine in Porthmadog. Every church and chapel needed an organ, as did the concert halls.

As Tom was an amateur in this specialised field, his book

was reviewed in a somewhat patronising tone: 'Mr Casson's well-considered organ schemes ... show much artistic thought ... [but] Mr Casson ... is something of a "free lance" still, individual thought and labour, on any given topic, has its value, and his book deserves to be read and thought over.'[6] His main thrust was to recommend improvements in the control of the pedal clavier, the keyboard that was played with the feet, and which sounded the lowest notes. It was a fairly recent addition to organ design. Before that, the manual keyboard had been longer, covering a wider range. In Tom's opinion, some musicality had been lost in recent developments, and he had strong ideas about adapting the pedal keyboard to give the organist more scope and variety of effects. His publication was prompted by his desire to get involved in organ manufacture, but although he was a proficient handyman, he did not have the skills to carry out his designs. His preface ended with the words: 'I have one enthusiastic disciple in a good builder of well-known name ... and I can now get organs built on this system.'[7] The man he had found was John Bellamy, whose fortunes would be bound up with his for the next few years.

Bellamy was a craftsman, two years younger than Tom. He had started off as a joiner in Staffordshire, but by 1869 was describing himself as an organ-builder. In 1875, he built an organ for a restored church at Cyffylliog, near Denbigh, and another for the Wesleyan Chapel in Alsager, Cheshire, near Sandbach.[8] Either of these installations could have brought him to Tom's notice. In 1881, by then based in Manchester, Bellamy built his 'magnum opus', a new organ for Holy Trinity Church in Ulverston. By this time, he had met Tom, seen his designs, and agreed that he could, given time, work out how to build the necessary parts. Tom arranged for the Bellamy family, consisting of his wife and two children, to spend some months on the Isle of Man, working up a prototype, after which they would move to Denbigh, and the two men would work together to build organs following Casson's patents. Tom wrote to his mother, 'I am still busy with my organ inventions, and there really seems to be a prospect of my making money from them.'[9]

Their first project was to rebuild the organ at St Mary's Church, Denbigh, where the Cassons worshipped. Tom persuaded W. T. Best to advise. His design had three manuals, controlling a 'great organ'; a 'swell organ'; and an 'echo organ', with a softer range of notes; and a pedal clavier (keyboard), offering a bass range. Tom's innovation was to introduce a mechanism (which he called the 'pedal help'), allowing the organist to shift the pedal clavier to connect with whichever organ he wanted. It was capable of a wider range of musical sounds than was usual in an instrument of this size. W. T. Best came to give an inaugural recital in June 1884.[10] Tom felt that he was now on his way to becoming a recognised organ-designer, though still an amateur, as his 'real' job was managing the bank.

At the time the new organ was installed at St Mary's, Tom read the announcement of an International Inventions Exhibition, to be held in London the following year. It would consist of two divisions, 'Inventions' and 'Musical Instruments', and it would take place in the garden and buildings of the Royal Horticultural Society, then situated in South Kensington. The Prince of Wales was its president, Queen Victoria a patron. By November, Tom had put in his application to enter. By December, he was one of 280 successful entrants. At first, the project went smoothly. In the spring of 1885, Tom announced that he would definitely be exhibiting. On the advice of Frederick Jardine – a well-reputed organ-builder in Manchester with whom Bellamy had worked – he went to a Mr Edward Wadsworth to take charge of the construction; John Bellamy was building the console; the keys would be made by a London firm.[11]

At the beginning of May 1885, the Prince of Wales, accompanied by the Princess of Wales, opened the Inventions Exhibition. Within the first week, there were nearly 100,000 visitors.[12] Tom's organ was to join other musical instruments in the central gallery. As the months went by, Tom found that Mr Wadsworth was alarmingly dilatory. By July, he was so frustrated that he took legal advice from a London firm of solicitors, and then dismissed Mr Wadsworth, who retaliated by claiming compensation. Tom wrote to ask Randal if he would defend the action if it came to court, but Randal was wary of mixing family and business. The dispute distracted Tom from the urgent need to get the organ completed. Eventually, mainly through the efforts of John Bellamy, it was almost, but not quite, finished. Constructed in a workshop in Denbigh, it was then dismantled and transported to London, where the newly built subway from South Kensington Station allowed exhibits to be brought into the gallery without local disruption. Tom and Bellamy then put the parts together again. In September, Tom met the jury. One of them, Robert Bosanquet, organist at St John's College, Cambridge, was particularly enthusiastic and suggested that he wrote up a description for *The Engineer*. Another, Dr Bridges, organist at Chester Cathedral, said that he would back Tom up in trying for an order from the Duke of Westminster.[13] They gave Tom the impression that he would have won the gold medal if he had managed to complete.

Despite not getting the top award, Tom now felt that his future was bound up with his organ designs. In December, Dr Bridges gave a recital on the organ at St Mary's, while Tom announced at the same time in *Musical Opinion* that

'An organ on Mr. Thos. Casson's Patent System is now being erected in Corwen Church by Mr John Bellamy.'[14] This would include his pedal system and was designed to sit on each side of the chancel, so as not to block up the transepts with an organ chamber. It was completed nearly two years later. This time, he lured Dr William Spark, organist at the Town Hall in Leeds, to come and try both organs, and elicited from him a letter to *Musical Opinion*:

Mr Casson should not, and must not, longer be neglected. I suggested to him some time ago, the formation of a small limited company which should build organs on his new principle and farm out the patented inventions to the organ-builders who are wise enough to use them.[15]

Upon this encouragement, Tom registered 'Casson's Patent Organ Co Ltd' in November 1887, with a capital of £6,000 in £10 shares and with registered offices at his bank. His main contribution was the patents he already owned, which he valued at £3,000, but this did not represent ready funds. He took a loan from the bank and hoped to raise the rest of the capital from friends and supporters in Denbigh. Some local people subscribed, including Dr Arthur Turnour, local magistrate and a beneficiary of the town, and Felix Watkins, music master at Ruthin School and organist at St Asaph. He drew on mortgages on his Cheshire properties. In the event, he raised less than £800 in shares. But he took over the two top floors of a local foundry, installed John Bellamy there and began to take orders for new instruments to be built along his system.

This venture coincided – and was the partial cause of – a serious rift with his mother. Over the last few years, Fanny had become more difficult, unable to deal graciously with the fact that she no longer had a household to rule, accusing Tom of mismanaging his part of the Cheshire estate. Now she decided that there was no point in paying him any rent for Cae Derw, as she had no intention of staying there again. She came to collect what she considered to be her belongings. At the time of the Plas Penrhyn sale, seventeen years before, Tom had offered to buy some things for his own new household, and his father had generously foregone payment. Now Fanny regarded these items as her own, as well as gifts William and she had made in the past. The whole visit was a disaster. She sniffed and sneered at the meals that were put in front of her – 'Better things,' Tom told Randal, 'than we can afford for ourselves.' He was particularly upset because she had treated Laura 'with marked and carefully studied offensiveness', and he had therefore found it impossible to be cordial. 'She leaves today,' Tom wrote, 'and I have no reason to suppose that I or my wife or children will ever see her again.'[16] The rest of her family in Wales offered no comfortable home for her. Galley was a widower, Maggie Casson having died suddenly of a heart attack, at the age of thirty-four, while her daughter Annie was increasingly frail. Fanny began to spend more time with her daughter Mary, by that time living in Surbiton, Surrey, where the Rev William Ranken was vicar of Christ Church.

Fresh orders began to come in regularly to Tom's company, but Fanny's apprehensions about the business were justified, for people did not pay promptly and Tom was always in need of money upfront to embark on a new instrument. And he was not the easiest of working partners. He often rubbed people up the wrong way. From the start of his enterprise he had relied on the skill of John Bellamy, who was foreman of the company, but Tom gave him little or no credit in public. He was also difficult on a day-to-day basis, as he often changed his mind about what he wanted, creating much pressure and extra work. A final break-up between them was caused by a squabble, after Bellamy went up to Ulverston to tune the organ he had built there. On his return, he found that Tom had hired a local clerk to be timekeeper – since he himself needed to be away at the bank much of the time. Bellamy found this offensive, as if he and his colleagues were being spied upon and he sent for his tool-box. He began working on his own, building a one-manual instrument for Llanfynydd Church, near Wrecsam. Tom wrote to the vicar there to say that Bellamy must have got the order under false pretences, while working for him. That was the final parting of the ways. Bellamy went on to build many organs under his own name, while Tom developed his own team.[17] Laura, however, made sure that the two families remained on friendly terms.

In February 1888, Tom announced that the company was expanding into additional premises in Denbigh.[18] This may have been a public relations exercise, to try to raise more capital in the town, for at the same time, he wrote to Randal: 'If I am not better supported here I shall transfer the works &c to Birmingham, as suggested by some eminent professional men there, and make a much larger thing of it.'[19] Frustrated that no-one in Wales seemed ready to give real support to his venture, he began to think seriously of setting up in London, as he knew of an organ-builder there who was in financial difficulties, whose enterprise he might take over. He would not need to leave employment at the bank, but simply invest some money, take a seat on the board and travel up to London a few times a year.

During this time, the lives of the three Casson brothers ran along separate paths. While Tom led a full life in Denbigh and was impatient to get national recognition for his organ inventions, Galley lived more quietly in Blaenau, still managing the bank, attending the Magistrates' Court, and being a keen member of the Cambrian Angling Association. Randal had a higher profile in Porthmadog, where his work in the law firm was his main preoccupation. It had its own dramas. Randal's protégé, David Lloyd George, completed his articles early in 1884, when he was eighteen. Randal, then in his thirties, wrote on that occasion, and included a gift of £5:

Bodawel, Portmadoc   24th January 1884

My dear George,

I observe that your term of service expires tomorrow, and as I shall probably not see you I write you a line to express a hope that you can look back now over the last five years with as much satisfaction as I can. I mean, of course, with reference to the connection and intercourse we have had together. Sometimes, as I told you the other day, a little apparent friction, but looking at it as I do, that one is under a considerable amount of responsibility in undertaking an articled pupil, I feel it better to err on the side of apparently requiring too much than the easier and more usual course which is adopted. It is a great satisfaction to me to be able to tell you that I am gratified thoroughly with the industry and capability which you have evinced, and I look forward to a good future for you. You can always count on me as a good friend I hope – and I shall always do what I can for your welfare.

I was sorry to hear you were rather complaining. Take my advice and run down to Llandudno and stay a week at the Hydropathic and make use of Dr. Roberts' name to Dr Thomas, the head of the place. It will fit you up very well for your final grind and accept the enclosed [£5] for the 'Xs' and as a small mark of your 'long service and good conduct'.

Remember me kindly to your Mother and Uncle and believe me,

Yours sincerely,
Randal Casson[20]

The young clerk replied in high-flown English that sometimes ran away with him:

> Morvin House
> Criccieth
> 24th January 1884

Dear Mr Casson

I received your kind note of todays with enclosure, for William [his younger brother, also articled to Randal]. Allow me to thank you warmly for this your last act of kindness towards me.

The sentiments which you are good enough to express concerning my behaviour in your employ are to me truly encouraging & I cannot but ever regard it as a triumph to have such expressions of esteem, from a gentleman whom I have always known to be sincere as well as discerning. As to the 'apparent frictions' you refer to, it behoves me to oblivionate [sic] them as much as possible, as I invariably, in the end, found that they were due to some blunders of my own; & I shall always appreciate the honourable motives which prompted you to take the pains you did to enable me to acquire competency in the profession you instructed me in.

Your assurances of friendship & help for the future are necessarily very valuable to me & I trust that my conduct will never be such as to give you cause to retract them.

I am afraid that a run to Llandudno, though very alluring, is at present entirely out of the question. I have been suffering from a very sharp attack of sore throat & as it has not quite healed, I am advised to keep in for some time to come.

My mother & uncle wish to join me in expressing deep gratitude for your very generous letter & gift.

Believe me
Yours faithfully
D Lloyd George[21]

Lloyd George took his final law examination that April, gaining a Third Class classification, and was admitted to the roll of solicitors that July. Randal offered him the post of 'assistant solicitor' in the Dolgellau office, but this did not satisfy the ambitious young man, who perhaps hoped to be made a partner at once.[22] At the beginning of 1885, his brother William went to London to take his intermediate law examination, with Randal paying for his holiday as he had done for David. When William George returned, he found that his brother had severed his connections with Breese, Jones & Casson and set up his own legal practice, a serious breach of professional ethics. Randal was understandably angry. The 'bitter controversy' and the 'spirit of unfriendliness thus engendered', as William

George put it, lasted for many years.[23] But Randal kept that last letter of his erstwhile protégé for the rest of his life, evidence of a time when he had been proud to be his mentor.

His own legal work was growing. The firm looked after several large estates in Meirionydd and Caernarfonshire. He was now the agent of the Tremadog estate, and in regular correspondence with its owner, William Roche. Appointed High Sheriff in 1887, Mr Roche made Randal Under-Sheriff. He did not have the same rapport with young William George that he had had with David before the rift. Most of the time, William found him like a 'standoffish headmaster in a posh private school.' But he also recalled a humorous side of Randal's character. The clerks' room was situated the farthest possible distance from Mr Casson's office, so that when he summoned a clerk to come up, his call frequently went unheard, at which point he would shout louder, 'with some choice expletives and stamping of feet to emphasize the urgency of the call.' One of the clerks was a very good mimic, and his party piece was his imitation of Mr Casson. Mrs Breese, widow of Edward Breese, persuaded him to perform it at her Christmas party, assuring him that Mr Casson was not present:

> ... he marched into the midst of the merry party. Of course he brought the house down, and never were there such roars of laughter in a Morfa Lodge party before. But when the laughter and cheers were at their height, who should march in from behind a curtain but Mr Casson himself. Bob was paralysed. But he noticed that Mr Casson was joining in the laughter as heartily as any of them, and to his credit, be it said, never afterwards did he show any signs of resentment.[24]

However, Randal's resentment was great indeed, when Lloyd George persuaded William to leave the firm of Breese, Jones & Casson and join his own, as soon as he qualified. Lloyd George wanted his younger brother to keep up the legal practice he had established, since he already had political interests he wished to pursue. Brought up by his uncle to be a fierce Welsh patriot, he was more radical than his early Liberal mentors, Edward Breese and Randal.[25] In the general election of 1885, when Samuel Holland stood down in Meirionydd, Lloyd George made a speech at Blaenau, condemning men like Holland as 'weak knee'd Liberals.'[26] In particular, he wanted to see land reform in Wales, and the disestablishment of the church. Personally ambitious, and encouraged by his uncle, he hoped to work directly for these causes by becoming an MP. At first, he sought to stand in Meirionydd, but the chosen candidate was T. E. Ellis, from near Bala, who was already secretary to a Liberal MP, and was elected to represent the county in 1886. At this time, the issue of Home Rule for Ireland was creating fierce political divisions and inspiring some Welshmen to adopt a nationalistic outlook for their own country. In London, a number of Welsh Liberals, including T. E. Ellis, formed *Cymru Fydd*, ('Wales Future'). Unlike the Irish movement, this group did not seek self-government, but promoted social reform and a legislative assembly for Wales.

Changes in the political landscape were matched by endings in the Cassons' family life. Lewis Holland Thomas was coming to the end of his life. He had never recovered from the death of his son Dickie, and then of his daughter Anna. He sank into melancholia and grew ill with encephalitis, which affected his brain, so that he often did not know where he was. 'We must set out, we must go on again,' he would say, and: 'Where shall we sleep tonight?', as if he was back on the *Laura Ann* with Winny and his two little girls.[27] He died at Caerffynnon at the end of September 1888, and was buried in the churchyard at Llanfihangel-y-traethau, on a headland looking out to sea. Reverting to his first language, he asked for the funeral service to be conducted in Welsh, with all his favourite hymns. He left money in trust to Laura and Ellen, which would be administered by their cousin Theodore and by Elizabeth's brother, Richard Roberts. He had written his will seventeen years earlier, soon after Dickie was born, in the expectation that he could leave Caerffynnon Hall to his son and heir. Now it was up to his widow to keep the household going.

The following year, Aunt Salisbury died at Betchton House. More unexpectedly, Galley died that summer of 1889, aged forty-eight. While fishing with a doctor friend, at Llyn Gamallt, on his own piece of land above Blaenau, he was taken ill, later went into convulsions, and died that evening. The doctor telegraphed the news to Randal, who informed the rest of the family. He arranged a simple funeral attended by their brother-in-law Robert Griffith, William Davies, their distant cousin in Ffestiniog and the doctor and his colleague. Tom wrote that he had sunstroke and could not attend, perhaps an excuse invented because of the uneasy relationship between his older brother and himself.

Although Galley had been the oldest of the three brothers, he had never taken on the role of family patriarch like his uncle George. His nieces and nephews gained the impression that there was something shady about this uncle, though this impression may have been unjust, since it was based on Tom's jaded view. If Tom hoped he would inherit something, allowing him to set up his organ company on a firm footing, he was disappointed. Galley left everything, including Betchton House and the Walker clock, to Randal, who, despite being the youngest brother, acted more and more as head of the family.

Notes

1   *NWC*, 26 August 1882
2   *NWC*, 1 Mar 1879
3   BBC Home Service, *Desert Island Discs*, interviewer Roy Plomley, castaway Sir Lewis Casson, pre-recorded 20 May 1965
4   *NWC*, 29 Apr 1882
5   *NWC*, 13 Jan 1883
6   Quoted in *NWC*, 23 June 1883
7   Casson, Thomas, *The Modern Organ*, 1883, p. 7
8   Information from articles by John Williams, Bellamy's grandson, in *The Organ*, 1990
9   Tom Casson to Fanny G D Casson, 25 February 1883, family papers
10 *NWC*, 2 August 1884
11 Williams, *The Organ*, August, 1990, p 97
12 *Morning Post*, 5 May, 1885
13 Tom Casson to Randal Casson, 26 September 1885, family papers
14 *Musical Opinion*, 1 September, 1887
15 *Musical Opinion*, 1 October, 1887
16 Tom Casson to Randal Casson 22 October 1887, family papers
17 Williams, *The Organ*, August 1990, p 99
18 *NWC*, 4 February 1888
19 Tom Casson to Randal Casson 16 Feb 1888, family papers
20 quoted in George, p. 119
21 Family photocopy, original held at LlGC/NLW
22 Grigg, John, *The Young Lloyd George*, 1973, p. 40
23 George, pp. 134-135
24 ibid, pp. 122-123
26 Price, R Emyr, 'Lloyd George and Merioneth Politics', *MHRS* Vol 7, 1976, p. 301
27 Isambard Owen, p. 106

Chapter 20

Childhood, Youth and Education
1882–1890

Amongst the lectures given at the National Eisteddfod in Denbigh in 1882 was one on girls' education, a topic which particularly interested Tom and Laura Casson, whose eldest child, Frances, was a bright ten-year-old. The speaker was Frances Hoggan. Originally from Aberhonddu ('Brecon'), she was the first female doctor in Wales, having trained in Zurich, before medical training was open to women in Britain. That year, she had published a pamphlet advocating women's education in Wales, believing this would help to build a 'strong Wales', in which 'the full measure of national prosperity, of national happiness and usefulness, and of national growth can be attained.'[1] 'Women, in Wales,' she said in her lecture, '[have] long been kept out of their birth right in the matter of education.' She went on to argue that 'girls and boys are pretty much alike in their capacity for learning'.[2]

For the early years of their education, Tom and Laura's children had an English governess. They spoke English at home, and heard Welsh spoken in the town, but none of them became fluent. Only Tom continued to use the language when dealing with monoglot customers at the bank. He could not afford to send Frances to boarding school in Liverpool, where the Holland Thomas girls were educated. Instead, she became a day pupil at Miss

Ridgeway's School in Penmaenmawr, on the coast opposite Bae Conwy. Laura and he planned that Will and Lewis would go to the local elementary school, established after the Education Act of 1880. According to a story later told by Lewis, Will attended for a time, but one night, when the boys were in bed, Laura overheard Will telling his younger brother the facts of life in graphic detail, as he had heard them from his schoolmates. Laura was shocked. She made the two of them come downstairs, kneel down before her and 'pray for chastity and purity of heart.'[3] Council school, she decided, was not suitable, but there was an excellent boys' school nearby. Ruthin Grammar School was an old, endowed foundation open to local boys who could speak English, with some places for boys from outside the town. Will and Lewis enrolled.

The family was almost complete. In the months leading up to the National Eisteddfod, Laura suffered a miscarriage, which Tom described brusquely to his mother as 'an event over which I do not think either of us grieve.'[4] The following year, 1883, she was pregnant again, and her next and last child, Annie, was born that September, quickly becoming the pet of the family. Tom now had seven children growing up in Denbigh. Of his siblings, neither Galley Casson nor Mary Ranken had offspring, and Randal Casson was still unmarried. Annie Griffith was also childless and was seriously consumptive. She died only two months after her namesake's birth. Once again, the middle son perpetuated the Casson line in Wales.

Music was naturally important in Tom's family life, and also theatre. Laura and he held regular musical evenings, attended by the bank clerks. They sang glees and applauded Tom's comic poems. Frances played the piano, Will sang, and so did Lewis, who also played the penny whistle, and could recite a large number of poems, while Esther was learning the violin. They were all familiar with Shakespeare's plays. Tom read *Macbeth* aloud, playing all the parts. They once presented a nursery version of *As You Like It*, though this had to be halted at one point as Rosalind, played by Frances, got cramp in her toe. Visits to the professional theatre were rare but Lewis would later describe how they went to see a Christmas pantomime in Chester, and how he particularly enjoyed the moment when 'Robinson Crusoe' picked up from the floor a cardboard footprint and showed it to the audience.[5] Sometimes, there were entertainments at the Drill Hall in Denbigh, including shows with 'Pepper's Ghost', an ingenious method of presenting the illusion of a ghost. Will and Lewis built a model theatre, an elaborate affair with a real auditorium. They bought scenes and cut-out characters by mail from Benjamin Pollock's toy theatre shop in London, choosing 'penny plain', which they coloured themselves, to avoid the expense of 'tuppence coloured', and writing their own scripts, to avoid further expense. They built lavish sets that would not have dishonoured the great Victorian actor, Henry Irving, at the Lyceum Theatre in London. Real gas jets lit the stage, ingeniously piped from the main supply in the house. When these lights once started a miniature conflagration, the boys solemnly let down a pretend 'fireproof' curtain before dousing the flames.[6]

Church was also important. Laura was deeply religious, consciously following the teachings of Christ in all that she did and bringing the children up to live a Christian life. The family supported the Church Extension Association (CEA), established in 1870 by Emily Ayckbourn, a clergyman's daughter from Chester, who wanted to alleviate the social deprivation she saw around her in the town. Charitable works were at the centre of the CEA's work. Out of it came a women's order, the Sisters of the Church. 'Mother Emily'

– as she became – founded schools for poor children, first in London, then in other towns, and later expanded the work abroad. In 1886, she established the Pinafore Society, for younger members of the CEA, to help fund her London school. Each member paid one penny a month and had to send a pinafore every six months for the children in the school to wear.[7] All the Casson girls became enthusiastic members, Annie waiting impatiently until she was six years old before she could join.

In 1885, Tom took his three sons to London for the first time, to visit the Inventions Exhibition. All three remembered the treat for the rest of their lives, especially the illuminated fountains, the display of electric lights, and such ingenious inventions as the first typewriter. Will began to dream of being an electrical engineer, and Lewis too thought some scientific vocation lay ahead of him, while young Randal decided to become an astronomer.

Tom Casson supported the Liberal Party, but the Holland Thomas girls in Talsarnau were brought up by their father to support the Conservative Party. In his prosperity, Lewis Holland Thomas threw in his lot with the party that had been dominant in his youth. His children copied his political stance with enthusiasm. Mabel, the third daughter, was said to have written home from boarding school in Liverpool: 'All the girls are Radicals! How glad I shall be to come home and be among good Conservatives again.'[8] In the spring of 1881, thirteen-year-old Ethel Holland Thomas wrote a lamentation on the death of Disraeli. It began:

O! Beaconsfield and art thou dead?
Has England's greatest spirit fled?
Has England lost her greatest, best?
And art thou peacefully at rest?[9]

Three days later, she penned another six-verse threnody, combining the same sentiments of praise and grief, assuaged by confidence that her hero was safe with Jesus. She had absorbed both her father's politics and his firm Christian faith. The Holland Thomas girls also developed a passionate and romantic strain of Welsh patriotism. Like many Welshmen, their father liked to claim, at least to his children, that they could trace their descent from the heroes of Welsh history, Llywelyn the Great and Owain Glyndŵr, that his family had seesawed through history 'now in high feather, now in dire poverty', that he used to stay at Castell Gwydyr, in Llanrwst, and hear the legend of Sir John Wynne's ghost, 'condemned to live behind the waterfall'.[10] Sometimes, he had to check their enthusiasm, when they started to speak of Queen Victoria as a thief and a usurper. His daughter Mabel remembered: 'We drew down such severe rebuke as effectually quenched all missionary spirit.'[11] They were enthusiastic Welsh speakers, having learnt the language from their various nurses and workmen. Mabel claimed – in English – 'If Wales has made me, body and soul, England no less has nurtured and informed my mind.'[12] Her sister Ethel also expressed her love for Wales in English, writing a description of a visit to Castell Harlech:

> I seldom, if ever, saw it look so lovely as it did then, the blue sea sparkling in the distance, the mountains made purple in the glowing light of the sunset and the crimson sky beaming above us, the green wood around us ... We passed under the old arched hall and then entered first Blodwyne's tower ... Oh, I can fancy how it all looked then! When 'Blodwyne stood upon the wall and saw the sea sparkling in the moonlight's beam' ... Oh, how my Welsh heart beats when I think of those days! of the beautiful Blodwyne ... of Queen Margaret of Anjou, of

her tears and agony, all her hopes fled! of the Noble Owen Glyndwr, of Llewelyn! What *Welsh* heart could behold such scenes *un*moved."[13]

Ethel and her sister Fanny were sent to a progressive school in London to finish their education. Later, Fanny studied singing in Rome and Germany, while Mabel, and the youngest daughter, Winnie, studied painting in Paris. Frances Casson, rising eighteen, did not have such opportunities. She successfully sat the Oxford and Cambridge local examination for over sixteen-year-olds, held in Bangor.[14] She was encouraged by her parents, particularly her mother, to pursue her education further, and decided to become a teacher. Colleges of education for women already existed but that route was too expensive. Instead, she applied successfully to become a pupil-teacher in the newly opened kindergarten at Wakefield Girls' High School in Yorkshire.[15] The independent school had been founded in 1878 by the governors of the local boys' grammar school, as they saw the growing importance of education for women.

Will and Lewis both did well at Ruthin School, with a particular bent towards science, while Lewis also gained a Distinction in French. In 1889, both boys passed the Oxford and Cambridge school examinations, and were entered for City and Guilds examinations in science and art, Will gaining a First Class in mathematics. They both gained certificates in inorganic chemistry, a school subject which would have been unheard of when Tom was at school, but of which his father would have heartily approved. Young Randal started at Ruthin, while Esther joined her older sister Frances, as a pupil at Wakefield.

Doors were opening in Wales and elsewhere both for privileged and less privileged young people to progress, as

279

older Randal's erstwhile pupil, David Lloyd George, had proved. The University College of North Wales opened, not in Denbigh, as Tom Casson had hoped, but in Bangor in 1884, joining colleges in Aberystwyth and Cardiff, all of which accepted women as students from the start. The 1880s were a period of ideals and aspirations, not only in terms of education but in terms of society as a whole.

In 1888, a novel appeared that proposed its own utopian vision of society in Wales. Called *Fraternity: A Romance*, and published anonymously in London, it was in fact written by Mabel Holland Thomas, then in her early twenties. Her story concerns a young idealistic teacher, Edmund Haig, with an ambition to teach the poor. He says: 'The death of a single aristocrat by guillotine will generally excite more sentimental compassion than the starvation of whole families of peasants, the burning of entire villages and the decimation of large provinces.'[16] He becomes second master in a village school in North Wales, and later begins teaching in a quarry village. Although the Cassons' quarry had been sold three years before Mabel was born, she would have heard stories about it, and her family knew the Greaves, owners of Llechwedd. In the 1880s, the Welsh slate industry was in a decline, the quarry proprietors trying to save themselves by lowering wages. Mabel perhaps knew of the North Wales Quarrymen's Union, established in 1874, but not yet very active. There were already signs of unrest at Penrhyn and Dinorwic in Caernarfonshire, and at least one short strike by men at one of the Ffestiniog quarries. But Mabel's hero advocates an alternative to industrial disputes. He aims to convince the quarriers that 'envy and greed are not the way', and that 'fraternity' is the answer.

Her hero bases his utopian vision on past traditions. While the ideal of 'fraternity' comes from the French

Revolution, he is inspired less by Robespierre than by the Gorsedd, the community of bards, supposedly based on medieval practice, which had become an important part of the *eisteddfodau*. He sees the different orders of bards, druids and ovates (the lay order) as the fulfilment of his ideal. 'For at the Gorsedd ... men and women are equal, princes and quarrymen meet on the same level ... [The Bardic rites unite] Tory and Radical, Dissenter and Churchmen, rich and poor, young and old; each and all following the light and truth through the systematic study of some science or art; each and all pledged to purity, truth, justice and brotherhood.'[17] He hopes that many of the quarrymen he teaches will be made ovates at the next Gorsedd. He abhors those who work their way up to being gentlemen and then break with their own people. He insists that money is unimportant, although, ironically, he himself is earning extra money by writing for a Radical journal. 'As long as we have shoemaker poets and musical carpenters, I think there is good hope for Wales,' he proclaims, believing that the arts would compensate for social inequality and the hardship of poverty.

In one passage, the narrator's voice breaks through, demonstrating that Mabel's vision of how society worked was based on the group dynamics she knew best, that of the family. Here too, her view was idealistic, taking no account of the tensions and rivalries of real life:

For the perfect type of society is a family – and even in an ideal family there is not absolute equality – one child is strong, another weak, one talented, another beautiful; but inequality hurts not where fraternity exists. In a family, the beauty of one is the pleasure of all, the strength of one supplies the weakness of another. All of us cannot live in large and beautiful houses. Shall we destroy them, therefore, and prevent our brother's enjoyment, because we cannot share it? Is it so in an ideal family? Is not the success of one the success of all?[18]

Years later, there would be a twist in Mabel's own history, lending irony to her idealistic outlook on property and family life. Yet, despite its vision of a society where wealth and social standing are irrelevant to happiness, *Fraternity* is constructed around a conventional romantic plot in which it emerges that Edmund Haig is the scion of a rich family, and a suitable husband for the young lady he has fallen in love with. *The Nation* was critical of the way this undermined the thesis of the novel:

> The doctrine of Fraternal Socialism will seem more pointedly put when some author shall be consistent enough not to make all his [sic] high-souled paupers turn out to be eldest sons of old families, and his renunciatory young ladies of rank unconsciously marry money. That Edward Haig proves to be a scion of an ancient Welsh family is clearly, in the author's mind, as triumphant a badge of superiority as ever was strawberry-mark upon the arm of rightful prince.[19]

What influenced Mabel to develop her vision of fraternity as a social system, and to break away from the Conservative values that informed her father's life? It was later claimed that she studied at Lady Margaret Hall.[20] However, neither that college, nor the other women's colleges in Oxford have any record of her attendance. Since she was later to study painting in Paris, it is possible that she was associated in some way with the School of Drawing that John Ruskin had founded in Oxford in 1871, perhaps attending classes or lectures, or meeting some of its students. There, she could have imbibed Ruskin's social and artistic ideals, as outlined in his *Fors Clavigera* pamphlets, published in the 1870s.

Tom Casson's children were not yet inspired with a vision of society, but the older ones enjoyed using their artistic talents for the benefit of those less fortunate than themselves. In January 1890, the *North Wales Chronicle* contained a report of a 'capital entertainment' mounted for the patients at Denbigh Infirmary:

> The programme consisted of a most mirth-provoking farce, the characters of which were sustained in an admirable manner by Masters W[ill] and L[ewis] T Casson, and the Misses F[rances] W and E[sther] Casson, and the whole performance was highly entertaining, Master L T Casson particularly distinguishing himself by the faithful manner in which he maintained the character allotted to him ... The second portion of the programme was introduced with a pianoforte solo by Miss F W Casson, and it was a pleasing performance. The song by Master L T Casson, 'Sold down south', was exceedingly well rendered and was deservingly applauded. The violin solo by Miss E Casson was well received, it being a clever performance.[21]

Their parents were giving them as rich a start in life as they could afford, full of homegrown theatre and music to complement their studies, and nurturing a firm belief in the need to contribute to society.

Notes

1   Hoggan, Frances, *Education for Girls in Wales*, [n.d] 1882, p. 31, quoted Aaron, p. 168
2   *NWC*, 26 August 1882
3   Casson, John, *Lewis and Sybil*, 1982, p. 78
4   Tom Casson to Fanny G D Casson, 23 March 1882, family papers
5   Personal communication to the author
6   Foss, Kenelm, unpublished biography of Lewis Casson.
7   Community of the Sisters of the Church, *A Valiant Victorian, The Life and Times of Mother Emily Ayckbourn*, p. 81
8   Isambard Owen, p. 113
9   eds Isambard Owen, Heulwyn and Hedydd, *My Welsh Heart*, Diary of Ethel Holland-Thomas [sic] of Caerffyynon, Talsarnau, 1881, private publication, 1969, p14
10 Isambard Owen, p. 5. In another version, he claimed that he was descended from King Louis IX of France
11 Holland Grave, *Some Welsh Children*, p. 36
12 ibid, p. 33
13 eds Isambard Owen, *My Welsh Heart*, p. 21. I have not found the source of her 'Blodwyne' quotation, but it may be drawn from Joseph Parry's opera *Blodwen*, which had been performed in Aberystwyth three years earlier.
14 The universities of Oxford and Cambridge instituted external examinations for boys in 1858, and for girls in 1868
15 The term 'kindergarten' had recently been adopted from Germany to describe the kind of early education developed by Friedrich Froebel.
16 *Fraternity*, 1888, Vol 1, pp. 90-91
17 ibid Vol II, pp. 44-45
18 ibid Vol II, p. 51
19 Review in *The Nation*, 11 October, 1888, unz.org
20 Isambard Owen, pp. 104-105
21 *NWC*, 18 January, 1890

Chapter 21

Then There Was One
1889–1892

Despite the precarious financial position of Tom's company, he expanded it. In 1889, as his older three children sat their public examinations, he took over an organ company in London, in order to have his designs fulfilled there, as well as at his Denbigh plant. At the Inventions Exhibition four years earlier, he had met two organ-builders, Carlton Michell and William Thynne, also showing an instrument. The two men had set up in Shepherds Bush, London, but the company failed.[1] Tom raised debentures and arranged a bank loan, which his brother Randal agreed to guarantee. By October 1889, Casson's Patent Organ Co had taken over the Shepherds Bush site. Orders soon came in, although W. T. Best wrote: 'It is of course a disadvantage to be so far away from the centre of operations.'[2]

Meanwhile, the plan was for Will Casson to go to college in London. He had turned sixteen in August 1889 and wanted to train as an electrical engineer at the City and Guilds of London Institute, starting that September. Tom, always hopeful that he would soon be making money, or that a mortgage on a Cheshire property would furnish him with funds, hoped to get a loan of £100 from his brother Randal, to cover the fees. 'I had intended writing Galley as to this as Will was his godson … Of course I would repay you when my capital is released.'[3]

In June 1890, a local newspaper carried an advertisement for the auction of Cae Derw. This was a drastic move of Tom's. He hoped to negotiate early retirement from the North and South Wales Bank, with a pension giving him a basic income, allowing him to move his family from Denbigh and set up house in London. But eighteen months later, the family was still in residence. Possibly, he sold Cae Derw and then rented it back, while continuing discussions with the Head Office of the North and South Wales Bank.

In January 1891, Fanny Casson died, while staying with her daughter in Surbiton. She had made her last will two years before, when Galley was still alive, confirming the division of the Cheshire properties between Tom and him. Randal now owned Galley's half, including Betchton House. Fanny was not likely to be much missed by Tom. Perhaps Mary would miss her, though her husband and she were already accustomed to turn to Randal with any problems, as he continued to take on the role of head of the family. Following Fanny's wish, her name was added to the memorial to her husband and daughter in Dolgellau.

At the time of his mother's death, lack of capital was still causing Tom grief, as he tried to fulfil a large number of orders, for which payment was never made early enough to provide a cushion against the next investment of labour and materials. One of the people working for him was Frederick Beale, an organist and organ-builder whose family had originally been manufacturers of pianos. He had much faith in Tom's designs and promised to put in £1,000 but could not do so for several months.[4] William Thynne was so keen to help that he too lent a few hundred pounds which he could ill afford. Tom was conscience-stricken. He turned to Randal yet again, who repaid Mr Thynne at once.

Later that year, the financial position of Tom's organ company deteriorated further. Frederick Beale wrote to

Randal, whom he had known years before in Liverpool, extolling Tom's patents, and assuring him that the company had a real future:

> Your brother is a man who thoroughly understands organ building & is looked up to as an authority on mechanism & arrangement, & there is no doubt that eventually his inventions must become very valuable increasing as they do the resources of an organ so considerably with but a small addition in price.
>
> Like all inventors he has had to bear much obloquy from those who are behind & it is amazing with what courage & perseverance he has stood it ... I am free to admit that mistakes have made, (when are they not?) & that through inefficient management & inexperience, work has been undertaken at too low prices & not carried out as economically as possible ... Certainly so long as I am here, no business shall be undertaken except upon carefully framed estimates including a fair profit ...
>
> The introduction of Electric action as patented by your brother is a great saving in material, labour, every way in fact, so will be a great help especially as it gives us the name of being in the Van of Business.
>
> Thus with your brother's supervision of the mechanics, Mr Thynne's voicing, and careful working of the business here, I have every confidence in the Co. developing a large and lucrative business.[5]

Mr Beale's eloquence led up to a request to help Tom raise another £500 – he had already managed £500 – to add to Beale's own £1,000, providing enough floating capital to complete the work they had in hand. Remembering the story of how John W. Greaves had been helped to uncover the rich vein of slate on his land, Tom suggested to Randal that the Greaves family might help: 'They owe us everything. Possibly they do not know their history however, as old Greaves always made himself the architect of his own fortune'.[6]

In October 1891, Lewis turned sixteen. He intended to study chemistry at the City and Guilds Central Institute, alongside his brother, but his father persuaded him to join the organ company instead. He began work in the foundry in Denbigh. Then he joined Will in London and started work at the Shepherds Bush factory.[7] At last, Tom succeeded in arranging early retirement from the North and South Wales Bank, with a pension of £300 a year. From then on, he was not a banker, but a designer of organs by profession, and a company director. In the spring of 1892, Tom, Laura and the two little girls, Elsie and Annie, moved

The Cassons at Cae Derw. Left to right, standing, Lewis, Will, Frances, Randal; seated on bench, Tom, Laura, Esther; seated on ground, Elsie and Annie.

into lodgings in Earls Court, London. Will and Lewis lived nearby. By that time, Frances was a full-time teacher in Derby, while Esther was at school in Wakefield. Young Randal remained in Wales, to finish his schooling.

The first few months in London went well. Laura, ever eager to promote the children's education and career development, persuaded Tom that Lewis should start his chemistry course that September. But within months, family life was shattered by the death of eight-year-old Annie. She fell ill with scarlet fever. Despite the devoted nursing Laura gave her in their lodging rooms, she died that June. For comfort, Laura retreated to Caerffynnon, recuperating in its beauty and comfort, and in the companionship of her stepmother and sisters. She little knew how much strength she would need in the ensuing months. Tom's company was in a state of financial collapse. He had left debts behind him in Denbigh. His friend Dr Turnour had started by supporting the organ business, putting money into it three years earlier, and making a loan of £300 (worth about £25,000 in 2019), which he now wanted repaid. In typical cavalier fashion, Tom asked him if he would treat half the loan as part of his interest in the company, but he declined. He did, however, agree to forgo the interest on the £300 and leave it in the company for the time being, if Tom's brother Randal would stand as security. In August, he discovered that Tom had not arranged that security, and he wrote to Randal: 'I don't like writing to your brother, for what with sorrow and worry I am sure he has enough to bear.'[8] There were other 'local liabilities', referred to in a letter to Randal from an inspector at the bank. At first, Tom kept the truth of the company's affairs from Laura, but when she returned to London he had to reveal it.

By the end of October, matters had reached crisis point. Letters flew between Tom in London and Randal in

Porthmadog. Frederick Beale, who had expressed optimism the previous year, in the hope of persuading Randal to invest, had lost faith in Tom's ability as a businessman, and offered to take over the company himself and run it with William Thynne. Tom wrote that Laura and he, with Elsie, were moving out of their furnished lodgings in Earls Court and looking for somewhere unfurnished and cheaper. In Denbigh, a warehouse where their furniture and many of their possessions were stored was 'attacked.'[9] One or more of Tom's creditors had insisted on his debts being paid, and called the bailiffs in. Laura wrote desperately to her brother-in-law:

> My dear Randal
>
> I do hope if you can help us in this terrible trouble, you will. We want so much to take a few <u>unfurnished</u> rooms & do without a servant, it is our <u>only</u> hope of keeping within our income and finishing the boys' training. – This last has been a terrible shock. Tom hoped it would not happen so did not tell me before, that he had feared it – I can only trust to your kindness.
>
> Yours affectionately
> Laura A Casson
>
> Please send us a line to say what we had better do. We cannot afford to stop here any longer.[10]

There was to be an auction of their household goods in Denbigh, and they tried to keep some possessions out if it. Laura telegraphed Randal: 'Can you advance 200 against my marriage settlement securing furniture for me paying interest furniture worth about that.'[11] And the next day,

Tom wrote: 'Can you not advise how to save at least Laura's little things and the children's? Also bedding & clothes?'[12] They were leaving Earls Court in two days' time to take cheaper lodgings. It was difficult to access Laura's funds quickly, as she needed permission from her cousin Theodore Williams, who was abroad. In the event, the Under-Sheriff allowed them to keep many of the chattels that could be considered as belonging to Laura or the children, and to sell some others for her benefit.

By the beginning of December, Laura's distress was still apparent: 'I am very much puzzled as I cannot understand your letter,' she wrote to Randal. 'I have been so upset by the shock & all the trouble that I have gone through that I should be truly thankful if you would send me a few lines to explain more clearly.'[13] Her concern was how she was to pay for the carriage of her belongings to London. She asked Randal to ensure that John Bellamy packed up the things and arranged for the unpacking. Whatever differences Tom and he had had when they were working together, she trusted him: 'he knows just what there is & warehoused everything. There is literally not one other person I could trust and I am not fit to go myself.' Randal quickly assured her that he would be paying for the carriage himself. Not only that, but he had bought 'certain articles of furniture and other effects' himself which he proposed to 'lend' her. One item of furniture she had been particularly keen to have brought to London was the piano, as she hoped that Esther, now fifteen years old, might be trained for kindergarten teaching, like her sister. The day that Laura was writing about the piano, Frederick Beale was in Bangor, presenting a petition for Casson's Patent Organ Co to be liquidated. Tom was declared bankrupt.

Randal stood staunchly by his brother and sister-in-law during these critical months and gave considerable financial help. But he was never persuaded that there was a rich future in organ-building, as there had once been in slate. In Porthmadog, he pursued his own concerns. In the summer of 1891, he had bought a house he had his eye on, none other than the Spooners' mansion, Bron y Garth.

Charles Easton Spooner had died two years earlier, leaving the house to his sons, Percy and Edwin. Percy had left Porthmadog over ten years earlier, banished to India under a cloud, having fathered a daughter by one of the maids at Bron y Garth. He was still in India at the time of his father's death, working as Superintendent for a railway company. Edwin Spooner and his family were Randal's particular friends. He too was away when his father died, working as a railway engineer in Ceylon (now 'Sri Lanka'). Only in that summer of 1891 did Percy return to Wales to tie up his father's estate, at which point Randal made an offer for the house. As Percy was short of money, he readily accepted, without consulting Edwin. It was later said that this caused a rift between the two brothers, but Edwin had plenty of capital, including two houses in Ireland, and seems to have reconciled himself to the situation.[14] Percy returned to India for the next few years, and Edwin spent the rest of his working life in Kuala Lumpur, while Randal remained friends with them both.

Randal had known Bron y Garth since he first joined his parents and brothers in Wales, over twenty years earlier, to be articled to Edward Breese. From Plas Penrhyn, his first Welsh home, looking across Traeth Bach and the Cob, he could see it directly facing him, above Porthmadog harbour: a three-storey, stone-built house, its three gables standing out proudly against Moel y Gest, the mountain behind, while its terraced gardens descended down the cliff. It was well proportioned, but not as generously sized as he could wish. He at once began to plan an extra wing to the west, to provide an elegant drawing-room. Elegant enough to suit Miss Nisbet, for that was what he had in mind. He was ready at last to end what had been virtually an engagement for nearly ten years. But just at that time her mother, Lady Susanna Nisbet, died at her Sussex home; they would wait one more year before getting married.

At last, in the autumn of 1892, while embroiled in his brother's disastrous affairs, Randal prepared for his wedding. A fortnight after Tom was made bankrupt, Randal travelled to Worfield, Shropshire, where Lucy Nisbet and he were married. Touchingly, in a letter Laura wrote him the day before the bankruptcy petition, desperate to hear when she might be able to access her own funds, and how her furniture and household possessions were to be brought to London, she also wrote: 'There are two electro fruit dishes with the things, will Lucy & you keep them, as from Tom and me.' She signed off 'With love & best wishes', as well as her more usual 'Yours affectionately.'[15]

The same year that Tom Casson's fortunes were at their lowest, the Diphwys Casson Slate Company was also in the hands of the liquidator and the quarry was auctioned. For the entire period of this company's life, the Superintendent had been Evan Parry Jones, the young man who had started his working life under William Turner. Now sixty-four years old, ready to retire, he looked for a suitable house for his wife and extensive family. The house he found was the Casson family home at Blaenyddôl, Ffestiniog, which he bought out of John Casson's estate in Chancery.

After a lengthy honeymoon, Randal, now the only Casson in Wales, brought his wife home to Bron y Garth, Porthmadog, to start a new phase of his life.

Notes

1 Beale, Griffin, *William Thynne's Forgotten Partner*, unpublished
2 W. T. Best to Tom Casson, 15 October 1889, private papers of Griffin Beale
3 Tom Casson to Randal Casson, 15 Apr 1890, family papers
4 Tom Casson to Randal Casson 16 January 1891, family papers
5 Frederick Beale to Randal Casson, 31 July 1891, family papers
6 Tom Casson to Randal Casson 15 January 1891, family papers
7 Devlin, Diana, *A Speaking Part: Lewis Casson and the theatre of his time*, 1982, p. 9
8 Arthur E Turnour to Randal Casson, 10 August, 1892, family papers
9 Tom Casson to Randal Casson, 2 November, 1892, family papers
10 Laura Casson to Randal Casson, undated, family papers
11 Post Office telegram, 3 November, 1892
12 Tom Casson to Randal Casson, 4 November, 1892, family papers
13 Laura Casson to Randal Casson, 3 December 1892, family papers
14 Wilson, D H, 'The Spooners up to Date', *Festiniog Railway Magazine*, No 77, Summer 1977, p. 20
15 Laura Casson to Randal Casson, 1 December, 1892, family papers

Chapter 22

The Cassons of Porthmadog
1893–1899

By the early spring of 1893, Randal and Lucy were settled in Bron y Garth and expecting their first child. A parlour-maid, cook and housemaid lived in, while a gardener and his wife were in the lodge at the bottom of the drive, together with a coachman who boarded there. A kitchen garden produced a rich crop of fruit and vegetables, while trees, shrubs and flowers enhanced the rest of the grounds. Lucy had a wide circle of friends and enjoyed entertaining them. She also offered hospitality to those less fortunate than herself. During her first summer in her new home, she had eight young women from the Soho Club for Working Girls to stay for a week, an organisation she had encountered while living in London herself.[1]

Lucy was a forceful woman, and she soon made her mark in the district. In June, she was at a ball held after the encampment of Randal's battalion, now the 4th Battalion of the Royal Welch Fusiliers. But she was eager to play a more public role. Within months, she had joined the Ladies' Committee of the workhouse at Penrhyndeudraeth, where George Casson had once sat on the board, and for whose inmates William and Fanny Casson had provided dinner on the occasion of Tom Casson's wedding. Lucy's colleagues on this committee were two members of the Greaves family. One was Mrs Richard Greaves, married to the younger brother of Ernest Greaves, once Tom's friend and groomsman. Ernest Greaves, now Lord Lieutenant of Caernarfonshire, owned half the shares in Llechwedd, and lived with his wife and family near Cricieth. Richard owned a quarter share, was general manager, and lived at Plas Weunydd, the house their father had built near the quarry.[2] Also on the committee was one of Ernest's sisters, married to Arthur Osmund Williams, son of David Williams, the Liberal MP whom William Casson had supported, and whose nephew Edward Breese had been Randal's partner. The Greaves and Williams family networks spread widely through Meirionydd and Caernarfonshire, in contrast to Randal's position as sole representative of the Casson family, although, as senior partner at Breese, Jones & Casson, and agent for a number of large estates, he was a recognisable figure throughout the district.

In October, Lucy gave birth to a son, Randal Alexander, known as 'Alec'. The prospect of motherhood did not bring her social activities to an end. In the late stages of her pregnancy, she was elected to the 'Portmadoc [Porthmadog] School District Governing Body', which oversaw the elementary schools in the town, an administrative position now open to women. Before Lucy was ready to get back into public life after her confinement, Randal attended a meeting to discuss the setting up of an 'intermediate school' in Porthmadog. The establishment of such schools was unique to Wales. The initiative had grown out of a report published in 1881 which showed that only a tiny proportion of the Welsh population were university students (one in over 8,000), compared to other parts of Britain. This was despite the fact that there were university colleges in Aberystwyth, Cardiff and Bangor.[3] Predating English legislation by a dozen years, the Welsh Intermediate Education Act was passed in 1889, its purpose 'to make further provision for the intermediate and technical education of the inhabitants of Wales and the county of Monmouth ['Sir Fynwy'].'[4] The new county councils would form boards to assess local need and establish the necessary schools. Royal assent was given in 1893.

At the exploratory meeting in Porthmadog in November of that year, Mr Jonathan Davies, acting as secretary, made his speech in Welsh. He was a slate merchant, a Calvinist Methodist and a Liberal, prominent in Porthmadog public life. The chairman was Mr William Roche, owner of the Tremadog estate. He apologised for not being able to address the meeting in 'the mellifluous language of the people of Wales.'[5] Randal offered £50 towards setting up such a school, Ernest Greaves offered 100 guineas. By the following year, the first intermediate school had been opened in Caernarfon, and Lucy Casson was appointed one of the governors of the projected school in Porthmadog. Mr Roche offered a ninety-nine-year lease of a site to build it, and meanwhile it was based in the Inn at Tremadog.

At the end of 1894, Lucy was elected to the Board of Guardians at the workhouse, another public position newly open to women. From then on, she was active and vocal on both the local intermediate school's Court of Governors, and the Board of Guardians. She had strong views, spoke her mind firmly, and was usually heard with respect. Her duties as wife, mother and hostess still occupied much of her time, and she took on the more conventional role of a charitable lady, providing tea and cakes at the workhouse on occasion, and inviting the children for an afternoon at Bron y Garth.

Randal's contribution to community life was less public, carrying out his duties as solicitor, agent and clerk to a number of organisations, such as the Caernarfonshire Lieutenancy, and the Western Sea Fisheries Commission. County councils had taken over some of the functions of the

Petty Sessions, while his firm acted as solicitors for Ynyscynhaiarn Urban District Council, the new local council for Porthmadog, named after the parish in which it stood. By 1895, Randal had given up his captaincy of the volunteers but remained a firm supporter of the movement. He still belonged to the Madoc Lodge of Freemasons, No. 1509. From time to time, he made trips to Cheshire, to oversee his estate there, where he rented out Betchton House and its farm.

Randal and Lucy's lives were in contrast to those of the Cassons in London. In February 1893, Tom's company's affairs were made public in the bankruptcy court. There was a 'total deficiency' of over £9,000. Tom explained that the insolvency was through 'accepting contracts at too low prices to be remunerative; the working expenses exceeded the receipts.' The official receiver commented unfavourably on the whole enterprise: 'None of the directors [who included Dr Turnour and Felix Watkins], except Mr Casson, had any practical knowledge of organ building.' He concluded: 'In my opinion it was never commercially or practically possible for the company to succeed, and the directors are to blame for having allotted upon so small a subscription and for having almost entirely neglected the business of the company.'[6] Frederick Beale and William Thynne took over the Shepherds Bush factory. Tom eked out his pension from the North and South Wales Bank by lecturing at the London Organ School, but his optimism was irrepressible. Although he could not be director of any company, he still explored ways of setting up some sort of organ business again. Within a year, he was applying for a new patent.

In their first seven years in London, Tom and Laura made at least five different moves. She no longer had a servant, so Esther, and later Elsie, were her 'maids-of-all-work'. Her wish to educate all the children was thwarted by lack of money; her own small income had to be spread between them. Lewis continued at the City and Guilds in South Kensington, but Esther was taken away from Wakefield High School and went to school in Kilburn. Much as Laura wanted her girls to be educated, she nevertheless put her boys first. Although their domestic life was straitened, and Laura never gained much cooking skill, none of the family pined for domestic luxury. Elsie began school in Highbury, and then went to a church school in Paddington. They all attended St Augustine's, Kilburn, a grand Anglo-Catholic church, often known as the 'Cathedral of North London'. There were still books and music. Museums were free, and gallery seats at the theatre were cheap. Sir Henry Irving reigned at the Lyceum, with Ellen Terry as his leading lady; Sir George Alexander at the St James, produced the plays of Arthur Pinero and Oscar Wilde. The Cassons' 'poverty' was relative, nothing like what they saw in the tenements in surrounding streets.

In Wales, Randal and Lucy also attended church regularly, often in Tremadog, Holy Trinity offering more English services than St John's in Porthmadog, which suited Lucy. Politically, Randal remained a Gladstonian Liberal throughout the 1890s. His erstwhile protégé, David Lloyd George, was now MP for Caernarfon Boroughs, and leader of *Cymru Fydd*, the movement promoting self-government in Wales. The Welsh Liberal MPs now formed a distinct group in Parliament, with their own chairman – ironically, an Englishman, Stuart Rendel – and their own agenda, including a wish to see the disestablishment of the Church in Wales.

How far Randal supported any independence movement in Wales is not known. Lucy, an Englishwoman brought up in England, had little reason to support Welsh nationalism as such. At some of the meetings she attended, there were undercurrents of unrest, as much to do with class as with national identity. Those in public positions were no longer drawn entirely from the gentry, or from men and women who had risen into it; they included Welsh tradesmen and those who had gained their education and social position through their participation in Nonconformist gatherings. High birth and wealth did not necessarily exert the same influence or deserve the same respect as Randal's father and uncles had been used to.

Her colleagues on the Board of Guardians recognised that Mrs Casson was of the gentry and better off than most of them. On one occasion, she argued for extensive alterations to the work-house, and was opposed on the grounds of cost: 'Such expenditure could not be tolerated when hundreds of ratepayers were out of employment and had to seek help.' One member urged the board to remember 'they were dealing with a workhouse and not a palace.' Her motion was lost by a large majority.[7] But she was praised for her kindness in arranging free breakfasts for the children of Tremadog, since some had attended school without a 'morsel' to eat. And she often gained her point because she had the time, and had taken the trouble, to investigate individual cases.

Many cases revolved around the question of 'outdoor relief', which was supposed to be given only on rare occasions, but the shame of entering the workhouse meant that paupers much preferred it. One woman appeared before the board and said that her husband 'would rather die on the roadside than enter the house and she was of similar opinion herself.'[8] Once, Lucy objected to relief being given to an elderly couple because she had discovered they had two sons who were perfectly able to take care of them, but had allowed them to live in dirty, squalid conditions.[9]

Another time, a widow was threatened with having her relief stopped because she was guilty of 'negligence to her children.' But Lucy also wanted relief stopped because the woman had an illegitimate child: 'It is simply subsidising immorality,' she said.[10]

In the summer of 1897, Lucy instigated a local scandal, by revealing corrupt practices in the handling of outdoor relief. She discovered that much of it was given in kind, and she hinted that some board members were profiting by illegally providing their goods to the workhouse. Some members were indignant, and at the following meeting, when she had to leave early and asked for the item on outdoor-relief to be adjourned, they did not agree. As she had made serious charges, they said, she would have to raise the matter as a new item, giving notice in the usual way; they were learning how to use procedure to their advantage. At the end of August, she made her accusation in full, and the chairman appointed a committee to investigate. In September, the board heard the committee's report, by which time her accusation was being reported as a main item in the *North Wales Chronicle*, as it had caused a sensation. She was proved right. It was confirmed that some on the board were supplying goods to the relieving officer, getting receipts signed by an assistant, or by their wife or child.

In Lucy's other area of public involvement, the intermediate school's Court of Governors, the question of the Welsh language arose. By the autumn of 1894, a Welsh headmaster and a mistress had been appointed. No-one suitable had applied for assistant mistress, and the court reported that they 'had had to appoint an Englishman as assistant master.'[11] The school opened with fifty-seven pupils, quickly rising to forty-nine boys and nineteen girls, and a total of eighty-two pupils the following September.

Religious worship and Bible instruction was to be given for twenty minutes every morning, 'to be free from anything in the nature of dogmatical theology or formulated creeds.'[12] One of the characteristics of the elementary schools was their freedom from sectarianism, in contrast to British (Nonconformist) and national (church) schools of earlier times. Whether or not Welsh was to be taught was a question less easy to agree on. Instruction in the intermediate school was in English (as it was in the elementary schools), but one governor was keen for the intermediate school to give instruction in Welsh grammar as a curriculum subject. He acknowledged that Welsh was taught to a certain extent in the chapel Sunday schools, 'but not the rudiments of grammar.' He pointed out that an examiner in Caernarfon's intermediate school had impressed upon the committee 'the importance of paying attention to this branch.'[13] The decision was left to the headmaster. When the same question was raised again, Lucy said that the question of Welsh language was far less important than the standard of education. The affection for all things Welsh that characterised the Holland Thomas women was not for her. She did not speak the language herself and believed that, realistically, command of English would open more doors for the Porthmadog schoolchildren.

By the spring of 1897, the new school building was complete. Lucy was given the honour of opening 'Portmadoc [Porthmadog] County School' on its site at the edge of town. There was a grand procession, including the (Volunteer) Battalion of the Royal Welch Fusiliers, the Friendly Societies, a corps of cyclists, councillors, ministers, teachers and representatives of the Welsh colleges, as well as all the members of the Court of Governors. John Bryn Roberts, Liberal MP for Eifion, the local constituency, chaired the event and there were speeches of praise for the Welsh initiative in forming the intermediate schools, of which this was the second in Caernarfonshire. Professor Anwyl from Aberystwyth made a speech in Welsh. Mrs Casson declared the building open, and was presented with a gold key, on one side of which was a red dragon, and on the other side 'Portmadoc County School, April 28th, 1897.'[14]

One person who was conspicuous by his absence was Mr Roche, who had given the site. He was too ill to attend, and that August, he died at his home at his home in Sir Frycheiniog ('Breconshire'), at the age of forty-three. This was a blow to the communities of Porthmadog and Tremadog, but of particular regret to Randal Casson. As agent for the estate he had worked closely with Mr Roche, inviting him to stay at Bron y Garth, so that the two could get to know each other. William Roche was described as a 'progressive Tory', being in favour of disestablishment, and had done much to encourage education in Wales, as manifested in his attendance at the first meeting to promote the school.[15] There were no children of the marriage, and the estate now passed to his brother, Major John Edward Fitzmaurice Hughes Roche. Randal discovered that this gentleman, an officer in the Dragoons, was a much more difficult customer.

Just after William Roche's death, Randal was in correspondence with the Sanitary Committee of 'Portmadoc [Porthmadog] Urban District Council' about some wooden cottages near the station of the Cambrian Railway. These were in such a bad state that they were considered to be uninhabitable and causing a public nuisance because of 'certain privies.' Randal explained that the late Mr Roche had decided some months ago to close them, giving due notice to the tenants, 'but where are the poor things to go, I cannot say.'[16] No doubt many of the houses in Porthmadog had been put up hurriedly as the town expanded and were falling into dilapidation. This matter was resolved satisfactorily, as far as Randal was concerned, but a few months later there was a complaint about another property, which escalated unpleasantly, and brought him up against his old pupil, David Lloyd George.

In November 1898, a new surveyor, Mr Thomas Harris, was appointed to the Urban District Council. He reported that 'the walls of certain houses in High-street were in a dangerous condition.' There were cracks and bulges rendering them unsafe. These 'certain houses' included the Australia Inn, built in the 1850s, when shipbuilding was first prospering. (It is unknown how it got its name, as Porthmadog ships did not carry slate to Australia.[17]) Randal had been in correspondence with the leaseholder about its condition, and as he could not afford any repairs, the Tremadog estate acquired ownership.

Randal was already reluctant to go on acting as agent for the estate, having found the new owner difficult to deal with. Major Roche had served in India and South Africa in the 3rd Dragoons, and left his regiment reluctantly, suffering from ill health. His brother's early death made him owner of an estate which he had not expected to inherit, and in which he took no interest. Soon after he inherited, he refused a request to be president of the National Eisteddfod, to be held in Blaenau the following year, writing to Randal that he preferred to be one of the audience paying half a crown than to fork out £500 required for the privilege of being a patron.[18] Randal asked Mr D. W. Thomas, a solicitor in Brecon, to be the Major's agent, but Mr Thomas replied, saying that he declined to act for a man who treated his tenants as badly as the Major did: 'His farm buildings are in poor repair while he wastes huge sums unnecessarily on his own house.'[19] During the following months, Randal tried to negotiate with Major Roche about the necessary repairs, but, as he would later report, 'a certain person' broke off negotiations in March.[20]

That month, Mr Harris asked the bench at the Petty Sessions in Porthmadog to make an order, compelling the owners (the Tremadog estate) to carry out the work, since they had not complied with the notices he had sent out. Richard Greaves was chairman of the bench and as he was also chairman of the local district council, he retired, to avoid a conflict of interest. Randal, as magistrates' clerk, remained present, but it is clear from the press report of the session that he did not succeed in keeping his interest as agent for the estate out of the debate that followed. With his agent's hat on, he told the bench that he had had instructions to carry out the work, but it would be dangerous to carry it out without proceeding with the work on the other properties. As Mr Harris agreed, the matter was adjourned for a month.

By the time of the next Petty Sessions, still no repairs had been done at the Australia Inn and the adjoining properties, and Mr Harris again applied for an order. This time, Randal objected to the procedure, claiming that the application should be by 'summons', not by 'order'. Mr Harris protested that it was the procedure he had adopted in other courts. Randal then muddied the waters by saying: 'I tell you candidly I shall disobey the order. I am not liable.' Unfortunately for Mr Harris, it transpired that he had not brought copies of the notices he had issued to the property owners, and the bench adjourned again, with Randal attempting to smooth things over by saying he was 'anxious to do all he could in the matter.'[21] At the next Petty Sessions, Richard Greaves took the chair, and Mr Harris tried to issue his order once again. Randal asked if he had taken any legal advice. This was disingenuous, as his own firm acted as solicitors for the district council. Mr Harris pointed out 'You are a member of that firm and you are an interested party', which Randal then tried to deny: 'I am not an interested party except that I am an agent for Major Roche.' Once again, he insisted, as magistrates' clerk, that the correct procedure was to issue summons on the parties.

Randal was at fault in not acknowledging that his role as magistrates' clerk was compromised by his role as agent for the Tremadog estate, and that the surveyor's situation was complicated by the firm of Breese, Jones & Casson normally acting as legal advisors to the District Council. The administration of affairs in Porthmadog was in few hands and some overlap of responsibility was bound to occur. It was also clear that the bench was allowing the matter to drag on for an unsatisfactorily long time. The practical difficulty was Major Roche's obstructiveness, which Randal did not wish to make public, hence his reference to 'a certain person' who had ceased negotiations. His next move was to involve the surveyor of the Tremadog estate, who recommended simply putting some boards up in front of the bulging wall.

Now the affair heated up. Mr Harris took legal advice from William George and they both attempted to serve a summons on Randal in his office, but he refused to accept it without his partner, David Breese (son of Edmund Breese), being present. At this point, William George must have written to his brother in London, complaining about Randal's intransigence, and about the endless delays the bench had allowed. At the end of May, David Lloyd George himself travelled up to Porthmadog, even though Parliament was sitting at the time, and took on his old employer, confronting him in the Court of Petty Sessions. He may have felt genuine concern for the inhabitants of the dilapidated housing, but he was also motivated by a wish to attack the gentry as a class. His manner and language were fierce and personal, and he clearly enjoyed making a drama of the occasion, twice rousing applause from the public area, which was quickly suppressed.

As the official business was the District Council's summons relating to the High Street properties, Mr Richard Greaves again withdrew. Lloyd George then said that he had a 'grave complaint to make against the Clerk of the Court', asserting that the people of Porthmadog had tolerated his conduct for years. He was sorry to have to tell their Worships 'that their clerk had disobeyed the order of the bench, and flagrantly deviated from the ordinary practice, and that purely and simply in order to protect his own interests.' He said that he would call witnesses to prove this, and when Randal interposed that he had no knowledge of witnesses being called, he retorted 'I must object to this interruption.' Randal then suggested that the chairman, Mr Greaves, should be present to hear the complaint. 'I object to this sort of interruption,' Lloyd George reiterated. He told the sitting magistrates that it was difficult for them to understand how Mr Casson treated the public; his manner towards his social superiors on the bench was totally different to his manner towards people like Mr Harris and Mr William George. The chairman, Mr Burnell, tried to stop these personal accusations: 'I think you are complaining of something we cannot take cognisance of.' After that, Lloyd George did address the question in hand, that 'certain premises were in such a dangerous condition that they might cause injury to life and limb and might come down at any minute.' There was further argument about procedure, and Mr Burnell acknowledged that 'injustice was done somewhere' but he was not prepared to say where the blame lay.

Finally, it was arranged that the summonses would be heard at a special court the following week, by which time,

Lloyd George had returned to London.[22] His brother William represented the District Council, Randal at last stood down from acting as magistrates' clerk 'as he ... had some interest in the case' and was himself represented in court by a solicitor from another Porthmadog firm. The two surveyors, Mr Harris for the District Council, and Mr Roberts for the Tremadog estate, gave conflicting evidence as to the hazard created by the buildings, and the bench suspended the summons order against all four defendants for three months, during which time the 'requisite alterations' were to be made. But before the three months was up, Randal had to apply for an extension, as he was summoned to the Roche home in Tregunter in the middle of August; the Major had died. The District Council received an indignant letter from Lloyd George & George, stating: 'We were very much surprised to hear that such an application had been made without giving us notice beforehand', but the Works Committee simply included the letter in their report, which was adopted without comment. The repair work continued to drag on, but Randal's role as agent was now easier. The next owner of the estate was a distant cousin of the Major, Edward FitzEdmund Burke Roche, 2nd Baron Fermoy, but he seems to have left decisions to his agent and to William Roche's widow, with whom Randal got on well.

Lloyd George's intervention in this local matter was vindictive, especially considering that Randal was not himself the owner of the Australia Inn, and that there were three local Welsh proprietors involved in the affair, as well as the Tremadog estate. But Randal did not deal with it straightforwardly, perhaps because of the recalcitrance of Major Roche. In several other local matters, he seems to have put difficulties in the way. There was a long drawn out delay over completing a lease of land for a recreation ground for Portmadoc County School, situated on the Tremadog estate. Randal stalled for months, because he was not satisfied with the design of gates into the ground. At one meeting of the Court of Governors, the chairman said that Mr Casson was 'the most cantankerous solicitor' he had ever come across.[23] Perhaps he simply enjoyed the cut and thrust of argument, and wrangling over legal niceties, as much as Lloyd George himself.

Randal was sometimes difficult in his professional life, and Lucy put some people's backs up. But for the most part, their life in Porthmadog was harmonious. They lived comfortably and enjoyed their social life. Although there were some who might carp at their enviable position, they were genuinely eager to work for continued social improvement in the town, according to their own lights. As the first century of the Cassons in Wales drew to an end, the grandson of Thomas and Esther Casson could look with considerable satisfaction at his situation.

Notes

1   Founded by the Hon Maude Stanley in 1880 to provide lodging and educational actitivities for working girls.
2   Drage, pp. 12-17 passim. The middle son of John Whitehead Greaves owned the other quarter share, and lived in England.
3   Davies, p. 435
4   quoted Carradice, Phil, *The Welsh Intermediate Education Act*, 1889, BBC Wales, 12 August 2012
5   *NWC* 4 November 1893
6   as reported NWC 18 February 1893 and in several other newspapers
7   *NWC* 16 Feb and 5 Mar 1895
8   *NWC* 14 Aug 1897
9   *NWC* 30 Nov 1895
10 *NWC* 10 Apr 1897
11 *NWC* 14 Aug 1894
12 *NWC* 1 Sep 1894

13 *NWC* 1 Sep and 3 Nov
14 *NWC* 1 May 1897
15 *North Wales Express*, 13 Aug 1897
16 *NWC* 14 Aug 1897
17 historypoints.org – The Australia, Porthmadog
18 F. (misreading for J) Roche to Randal Casson, 26 December,1897 (Gwynedd Archives, as listed at the National Archives)
19 D. W. J. Thomas to Mr R. Casson, 23 Dec 1898, Breese Jones and Casson, NA catalogue, XD8/4/56
20 *NWC*, 3 June, 1899
21 *NWC*, 22 April 1899
22 *NWC*, 3 June 1899 for account of Petty Sessions 26 May and special court 1 June
23 *NWC*, 15 September 1900

Chapter 23

Home and Away
1893-1914

Randal and Lucy Casson

When Lucy took up residence at Bron y Garth, in 1893, she started a visitors' book, in which her houseguests signed and dated their visit, and where she noted major events, such as the birth of her son. This black leather-bound volume, now patched and worn, provides something of a record of her domestic life. Family and friends came from near and far. In fine weather, her guests could leave the West Room, part of Randal's extension, walk out onto the terrace and look out across the Traeth, and beyond to Bae Ceredigion. To the south, the outline of Castell Harlech stood out against the sky. The tide came in past Cei Balast [Ballast Island], mingling seawater with the outflowing river Glaslyn. As it ebbed, it left ever-changing patterns on the sand. The smells and sounds of shipbuilding, the voices of workmen and crews, wafted upwards from the wharfs and decks in the harbour below. Ships sailed out on the full tide, vying with the increasing number of steamers. Some had names familiar to Randal, the schooner, *C E Spooner*; and the steamship, *George Casson*. The hooting of the Ffestiniog train drew eyes to the Cob, to watch it trundle in and out of Porthmadog. On the east side of the house, the garden rose steeply towards a flagpole at the top, giving a clear view of the slopes and crags of Moel y Gest, a mountain of less than 900 feet. From the harbour, a small road, Ffordd y Clogwyn, wound westward below the house to the harbour of Borth-y-gest. Beyond that lay Ynys Cyngar, from where his grandfather had sent out ships loaded with slate.

The visitors' book bears witness to the friendship Randal and Lucy maintained with Edwin Spooner, to whom Bron y Garth had once belonged. His wife Martha, on annual trips back from Kuala Lumpur, brought her children, Molly and Jack, to stay in their old home during the summer holidays, sometimes with their mother, sometimes on their own. Randal and Lucy had just one child, Alec, and their willingness to take on this quasi-parental role suggests that it was not through choice. Lucy's cousin, Margaret Davenport, was a regular visitor, and Lucy made return trips to her old neighbourhood, Worfield, in Shropshire. Another frequent visitor was Lucy's half-brother, Henry Kitching, a Royal Navy officer.

There are no signatures of Tom or Laura. Tom was firmly based in London, and Laura was always welcome at

Caerffynnon Hall, where Elizabeth Thomas offered generous hospitality during the months she was there. The first winter after her husband's death, she had taken her daughters to Italy, to avoid the sadness of Christmas without him. After that, she spent most winters on the Continent, visiting France, Italy, Germany, Spain, Switzerland – and Algiers on one occasion. The girls' lives became cosmopolitan. Mabel and Winnie both studied painting in Paris, and Mabel settled there, while Winnie married a diplomat and moved to Singapore. In Paris, Mabel met Jean Grave, a prominent figure in the French anarchist movement.[1] They fell in love, and she absorbed most of his ideas, completing her journey from Conservatism, through 'fraternity' to a radical political creed. Her older sister, Lily, died. Her younger sister, Fanny, who had trained as a singer, gave up her career, married Claude Haigh, a long-time neighbour in Penrhyndeudraeth, and settled there. Ethel, the sister who had written so feelingly of Disraeli and Wales, had not settled to any career, though she had published two novels.[2] All four surviving sisters continued to regard Caerffynnon as their home, holding it in great affection and bringing friends to enjoy the pleasures of Wales.

The Cassons in London led a less luxurious life, living off Tom's small pension from the North and South Wales Bank and whatever freelance work he could pick up. But in the second half of the 1890s, his financial affairs began to improve. Although his bankruptcy was not discharged until 1901, he began to achieve success with his organ-building. He found a sponsor in Mr William Raeburn Andrew, a barrister, grandson of the painter, Sir Henry Raeburn. Mr Andrew bought some of Tom's patents and set up a workshop for him. Tom started to specialise in what he called the 'positive organ', taking the name from the small chamber organs built for medieval chapels and small churches. He incorporated many of his earlier ideas, but on a smaller scale. Soon, orders were coming in, but unlike the larger ones he had built previously, these could be completed reasonably quickly, and payment received. By 1897, he was getting an order every week. Mr Andrew took on larger premises. In the summer of 1898, an advertisement appeared in *The Church Weekly* for 'THE POSITIVE ORGAN (Casson's Patent)', for which specifications and full particulars could be obtained from 'W. R. Andrew, Organ-builder, at 8 Berkeley Road, Chalk Farm.' It was puffed as 'THE GREATEST MUSICAL SUCCESS OF THE JUBILEE YEAR.'[3]

Early in 1899, Mr Andrew registered the business as 'The Positive Organ Company'. The directors were Dr E. J. Hopkins, a well-known musicologist; John Mewburn Levien, a singing teacher who had known Tom's mentor, W. T. Best; and Mr Andrew himself. The first two were of some standing in the musical world, unlike the directors of the earlier Denbigh company. Though no longer a company director, Tom was managing director, and all the instruments he produced carried a plaque reading 'The Positive Organ Company', and underneath 'Casson's Patent.' Positive organs were sent to all parts of Britain, to North America and to the Empire. In the long run, his decision to move to London from Wales had proved right, putting him in close touch with the musical world of the capital, and in contact with people who appreciated his innovations. His reputation grew. He opened a showroom in Hanover Square, and was interviewed for an article in a church magazine. Tom attributed his new success to Laura, just as his grandmother Esther was given the credit for the post-war recovery of William Turner & Company. 'Mrs Casson,' he told the interviewer, 'suggested that instead of prosecuting organ reform generally, I should undertake the necessary, but less grandiose, task of producing a small real or pipe-organ to supplant the reed instruments.'[4]

In the summer of 1900, marking a thaw between the brothers as Tom became more prosperous, his son Lewis stayed for the first time at Bron y Garth. He was on a walking holiday with a friend, eager to show off his childhood land, unaware that his life would one day become closely bound up with his uncle's home. His ambitions had by that time taken several turns. Uninspired by his studies in chemistry, he decided he wanted to become a priest, and to that end became a pupil-teacher at St Augustine's, Kilburn, where the family worshipped. He then won a Queen's Scholarship to St Mark's College in Chelsea, where he became inspired by the ideas of Robert Blatchford, who developed an English version of socialism, which did not depend upon any theory of economics but on humanity and common sense. Lewis was drawn to Blatchford's pursuit of 'frugality of body and opulence of mind.[5] He gave up his ecclesiastical ambition, and agreed to join his father's organ company.

Two weeks after Lewis was at Bron y Garth, Will Casson stayed. He was a successful electrical engineer and had worked on the newly opened 'Tuppenny Tube' that ran from Shepherds Bush to Bank. Will and Lewis each enjoyed their return to Wales. There were walking expeditions, swimming, cricket and sailing outings. On wet days, the bookshelves in the West Room offered a wide range of reading, as Randal and Lucy were amassing a full and eclectic library. A catalogue of Bron y Garth books compiled many years later lists fiction, poetry and plays, history, biography and travel, natural history, religion and theology. A collection of John Ruskin's writings manifested Lucy's interest in art, dating back to her student days, while a small number of books of Welsh interest owed more to Randal's background. It included Charlotte Guest's translation of

The Mabinogion and the *Kalendars of Gwynedd*, compiled by his old partner, Edward Breese.

That year saw the 'Khaki Election', fought on a wave of enthusiasm for the supposed British victory in the Second Boer War, giving Salisbury's Conservative government a large majority. Both David Lloyd George and John Bryn Roberts, Liberal MPs in Caernarfonshire, had opposed the war. Both stood again and won. T. E. Ellis, Liberal MP for Meirionydd had died the previous year; at this election, Arthur Osmund Williams, husband of Lucy's colleague on the Board of Guardians, was elected as Liberal MP. The foreign war had little effect on the Casson or Holland Thomas families, but all three of Tom's sons continued the

Randal , Will, Lewis, Tom – the Casson soldiers

tradition of peacetime soldiering, first taken up with such enthusiasm by their great-uncle John.

In 1901, Randal's third nephew, the young Randal Casson, made his first visit to Bron y Garth. He had stayed on at Ruthin School when the family moved to London. He had the most successful academic career of the three brothers, gaining an Open Scholarship to read mathematics at St John's College, Cambridge, the first member of the family to attend university. Again, Laura chose to put her sons' education before her daughters, withdrawing Esther from her training as a kindergarten teacher in order to support Randal's time as an undergraduate. He graduated as 9th Wrangler (the term used for those who gain First Class Honours in mathematics at Cambridge). He then set off for Burma (now 'Myanmar'), where, having given up his early ambition to be an astronomer, he had been appointed assistant commissioner in the Indian Civil Service, the first member of the family to work overseas.

In England, Frances Casson continued to teach, and Esther began to teach kindergarten as well, while Elsie started work in her father's office in the organ factory. Esther scolded her father for not ensuring her younger sister had 'a proper clerical training.'[6] Music and drama played an important part in all their lives. Frances was a fine pianist, making practice a daily routine. In 1900, a month or so before Lewis stayed at Bron y Garth for the first time, Esther and Elsie were asked to take part in a performance of Racine's *Athalie*. Written in 1691, for a girls' school, it included a female chorus. Mendelssohn's incidental music for it had become part of the classical repertoire, especially the thrilling march he wrote, a staple in Tom Casson's repertoire. This performance, in St George's Hall, Langham Place, was a rare revival mounted by the London Organ School, for which Tom Casson had installed an organ, and where he gave classes in organ construction. That was how Esther and Elsie came to be involved, and when Mr Charles Fry, who taught elocution and drama classes at the school, required an extra actor, they suggested Lewis. His participation would lead to another twist in his career path.

Tom was now very much a Londoner, immersed in its musical world, while his positive organs made their way to churches all over the world. In the summer of 1903, he felt prosperous enough to take his family on a short holiday to the Lake District. It was their first opportunity to explore the region where his paternal grandparents had grown up. He described the trip enthusiastically to his brother Randal. The country was green and 'very like Wales, the houses & walls of slate stone & roofed with grey slate.' But it was on a smaller scale: 'Looking at a map one judges of things as in a map of Wales & it is startling to find oneself at a lake one imagines to be miles away.'[7] The highlight of the trip was a visit to Seathwaite, to see the old haunts of the Cassons and Walkers. The family group, consisting of Tom and Laura, Frances, Will, Esther and Elsie, went by horse-drawn coach from their hotel in Ambleside to Coniston. There, Tom and Laura took a train to Broughton, and then hired a trap to go up the Duddon Valley, while the younger ones walked over to Walney Scar from Coniston, passing the old quarry. Tom visited the churchyard, picking out Robert Walker's gravestone, made from Ffestiniog slate, and seeing many others 'of those whom we knew or heard much of', including two 'Miss Dawsons' whom he thought Randal might remember as 'two very sweet old gentlefolk', cousins of their father, who had visited Blaenyddôl. He saw the grave of 'Mrs Harrison', another cousin of their father's, 'whom you may remember,' Tom reminded his brother, 'as "visiting" Blaenyddôl for a fortnight & staying for a year or so.' He picked out the grave of William Turner's father and visited Newfield Inn. This former Casson home was owned by Dawsons, also connected through his father's cousin. Tom was particularly taken by seeing an old oak '*cwpwrdd*', as he termed it, carved with the names of 'Robert Casson and Agnes Casson, 1687.'[8] He was enthused by the whole trip, and hoped that Randal would be motivated to make his own journey there.

The year 1904 saw several changes in the lives of the Casson and Holland Thomas families. That summer, Lewis Casson left the organ factory to become a professional actor. In retrospect, it would not seem a surprising decision. 'During the whole of my life,' he later explained, 'I'd been an actor.'[9] Other events that year were the marriage of Esther to Lewis's friend Arthur Reed, whom he had met at St Mark's College. On Christmas Eve, Elizabeth Holland Thomas died from a stroke, while wintering in Cannes with her daughters Mabel and Ethel.

A difficult situation now arose with regard to Caerffynnon Hall. Lewis Holland Thomas had specified in his will that, failing a son inheriting, after his wife's death it was to go to 'their eldest unmarried daughter.' If all were married, they were to take equal shares. Mabel was in a settled relationship with Jean Grave, and enjoyed dividing her time between Paris, England and her old Welsh home, but her partner did not believe in the legal institution of marriage. The ideal harmony of family life which Mabel had described in *Fraternity* was sorely tested. She acquired the title deeds of Caerffynnon, but her sisters felt that her sole ownership of it was not what their father had intended. They had to persuade Jean Grave to betray his principles. Eventually, four years later, the couple went through a civil marriage ceremony; Mabel took French nationality and became legally 'Madame Grave'. The four sisters then inherited their Welsh home in equal shares.

A few months after her mother's death, Ethel Holland

Lewis and Sybil

Thomas married Sir Herbert Isambard Owen, who had been a major figure in the creation of the University of Wales and was its deputy chancellor. At the time of their marriage, he was principal of Armstrong College, in Newcastle, a constituent college of Durham University. They settled there. Fanny Haigh was the only sister living in Meirionydd. Ethel and Winnie persuaded Mabel that the three of them should sell their shares in Caerffynnon to Fanny. She and her husband moved in. Once again, it was a lively family home, offering open house to the other sisters, including Laura and her family.

No such complications ruffled the calm at Bron y Garth, where Randal and Lucy continued to entertain her grand Davenport relations, the humbler Cassons, and their numerous friends. In 1906, young Randal, home on leave from Rangoon, stayed twice, the second time accompanied by Lewis, already by that time a successful working actor. In 1907, came the warmest expression of Randal and Lucy's friendship with Edwin Spooner. His daughter Molly was to be married, but her father's work in Kuala Lumpur meant he was unable to be in Wales, and so Randal gave the bride away, Lucy and he hosting a house-party and a reception afterwards.

At the beginning of 1909, two more newly-married couples stayed at Bron y Garth. Just before Christmas, Lewis had married a young actress, Sybil Thorndike. The elder daughter of a clergyman, she had first set out to be a concert pianist, but strained her wrist, and turned to her second love, the theatre. Like Lewis, she had been acting since childhood. Eager to share his love of North Wales with his bride, Lewis brought her to Bron y Garth at the end of their honeymoon, before they returned to the Gaiety Theatre, Manchester, where they were playing in the first regional repertory company in England. Then young Randal came with *his* bride, May Man, whom he had met in Burma. Several times, the name 'M. Ethel Casson' appeared in the visitors' book, she being the daughter of Tom and Randal's uncle John. She was the only remaining link with him, since his posthumous son, John George Walker Casson, had died abroad a year or so earlier.

Randal and Lucy settled into a routine, usually away from Wales for part of February, March and April, and again in May or June. Their son Alec was at Winchester School, an establishment with which Lewis and Randal's headmaster had once favourably compared their own *alma mater*, Ruthin School. In Porthmadog, Randal and Lucy continued to sit on a number of committees, and to lead a busy social life. Not many days went by without the sound of horses' hooves and the rattle of harness on the drive, sometimes the rumble of a motor-car engine, and the scurrying around of Lucy's devoted housekeeper, Sarah Bailey. All the conversation round the dining table was in English, but Sarah, who was from Shropshire, had had to acquire enough Welsh to deal with tradesmen, for the only Welsh member of staff was the coachman.

Randal turned sixty in April 1910. In July, Tom died in Putney, where he and Laura lived with Esther and Arthur Reed. He had seen the birth of six grandchildren: two daughters and a son to Esther, with another on the way; a son to Lewis; a daughter and son to young Randal. Frances Casson, enjoying a successful career as a teacher, was unmarried, though she had had a shipboard romance while on a voyage out to visit Randal and May in Burma. Will, too, was unmarried. Elsie Casson was forging a new career. She had left the organ company and begun working for Octavia Hill, the housing reformer, who trained many young middle-class women as rent-collectors. She put Elsie in charge of Red Cross Hall, attached to one of her estates for working people in Southwark. Red Cross Hall was to provide recreation and education for the residents, which Miss Hill, strongly influenced by John Ruskin, considered an important part of her work. Like her brother Lewis, Elsie believed that encouraging music and the arts was as important as providing adequate housing.

From the end of 1910, Randal and Lucy attended no meetings for eighteen months. Randal was ill, and the visitors' book shows a blank, as they spent the time in warm climates. He resigned from many of his positions, including that of agent to the Tremadog estate. By the summer of 1912, they were back, receiving visitors through the rest of that year. In August, Will Casson stayed. He had to tell them about his mother Laura's illness and death a month earlier. In the spring of 1913, Randal and Lucy were on their travels again, this time sailing as far afield as Port Said. In July, just after their return, Randal's sister Mary Ranken died, leaving him the sole surviving child of William and Fanny Casson.

During the fine summer of 1913, several of the family stayed at Bron y Garth. Elsie Casson made her first visit. She was a frequent visitor to Fanny and Claude Haigh at

Caerffynnon, but she spent time with Randal and Lucy, to tell them about her new career. For some years, she had nursed an ambition to study medicine, still a bold choice for a woman. Being needed to help her mother at home, she had waited until after Laura's death. Then, much encouraged by her uncle-in-law Sir Isambard Owen, who was now the vice-chancellor of Bristol University, she had enrolled there, and was now embarked on her training, at the age of thirty-eight.

For the rest of the year, there was a regular flow of visitors at Bron y Garth, including a flying visit from Lewis and Sybil, arriving on a Saturday in their battered 'Tin Lizzie' car, and leaving the next day. Lewis was now running Miss Horniman's Gaiety Theatre, Manchester. Henry Kitching was also a guest on that occasion, serving on HMS *Warrior*, assigned to the Royal Navy's torpedo training fleet. More visitors came in the first two months of 1914. After that, the book has a double black line ruled across the page. Underneath, in Lucy's handwriting: 'Randal died at Taormina Ap. 2d [2 April] Thursday.' He had contracted pleurisy while on holiday in Sicily with Alec and herself. He was buried in the graveyard at Taormina.

When the news of Randal's death reached Porthmadog, flags were lowered to half-mast at the Town Hall, at other public buildings and business premises in the town, and on all the ships in the harbour. An obituary in *The Cambrian News* listed Randal's many offices. The writer pointed out that Randal had never sought a seat on the local governing bodies. Nevertheless, 'he filled a big space in the public life of the town, and there is a consensus of opinion that Portmadoc [Porthmadog] has lost a strong and dominant personality.' There was a hint that Randal had not been universally popular: 'Even those who did not see eye to eye with him on questions have to acknowledge that he was of an exceptionally kind disposition and possessed lovable and noble qualities, whilst those who knew him intimately feel that they have lost a true friend.' Soon, Lucy was back in Wales, and Alec, now a student at Christ Church, Oxford, returned there for the Trinity term.

Notes

1   One version of how they met was that Mabel was acquainted with the Russian anarchist, Peter Kropotkin, who introduced her to Jean Grave in 1895, see Patsouras, Louis, *The Anarchism of Jean Grave*, 2003, p. 65.

2   Presumably, these were anonymous, like *Fraternity*, for there is no record of them.

3   *The Church Weekly*, 1 July, 1898

4   Wilcox, Alfred, 'The Organ in the Church: interview with inventor of the "Positive Organ"', *Church Bells and Illustrated Church News*, 26 September, 1902

5   Blatchford, Robert, *Merrie England*, 1893, p. 15

6   Personal communication to the author from Esther's daughter, Marjorie Reed

7   Tom Casson to Randal Casson, 14 August 1903, family papers

8   There is no modern trace of this cupboard, nor any genealogical record of the Cassons named on it.

9   Lewis Casson, interviewed by Elizabeth Sprigge, for *Sybil Thorndike Casson*, 1971. The background to his decision is covered in Devlin, Diana, *A Speaking Part: Lewis Casson and the Theatre of his Time*, 1982

Chapter 24
Soldiers of War
1914-1919

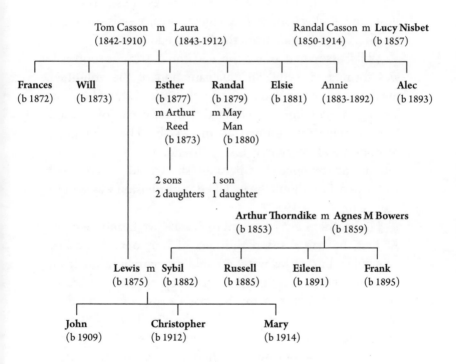

The Casson/Thorndike Family 1914

Four months after Randal Casson's death, war broke out, changing the course of life for the family, the country and the wider world. For the first time, Casson men were involved in active service, required to fight on the battlefield. An early casualty was not a man, but a namesake, the steamship, *George Casson*, interned in Germany on 4 August, the very day war was declared. In Penrhyndeudraeth, the factory that William Casson had established, was now 'Cookes Explosives Ltd', and began supplying nitro-glycerine explosives to the Army. The slate industry declined, constricted through shortage of men, many joining the Armed Forces, or taking up jobs in war factories. A shell-making factory was established at the Festiniog Railway Boston Lodge Works, requisitioning a steam haulage engine from the Llechwedd quarry.[1]

Will Casson had joined the Territorial Army as soon as it was formed in 1908, an amalgamation of the volunteer movement and the Yeomanry. In 1914, the City of London Territorial Battalion he belonged to became part of the 2nd London Division, known as the '47th'. His immediate response was to marry his girlfriend, not so much for reasons of romance, but because she would be provided with a pension, should he be killed. The division was sent to France in March 1915.

His brother Lewis was sent to France two months earlier. At first, he had resisted the idea of war, out of socialist principles, but as he watched soldiers marching off from London, he was caught up in a wave of patriotic enthusiasm and enrolled in the Army Service Corps. Transferred to Mechanical Transport, also part of the 47th Division, he left for France in January 1915. Their brother, the younger Randal, remained in Burma, where he was a district judge. His contribution to the war effort was as adjutant in the Volunteer Mobile Battery, giving instruction in gunnery. All three brothers were abroad, therefore, when their older sister, Frances, died of cancer in April 1915. At the end of August, Lewis returned to France from leave, and was stationed close enough to Will to see him a couple of times, preparing to lead his company into the Battle of Loos. On the 25 September, Will was shot dead by a sniper, one of ten officers out of eighteen who were killed. 'His gallant company,' ran the official account, 'was cut to pieces, but he had, by a very bold piece of soldiering, held the German counter-attack till reinforcements arrived.'[2]

Five days later, Lewis managed to talk to a Captain who had witnessed Will's conduct in the battle. He described how Will, having some difficulty in controlling the men from the trench, 'got out on the parapet and strolled about smoking a pipe, bucking the men up.'[3] He described Will's work as 'magnificent' and assured Lewis that it would have won him the Distinguished Service Order (DSO). The whole battalion had lost heavily. Every officer in the first three companies was either killed or wounded. Lewis stayed to speak a few words to some of Will's men and was cheered by their pride in him. He took their father's signet ring, with its Casson crest, from Will's body. Feeling that he too should be risking his life, he applied for commission, which came through in the spring of 1916, when he was appointed 2nd Lieutenant in the Royal Engineers (Special Brigade). Because of his knowledge of chemistry gained twenty years earlier, he was assigned to work on poison gas. Within six months, he was promoted to Captain, with his own company, carrying out the deadly work of preparing and laying cylinders and projectors of poison gas along the enemy line. It was a horrific task which he hated but carried out conscientiously. The work continued through the Battle of the Somme.

By 1917, Lloyd George had become Prime Minister, determined to bring the war to an end. Sir Douglas Haig had replaced Sir John French in command of the British troops in France. Lord Kitchener was dead; the Tsar was overthrown; the Americans were about to join the Allies. But trench warfare continued unchanged, with its casualties and sickening conditions. That summer, Lewis was sent on a mission to lay cylinders of phosgene with a party of Australians. The Australians failed to turn up, so Lewis set off with his Sergeant and a few privates. He succeeded in the mission, but at the cost of a shrapnel wound. After a short spell in hospital in France, he was sent home. In August, he learnt that this exploit had earned him the Military Cross, but he also heard that his brother-in-law, Frank Thorndike, serving in the Royal Flying Corps, had died after crashing his plane. Sybil's older brother Russell was out of the war by then, having been badly wounded at Gallipoli.

Lucy Casson's son Alec was the same age as Frank Thorndike. He was a student at Christ Church College, Oxford, when war broke out, a member of the Officer Training Corps. He enrolled on a shortened course at the Royal Military College, Sandhurst. His health was not good, and he was barred from active service, but in the climate of patriotism that was sweeping the country, Lucy was determined to have his disqualification overturned. She pulled every string she knew how, to get him a commission, and succeeded. He was appointed 2nd Lieutenant in the Royal Welch Fusiliers. In the spring of 1917, Alec found himself reporting as assistant adjutant to the poet, Siegfried Sassoon, who described him as 'a sensitive, refined youth and an amusing gossip.' He wrote an account of one particular experience they had shared:

When Casson was at Winchester he did not anticipate that he would ever be walking about on a fine April evening among a lot of dead men. It struck me as unnatural at the moment, probably because the stretcher-bearers had been identifying the bodies and had arranged them in seemly attitudes, their heads pillowed on their haversacks. Young Casson was trying to behave as if it were all quite ordinary; he was having his first look at 'the horrors of war'. While we were on the hill there was a huge explosion down by Fontaine Wood, as though a dump had been blown up. On our way home we stopped to inspect a tank which had got stuck in the mud while crossing a wide trench. But I was thinking to myself that sensitive people like Casson ought not to be taken to battle-fields. I had grown accustomed to such sights, but I was able to realize the impact they made on a fresh mind. Detached from the fighting, we had merely gone for a short walk after tea, so to speak, and I couldn't help feeling as if I'd been showing Casson something obscene.[4]

Sassoon was wounded and sent home. They had got on so well, that Alec tried, vainly, to meet the poet again, when he was on leave. Back in Porthmadog, in contrast to his war experiences, Alec found his mother preoccupied with the memorial she had commissioned for his father, to be installed in the church at Tremadog, a welcome distraction from thoughts of war. It was designed by Charles Robert Ashbee, a prime mover in the Arts and Crafts movement, whom she had met in Taormina and who had worked on the cross over Randal's grave there. There was a service to celebrate the installation, but Alec had to return to France before it took place. The Rev Llewelyn Hughes, rector in Porthmadog during many of the years since Lucy's marriage, praised Randal as a member of a family 'not originally of this district, but who for the last hundred and fifty years had been so closely and honourably connected with this place', mistakenly extending the Cassons' residence by fifty years. He pointed out that 'the terrible events of the last three years have taught us to look at death in another light.'[5]

That autumn, Alec took part in the Passchendaele Campaign, aimed at controlling the ridges around Ypres, Belgium, and cutting the supply line of the German 4th Army. Lloyd George opposed the offensive, as did General Foch, French Chief of General Staff, for some of the Allied forces had been diverted to Italy, but Field Marshal Douglas Haig received approval from the War Cabinet in July. At first, the Allies were hampered by heavy rain. In September, the weather improved. Alec was at Polygon Wood, where another advance was made. Alec and his commanding officer were in a concrete, dug-in guard post which was their battalion HQ. Such posts were named 'pill-boxes' because they looked like giant versions of the boxes in which medical pills were sold. When the Germans began to bombard the position, Alec and his commanding officer left the pill-box and took shelter in a large shell-hole with a trench dug in the bottom of it, thinking they would be safer there. Another officer came by to talk to them. At that point, a howitzer shell pitched into the hole, killing all three men. 'During the day,' wrote the soldier witness, 'shells fell all around the pill-box, but not one made a direct hit on it.'[6]

Lucy recorded a second death in her visitors' book: 'Oct.3 [3 October] Alec killed in action. Black Watches Corner, Polygon Wood on Sep.26 [26 September].' Again, she drew heavy black lines underneath. There are no further entries until March 1918, and none for that summer. Her loss was made worse by the fact that Alec's burial place was not identified for some years. It was thought that all three who were in the crater were buried where they died. In 1923, long after the war ended, a group of searchers, either having a note of the site, or simply stumbling across it, found the skeletons of the three officers and a private. There was no marker. Alec was identified by a signet ring with the Casson crest, and was finally buried at Poelcapelle British Cemetery, with an epitaph chosen by his mother: 'He did his duty gallantly.' She had had his portrait painted in uniform, and she later presented the picture to the Royal Welch Fusiliers, together with his medals, his bronze memorial plaque, his Scroll of Honour and a silver tankard carrying the Casson crest.[7]

A month before Alec's death, Lewis had been shipped home with a shrapnel wound, and put on light duties. Later, he returned to France, where, much to his chagrin, he invented a mechanism that increased the efficiency of gas missiles. He was recalled to the Ministry of Munitions, and appointed Secretary of the Chemical Warfare Commission, continuing to do work which he abhorred, but which kept him safe for the rest of the war. Four weeks after the Armistice, he at last came for a two-day visit to his widowed and childless aunt. The casualties of war had made him her heir. The first decision they made was to sell Betchton House and the rest of the Cheshire estate. There remained Bron y Garth, and Hafod Ysbyty, the land Galley had bought out of John Casson's estate.

Notes

[1] Richards, *Slate Quarrying in Wales*, p. 207
[2] 'The 2nd London Division at Loos', *47th (London) Division, 1914-1919*, London, 1922, greatwarlondon.wordpress.com
[3] Lewis Casson to Esther Reed, 1 October 1915, family papers
[4] Sassoon, Siegfried, first draft for *Memoirs of an Infantry Officer*, entry for 3rd April 1917, quoted in www.winchestercollegeatwar.com/archive/randal-alexander-casson. When it was published, 13 years later, Alec appeared under the fictional name 'Shirley'. Draft contained in Dunne, Captain J C, *The War the Infantry Knew*
[5] *Portmadoc Church Magazine*, June 1917

6   Richards, Frank, *Old Soldiers Never Die*, 1933, quoted in www.win-chestercollegeatwar.com/archive/randal-alexander-casson

7   Information provided by Clive Hughes, Volunteer, RWF Archives, Wrexham Museum, 24 February, 2016

Chapter 25
The New Heir
1920-1950

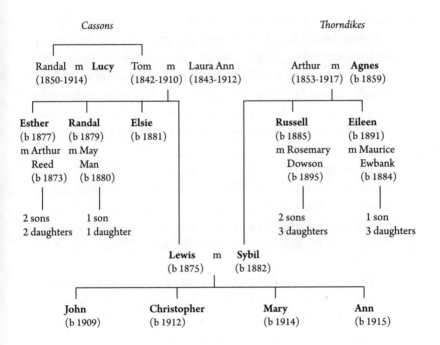

Cassons   *Thorndikes*

Randal m **Lucy**   Tom   m   Laura Ann   Arthur   m   **Agnes**
(1850-1914)   (1842-1910)   (1843-1912)   (1853-1917)   (b 1859)

Esther   **Randal**   **Elsie**   **Russell**   **Eileen**
(b 1877)   (b 1879)   (b 1881)   (b 1885)   (b 1891)
m Arthur   m May   m Rosemary   m Maurice
Reed   Man   Dowson   Ewbank
(b 1873)   (b 1880)   (b 1895)   (b 1884)

2 sons   1 son   2 sons   1 son
2 daughters   1 daughter   3 daughters   3 daughters

Lewis   m   **Sybil**
(b 1875)   (b 1882)

John   **Christopher**   **Mary**   **Ann**
(b 1909)   (b 1912)   (b 1914)   (b 1915)

The Casson/Thorndike Family 1928

Once her son Alec's remains had been given a suitable burial, Lucy was ready to start a new phase of life. Now in her sixties, she no longer sat on committees, but she made new friends, both at home and abroad, and entertained old ones. Henry Kitching and his family were frequent visitors. At first, there were no visits from her Casson in-laws, except Lewis' snatched visit soon after the Armistice, but she helped him to buy the lease of a family house in Carlyle Square, Chelsea, and took tea there once a year, his four children impressed by the tall gracious lady, in front of whom they had to be on their best behaviour.[1]

By the time Lewis visited again, in 1924, he was at the forefront of the London theatre, and Sybil was making theatrical history in Bernard Shaw's *Saint Joan*. During that summer, after its first run, he spent over two months at Bron y Garth, his first opportunity to get to know his aunt well and re-acquaint himself with the country of his birth. He went up Snowdon and the Glyders ('Glyderau'), crossed the Traeth, just as his father had done, over fifty years earlier, to visit Caerffynnon Hall. Later, when Sybil and he stayed one Sunday night while touring, Lucy encouraged them to bring their family for a proper stay.

So, in August 1927, Lewis and Sybil arrived for nearly a month's holiday, bringing their four children: John, aged seventeen; Christopher, aged fifteen; Mary, aged thirteen; and eleven-year-old Ann. John, by then a naval cadet, came direct from his ship and remembered their arrival:

> Aunt Lucy was at the front door to greet the 'cavalcade' when we drove up the drive. 'Come along in,' she cried with a beaming smile of welcome. 'Tea will be ready in a minute, and then there will be time before we all go to change for dinner.' Change for dinner! that was something we had never done at home.[2]

They were used to the usual pleasures of the seaside and countryside, having spent summers in Dymchurch, on the Kent coast. But mountains were new to them. Sybil wrote to her mother: 'We climbed Snowdon yesterday, 3,600 ft – and had tea at the top right in the clouds and thick fog. But then a little lower down the view was simply magnificent. The children all climbed marvellously – we did the whole thing in five hours.'[3] They went to Castell Caernarfon and on to Cae Derw, in Denbigh, where Lewis showed them the oak trees his father had planted in the garden there. They spent hours on the beach at Morfa Bychan. Aunt Lucy took them to a Conservative Party fête, where they had to keep their socialist views in check. The Conservatives had little support in Wales. In 1922, Caernarfonshire had returned a Labour Party candidate for the first time, but it was regained by the Liberals in the following elections. Despite political differences, Lewis' family ended their stay 'enamoured of Aunt Lucy and not so much in awe of her.'[4]

Just before this stay, Lewis' sister Elsie had arrived at Bron y Garth. She was harbouring a new ambition. Having graduated as Bachelor of Medicine in 1919 (the first woman in the family to gain a degree), she had then worked as a clinical assistant at West Herts Hospital, in Hemel Hempstead, where she had had a formative experience:

I found it very difficult to get used to the atmosphere of bored idleness in the day room of the hospital. Then, one Monday morning, when I arrived at the women's wards, I found the atmosphere had completely changed and realised that preparations for Christmas decorations had begun. The ward sisters had produced coloured tissue paper and bare branches, and all the patients were working happily in groups making flowers and leaves and using all their artistic talents with real interest and pleasure. I knew from that moment that such occupation was an integral part of treatment and must be provided.[5]

From then on, she devoted her career to mental health, eventually opening Dorset House, on Clifton Hill, Bristol, as a residential centre for women suffering mental illness, with a training school in occupational therapy. While Lewis had discovered his vocation by a circuitous route, Elsie's was more direct, though delayed by domestic duties. The seeds of her interest in mental health had been planted when, as a child, she visited Denbigh Asylum and took part in entertainments for the patients. Later, working for Octavia Hill, she had recognised that 'it was Londoners themselves, as well as their tenements that needed 'first aid'.[6]

As Lucy Casson entered her seventies, she continued to take an interest in her family's activities. Visits to London allowed her to see Lewis and Sybil in the theatre. She made occasional descents on Randal and May in Southampton, where, having returned from Burma for the sake of his health, he was lecturing in mathematics at the University. She visited Esther Reed, whose husband was an academic at King's College, London, doing ground-breaking work on early English drama.[7] At home, Lucy's half-brother, Henry Kitching, retired from the Navy and moved into Plas Penrhyn, the house on the other side of the Traeth, above Penrhyndeudraeth, where William and Fanny Casson had lived with their family, sixty years earlier. Lucy enjoyed the company of the younger generation. Randal and May's two children stayed, as did John Casson. In 1930, Lewis and Sybil paid another visit, with daughters Mary and Ann, while they were on a provincial tour. The following year, fifteen-year-old Ann Casson spent twelve days with her great-aunt, swiftly followed by her Reed cousin, Owen, who brought poignant memories of Alec to Lucy's mind, as he was up at Christ Church, Oxford.

Local life around Lucy was changing. The church where she worshipped was no longer Anglican; after the war, the implementation of the Welsh Church Act had finally separated and disestablished the Church in Wales. She was witness to the end of Porthmadog's prosperity. Shipbuilding had begun to decline before the war, with the advent of steam. Steamers ran to schedule, instead of being dependent on winds, and carried larger loads. The competition proved too much for sail. Some ships continued to trade; there were still repair workshops, but, as local historian Henry Hughes wrote: 'the age-long propulsion by means of the breezes of heaven, had little chance of survival. The end of a romantic and glorious era had come.'[8]

After a brief post-war boom, the slate industry too declined, in competition with tiles, which could be mass-produced in quantity to precise specifications. Production costs rose, since most of the accessible, good-quality slate had already been extracted. There was competition from Belgian, Norwegian, Italian, German and, especially, French slate, which was of as fine quality as the 'blue veins of Merionethshire.' The North Wales Slate Quarry Association, a group of quarry owners, kept prices stable for some years, just as in the time of William Turner, negotiating from Dinorwic, but it had now broken up. Prices fell as owners undercut each other; and when they lowered wages, industrial disputes broke out. In 1926, the Quarrymen's Union, founded in 1874, had affiliated with the Transport and General Workers' Union, the year of the General Strike. Lewis Casson was a fierce supporter of the strikers. He had to keep a hold on his tongue if he found himself in conversation with any of the Greaves family, whose Llechwedd quarry was one of those that survived partly by lowering wages.

The Diphwys Casson Slate Company had reopened after its liquidation in the 1890s, closed during the war, reopened in 1920, but closed again in 1927. In 1936, it would reopen

337

as a subsidiary of the Oakeley Slate Quarries Company, but the Casson name would be lost, except as it referred to a part of the gorge. The Blaenau quarries were amongst the strongest to survive, some loads still carried on the Festiniog Railway. The local banks no longer carried the name 'North and South Wales Bank'. They were now part of the Midland Bank. But the law office, Breese, Jones and Casson, continued to do business in Porthmadog High Street.

In the spring of 1932, Lewis and Sybil set off on an international tour. Later in the year, their son John arrived at Bron y Garth in his 'Baby Austin'. He was twenty-two years old, excited at having joined the Fleet Air Arm, and full of a new enthusiasm for rock-climbing. When he was not roping himself up on Snowdon, Lucy enjoyed parading her handsome great-nephew round the neighbourhood. As he left, she handed him the silver signet ring that had belonged to Alec. Early in 1933, Lewis and Sybil began the journey home. Just before they docked at Southampton, Lewis received a telegram from his brother Randal: Aunt Lucy had died suddenly in her sleep on the night of 10/11 April. He hurried up to Wales, taking his sister Elsie and his secretary. *Portmadoc Church Magazine* published an obituary:

> With the old-fashioned courtesy of the Victorian age she combined a deep spiritual earnestness, a selfless devotion to duty, and a determination to carry to success any undertaking on which she had set her heart ... The death of her husband and the loss of her only son in the Great War were hard blows which might have brought collapse, but she endured them with exemplary patience and courage. And not only that, but she grew in largeness of heart, in kindness, in sympathy and in love.[9]

Others had memories of a formidable woman. Sam Beazley,

a member of the Greaves family, remembered how she reserved a whole carriage when she took the train to Paddington.[10] In public life, her views had been too autocratic for some, her manner sometimes high-handed. At home, she had held sway, receiving friends and family in the West Room, combining formality with genuine affection, offering a warm welcome, despite the grandeur of her style.

Lucy had made Lewis her residuary heir. She left £6,000 to one of her Davenport cousins, together with jewellery, plate and some Red Worcester china. She left £2,500 each to her nieces, Esther and Elsie, the second of whom was particularly appreciative, as she could put it towards Dorset House. A touching bequest was £50 to Gertrude Casson, widow of Will Casson, her nephew killed at Loos. She left £100 to Henry Kitching, and the same sum to nine other friends. Other bequests included £200 and an annuity of £1 a year to her gardener, and to her housekeeper, Sarah Bailey.

'Hafod Ysbyty and Gamallt', the last remaining Casson property in Wales besides Bron y Garth, came into the ownership of its tenant farmer, Griffith T. Jones, at this time, the sale releasing funds to pay for some of Lucy's bequests. In July 1933, probate was granted, and Lewis became the owner of Bron y Garth. He soon found the visitors' book. Following her custom, he noted her death, with a heavy ink line below it.

Lewis knew, as Lucy must have known, that he would not be taking up residence. Bron y Garth became a holiday home, for family, actors and other friends. His brother and sisters came, renewing memories of their Welsh childhood. Sybil's brother Russell brought his wife and five children, and her sister Eileen, recently widowed, came with her four children, all of them discovering the delights of Wales for the first time. One eminent early visitor was Douglas Fairbanks Jr, another was Paul Robeson, while Sybil set about learning Welsh and enjoyed practising on the local shopkeepers. Lewis noted the death of a dog, succeeded by another, Jafna, a thick-haired black Dutch Barge Dog. There must have been many dogs that were part of the Casson households over the years, but this is the first whose name is known. Rescued from Battersea Dogs Home, he was named after a role Lewis had been playing, Sir Jafna Pandraneth, in Shaw's *On the Rocks*.

In 1934, Lewis noted the improvements he had made, including new bathrooms and mains electricity supply. He asked his brother Randal's son Hugh to suggest further changes. Hugh was just starting the architectural career that was to bring him fame[11]. His most dramatic innovation was to have several ground-floor walls taken out, so that anyone entering the house walked straight into a large hall that stretched across to the windows and terrace, revealing the spectacular view across the Traeth. The book-lined West Room retained its formality, but the house became more spacious and airy, and the atmosphere more informal.[12]

While much had changed since Lewis' childhood, the beauty of North Wales had not diminished. More tourists, holiday-makers, hikers and climbers made their way there. Sybil, who had seen the Alps, commented: 'The Welsh mountains are not very large, but they're very well stage-managed.'[13] Just as the railway had brought the age of coach-travel to an end, motor-cars were beginning to rival trains. In March 1935, Lewis made a marathon journey from London to Porthmadog. He was playing the Welshman, 'Owen Glendower', in Shakespeare's *King Henry IV, Part I*, at His Majesty's Theatre, Haymarket. Eager to show Bron y Garth to his son John, just back from the Far East, he set off with him after a Saturday-night show, with a bust of Sybil, recently completed by Jacob Epstein, in the back of the car. They drove 250 miles through the night, sharing the driving, the roads lit only by dim headlamps. Stopping near the foot of Snowdon, they sniffed the mountain air, and watched the dawn light catch its top, arriving at Bron y Garth at six o'clock in the morning. After breakfast and a short nap, they went over the house, looking at what had been done and what was still to do, choosing a suitable place to display the bust. Next morning, they set off before dawn and drove back again in time for Lewis's Monday night performance. Before setting off, Lewis gave the interview to the Welsh journalist in which he expounded on his great-grandmother Esther's achievements. Playing a Welshman, and relishing his ownership of Bron y Garth, he was particularly conscious of his Welsh identity:

> It is more than seven weeks since I have been down there, and even a short stay of a few hours is well worth having. I love that country, and I certainly have my roots there, for when my parents married, my father came from Portmadoc [Porthmadog] and my mother from Talsarnau, on the other side of the Traeth.[14]

His two sisters, Esther and Elsie, encouraged this interest in their Welsh roots. Esther had recently visited San Francisco, and shared discoveries she had made about their grandfather Lewis Holland Thomas' properties there, while Elsie was president of the Bristol Cambrian Society.

Lewis and Sybil soon made the acquaintance of another Welshman, with more Welsh blood than Lewis, who was making his mark on the local landscape. Bertram Clough Williams-Ellis, was a grandson of John W. Greaves, and nephew of Sir Arthur Osmond Williams, MP, of Castell Deudraeth. He had trained as an architect. In 1908, his father gave him Plas Brondanw, a run-down estate overlooking the Glaslyn valley, which he proceeded to

341

restore. In 1925, he bought the peninsula behind Castell Deudraeth, known as 'Aber Ia', 'ice estuary', and began the project by which he would be best known, the creation of the Italianate village known as 'Portmeirion'. Like William Madocks, who had created Tremadog, and David Williams, who had developed Penrhyndeudraeth, he wanted to design and build a town from scratch. Already, he had marked out the site and put up several buildings in distinctive Arts and Crafts style. Lewis and Sybil were unsure if they entirely approved of this showy outcrop on the Welsh coast, with its sense of 'make-believe', but Sybil's ebullience overcame any scruples. The actor Sam Beazley, of the Greaves/Williams family, remembered her arrival on one occasion: 'She said "I've come! By boat!" as if she was Iphigenia in Aulis. We all clapped.'[15]

The inhabitants of Porthmadog grew used to the regular influx of the theatrical Cassons and their friends, and enjoyed hearing 'Dame' Sybil, as she now was, rehearsing her lines with Lewis, in the Bron y Garth garden, their voices reverberating down the hill. While Lewis was the only one of his siblings to go into the theatre, Sybil's brother Russell and sister Eileen had both done so, while six of the next generation also had theatrical careers. Soon there were more young visitors, as girlfriends, boyfriends, fiancés and fiancées, wives and husbands made their first visits, filling the house as in the heyday of Aunt Lucy's social life. There was Patricia Chester-Master, from Shanghai, who married John Casson in June 1935, at a grand wedding in Knightsbridge, which Lewis duly noted in the visitors' book. They stayed at Bron y Garth during their honeymoon. In September 1935, Eileen brought William Devlin, an actor she had trained, and who had played King Lear at the age of twenty-three and been in John Gielgud's *Hamlet*. He had met Lewis' older daughter, Mary, and fallen in love with her.

Bron y Garth terrace, 1937, left to right: Anthony, John, Patricia,
Sybil, Lewis, Ann & Christopher Casson, Mary & William Devlin

Lewis recorded their London wedding in March 1936 and
added the birth of his first grandson two weeks later,
Anthony David, son of John and Patricia Casson, later to be
followed by two daughters.

In the second half of the 1930s, while many visitors came
and went, Lewis and Sybil spent more peaceful times there
together. John and Mary were married, Christopher was
living in Dublin, acting at the Gate Theatre, and Ann was
making her own career as an actress. They no longer needed
the large family house in Chelsea, which they had bought
when the lease at Carlyle Square ran out, the loan from Aunt
Lucy long ago paid off. They moved into a two-bedroom flat
nearby and spent Christmas 1938 at Bron y Garth. Early in
the New Year of 1939, Sybil had appendicitis and went there
to convalesce. She wrote to her sister-in-law Elsie: 'No place
is so dear and beautiful to me, I suppose because it's all
mixed up with Lewis and walks and the glorious smells
there.' Lewis himself, about to lead an Old Vic tour to the

Mediterranean, wrote: 'Think of me when you get to Bron y Garth. I'll be there with you. I shall think of you always.'[16]

This period of restful retreats at Bron y Garth came to an end that September, at the outbreak of the Second World War. Lewis joined the Chelsea Air Raid Precautions (ARP). John was in the Fleet Air Arm; Christopher, a pacifist, like Sybil and her sister Eileen, had settled in Dublin, away from the fray, invoking Sybil's indignation that he did not return to proclaim his pacifism and face the consequences. Mary's husband, William Devlin, volunteered for the Royal Wiltshire Yeomanry, and served in North Africa and Italy throughout the war. In the late spring of 1940, John, in command of a squadron of dive-bombers stationed on the Firth of Forth, was shot down while attacking two German battleships at Trondheim, Norway. He and his observer were reported as 'missing believed killed.' For his wife, Patricia, this was a second devastating blow, since her elder brother, who was in the RAF Volunteer Reserve, had just been killed flying a Wellington bomber over northern Germany.

Patricia retreated to Bron y Garth, with her three children. After four weeks of suspense she heard news. 'Lord Haw Haw', the Nazi sympathiser, William Joyce, announced in one of his broadcasts from Germany that the son of Dame Sybil Thorndike was now a prisoner of war. A month or two later, correspondence began, and John remained in prison camp until the end of the hostilities.

Bron y Garth offered a wartime refuge. Russell Thorndike's family spent time there when their house was bombed. In the autumn of 1940, Sybil and Lewis prepared to embark on an Old Vic tour that would take them to the mining valleys of South Wales. While they were rehearsing, their flat in Chelsea was bombed, and they camped out for some time with Eileen's family in Bayswater. Tyrone

Guthrie, who was directing them in *Macbeth*, decided to finish rehearsals in Wales: 'Leaving Paddington at noon,' he announced, 'if Paddington is still there.'[17] In January 1941, the tour was extended and included North Wales. They stayed at Bron y Garth, where Mary, now pregnant, had joined her sister-in-law, when William Devlin was posted abroad. In April 1941, Patricia, following Lewis' custom, made the appropriate entry in the visitors' book: 'Diana Mary Devlin to William & Mary Devlin', the only member of the Casson family to be born at Bron y Garth.

In January 1942, Sybil and Lewis set out on another Welsh tour. The mining communities particularly relished the Greek tragedy *Medea*. 'This is the play for us. It kindles a fire,' one miner was reported as saying to Sybil; and Lewis told Gilbert Murray, whose version they played: 'The big emotional sway and the beauty of the poetry really do give these Welsh people what they want. An old miner said after a performance that if he hadn't known a word of English, the music of it would have made him understand it.'[18] Their director Tyrone Guthrie and his wife Judy stayed at Bron y Garth during this tour. She described it to a friend: 'It's unbelievably beautiful and I think the situation of the house is the loveliest I've ever seen ... The house is quite full – ailing relatives, healthy grandchildren, maniacal PGs [paying guests] incarcerated upstairs ...'[19]

The last phrase was fanciful, but she had caught something of the ambivalent atmosphere of

Lewis Casson & the author at Bron y Garth.

the house. Randal, despite his eagerness to buy the house from the Spooners, had found it depressing, hence his frequent trips abroad to sunny spots like Sicily. To many it was a beautiful, happy, welcoming home, with convivial evenings, often ending with music, inspiring a romantic attachment to the place. One evening sang Paul Robeson;[20] Mary Devlin had learnt enough Welsh to sing some of the folksongs, accompanying herself on the piano. But for others, including Mary herself, the house roused a powerful melancholy. There was a rational explanation in her case. Her marriage was shaky, and she was looking after her aunt, Eileen, who had come to Bron y Garth to recover from a nervous breakdown. There was also the presence of Sarah Bailey, the housekeeper. Sarah had started as a housemaid there in 1898, when she was eighteen years old. She had stayed ever since and become totally devoted to Lucy Casson. Lewis had promised his aunt to keep her on, but she was a sinister figure in the house, drinking, brooding and sending unpalatable, meagre dishes to the table; more practically there was some suspicion she was cheating over the food rations. Lewis felt the oppressiveness, and even considered exorcism, while Sybil was undisturbed. 'I feel I want to pack up and go to Bron-y-Garth and never move. I will one day too.'[21] Perhaps the house reflected back the mood of its inhabitants.

As the war dragged on, Patricia and Mary, the main occupants, felt isolated and began to plan a move to somewhere nearer London. In the summer of 1942, Sybil and Lewis were in contact with Dora Harvey, a woman living near Borth-y-gest, whose husband was the retired manager of a metal-working company in Greenwich. She was anxious to get the employees' children out of London and into the safety of the countryside.[22] Sybil was enthused by the idea and wrote from Wales to her friend Vera Brittain, a colleague in the Peace Pledge Union: 'I am desperately working now to get our house here turned into a Children's Home. We will take forty and they come in next week with matrons and nurses – all from bombed places. I'm so excited for them to use this darling house.'[23] She worked hard to get the place ready by the autumn. It would be a wrench for Sarah Bailey, who, with a macabre sense of humour, made the following entry in the visitors' book:

Date of Arrival	Name	Address	Date of Departure
Sep 15th 1898	Sarah A Bailey	Bron y Garth	Aug 24th 1942

Lewis did not make another entry until after VE Day:

Between these dates [16 November 1942 and 22 June 1945] the house was a home for about 30 babies evacuated from Greenwich district, with staff and nurses. On July 9 John & Patricia Casson took the house over and with the help of Jennie Jones restored most of the furniture there by that date.

John and Patricia's son Anthony, aged nine, later remembered being at the house that August with his father and grandfather, when they heard the news of the Hiroshima bomb.

At first, it seemed that life at Bron y Garth would continue much as it had before the war. John returned from prison camp. The 1945 Labour victory delighted Lewis, and in that year's Birthday Honours, he was knighted for his services to the theatre. Sarah Bailey returned, her weird presence offset by the commonsensical above-named 'Jennie' (more correctly 'Jinnie') Jones. Lewis installed Patricia Casson's parents in the house, Reggie and Betty

Chester-Master, who had lost all their money and possessions when the Japanese invaded Shanghai. Many visitors came that first summer and autumn. But there had been much wear-and-tear while the evacuees were there – some pictures were damaged irreparably. Few visitors came during the winter, making it lonely for the Chester-Masters. Elsie Casson continued to visit, but the other branches of the family – the Reeds, the Randal Cassons, the Russell Thorndikes, the Eileen Ewbanks – all had their own lives and took holidays elsewhere. Christopher Casson's home was permanently in Dublin. He had married Kay O'Connell, a stage designer at the Gate Theatre. He brought her, with his two little girls, for one holiday there, but they too had their own favourite places nearer home. Ann, now married to Scottish actor Douglas Campbell, brought her baby son, and added to the superstition that there was something strange about the house, when she related how, on one occasion, she watched his gaze steadfastly follow an invisible someone, or something, round the room.

Still, Patricia Casson made Bron y Garth an idyllic holiday home for her own children, for me, her niece (my parents having split up after the war), and for several other families with children: long days on the beaches at Carreg Wen and Morfa Bychan; climbs up Moel y Gest, Cnicht and Snowdon; birthday parties in the garden; camping on the lower terrace; mah-jong and board games on wet days, or exploring the attic, with its collection of toys and exotic treasures, and a trunk full of dressing-up clothes, the remains of Aunt Lucy's extensive wardrobe.

It came as a shock to the family, when, in the summer of 1949, Lewis announced that he was selling Bron y Garth. He had had an offer to buy, from Sam Beer, a local businessman in Porthmadog, and had accepted it. Mr Beer was the owner of the local laundry, quite unconnected with any of the families with which the Cassons had been associated over the years, and a Conservative councillor, unsympathetic to many of Lewis's views. Although the news was unexpected, and his decision seemed precipitous, Lewis had been worrying for some time over the problem of maintaining a large, rambling house, in need of repairs, many miles from London, weighing up how much use would be made of it in the coming years, as Sybil and he, now well into their seventies, grew older. Earlier that summer, Patricia and John had gone off on holiday with Mary Devlin, choosing Brittany, rather than Wales. That, and Mr Beer's offer, decided him. He wanted to be shot of the responsibility, and acted precipitately, without consulting his siblings or children. Agreeing the sale so quickly was an act of impatience and frustration. But perhaps he had never quite accustomed himself to being the owner of a mansion. The poverty of his early days in London had stayed with him, and when he did become wealthier, he used the money to give other members of the family a lift up, rather than spending on himself.

At first, Lewis was ready to sell Bron y Garth with all its contents, a decision he would have regretted, since in calmer moments, he valued the continuity of Casson family history. Instead, as Sybil and he began to rehearse their next play, *Treasure Hunt*, which, as it happened, was about a family trying to make ends meet in a ramshackle country house, he asked his daughter-in-law Patricia to deal with the contents. It was a mammoth task which she undertook over the next few months. She chose which articles of furniture and other chattels to save, which to discard, which to send to auction, which to give away. She saved the Walker clock, and the family portraits. She saved a miscellaneous collection of family papers and documents which Lucy's Randal had kept, and some of the books. She was left with the problem of what to do with the rest of the library, since the shelves in all the family houses were overflowing. She wondered if she dared make a gift of them to Porthmadog Council, and received the following letter from her father-in-law:

15th February 1950

My dear Patricia

Your idea for the books was an inspiration, and we're both delighted with the Council's acceptance. Anyway why should you have been afraid of my wrath? I really meant it literally when I put the whole thing in your hands and said that your decisions should be final. I shall never be grateful enough for all you have done and are doing. Judging by the worry and depression I got in dealing with the infinitely easier decisions and work at Cedar Cottage [the smaller house in Kent he had bought], dealing with Bron y Garth would have killed me off! So I owe you what remains of my life.

Love,
Lewis[24]

Porthmadog's local library received about 1,500 books. The following May, Lewis wrote again, saying 'Beer has paid up and all is signed and sealed.'[25] One hundred and fifty years of the Cassons in North Wales had ended.

Notes

1   Casson, p. 140
2   *John Casson: Sailor and Airman, A memoir,* unpublished
3   Croall, Jonathan, *Sybil Thorndike: A Star of Life,* 2008, p. 207

4   Casson, p. 140

5   Casson, Dr Elizabeth, OBE, written in 1950, published in *The Story of the Dorset House School of Occupational Therapy, 1930-1986*, private publication, 1987

6   AWR (Arthur W Reed) ibid p.7

7   Reed, A W, *Early Tudor Drama: Medwall, the Rastells, Heywood and the More Circle*, 1925

8   Hughes,Henry, p. 240

9   *Portmadoc Church Magazine*, undated cutting

10 Sam Beazley, personal recollection via Charles Duff

11 Sir Hugh Maxwell Casson CH KCVO PRA RDI

12 One of Eileen's children later maintained that the exterior of the house was painted bright pink, visible from across the Traeth, but there is no evidence that this was done.

13 Personal recollection of the author

14 Roberts, Glyn, *Western Mail*, op cit

15 Sam Beazley, quoted Croall, p289

16 Croall, p. 296

17 Devlin, pp. 206-207

18 Croall, p. 318

19 Croall, pp. 322-333

20 Paul Robeson had appeared as Othello, with Sybil, and fell in love with Wales when making *The Proud Valley* in 1940.

21 Croall, p. 322

22 Research and notes by Veronica Millington

23 Croall p. 327

24 Lewis Casson to Patricia Casson, 15 February 1950, family papers

25 Lewis Casson to Patricia Casson, 24 May 1950, family papers

Chapter 26
Revisiting the Past

Bron y Garth

In the years after the Cassons left Wales, their descendants made occasional pilgrimages to Seathwaite, now in Cumbria, and to Porthmadog, now in Gwynedd. Some explored the churchyard of Wonderful Walker, supped in the Newfield Inn and looked up at Wallowbarrow Crag, which they still commemorated every Christmas. Some pitched tents on campsites close to Porthmadog, climbed Snowdon, and other peaks, took the road from Porthmadog to the harbour at Borth-y-gest, and followed the path to Carreg Gwen beach. One summer, some years ago, two of us set about re-exploring our Welsh heritage. We walked up the drive to

Bron y Garth and knocked at the door, hoping not to be turned away by whoever had bought it after Mr Sam Beer's widow died in the 1990s. The owner turned out to be Dr Gwyn Jones, a successful entrepreneur and academic, whose father had once run the Australia Inn, cause of the bitter altercation between Randal Casson and David Lloyd George in 1899. For the first time in its history, life in Bron y Garth was being conducted in Welsh.

Modern Wales has a stronger national identity than when the Cassons left. In 1974, Meirionydd and Caernarfonshire became part of Gwynedd, the old kingdom. After the years when Welsh nationalists desecrated English road signs, Welsh place names prevailed. In 1982, the Welsh television channel, S4C, was launched; in 1993, the Welsh language was given equal status with English in the public sector. In 1999, after a closely run referendum, the Welsh Assembly was established. There are still debates about how much independence it should seek, and about the status of the Welsh language, but Welsh men and women undoubtedly have a greater confidence in their nation and its future, than when the Cassons were part of it.

Since first returning to Bron y Garth, I have stayed on many occasions with cousins, in one of the holiday flats at the east end of the house, or in the old coach-house. From what was once our grandparents' bedroom, we look out over the terrace and across the Traeth towards Harlech. We revisit childhood haunts and show them to the younger generations. At first, we did not know the places where our ancestors once lived and worked. I wanted to see and learn more than what family lore had taught me. In Shakespeare's *King Henry IV, Part I*, the Welsh prince, Owen Glendower, the role once taken by my grandfather, boasts: 'I can call spirits from the vasty deep', but the prosaic Harry Hotspur retorts: 'Why, so can I, or so can any man; But will they come when you do call for them?' We may not be able to conjure up the spirits of bygone times, but the urge to connect with our history is strong. 'By recreating the past,' biographer Michael Holroyd has written, 'we are calling on the same magic as our forebears did with stories of their ancestors round the fire under the night skies.'[1]

Out on a walk, a cousin and I met Bill Jones, a local industrial archaeologist who asked what had brought us to the neighbourhood. We mentioned the Casson name and confessed that we did not know where the first who came to Wales had lived. 'I know *exactly* where they lived,' he told us. The next day, in pouring rain, he met us in Llan Ffestiniog, so called to distinguish it from the larger town of Blaenau Ffestiniog. He showed us the Casson graves in St Michael's churchyard. He pointed out a small car park, where Tŷ Uchaf, Thomas and Esther Casson's inn, once stood. The church is closed, and the village quiet, off the beaten track. He indicated the drive, leading to the lodge, stables, house and gardens at Plas Blaenddol, once Blaenyddôl. It's a more substantial house than when Thomas and Esther moved in, offering holiday accommodation. The first time we called, there was a longcase clock standing inside the front door, reminding us that the ticking and striking of the Walker clock marked the passing of their days. In the slate-flagged kitchen, it was easy to imagine family gatherings, when George, Bess, Ann, William and John Casson were children.

There are other Casson houses to explore, each with its own story. Nearby Pengwern Hall, where the first William Casson took his wife to live, is privately owned, and its mixture of architectural periods has caught the attention of local historians. Saddest of the houses associated with the family is Caerffynnon Hall, designed and built by Lewis Holland Thomas. After his granddaughter Elfrede Haigh, sold it, the house became a hotel, later lodging workers who were building a nuclear plant at Trawsfynydd, to the south. After that it offered holiday accommodation, but in recent years it has suffered neglect and shoddy alterations; the front hall from which the double staircase rises has been partitioned, obscuring the great stained-glass window on the landing. But the view from the front of the house still offers a spectacular view of Bae Ceredigion.

Sometimes, finding traces of the Cassons is a matter of serendipity. Once, in search of a church featured in Simon Jenkins's *Wales: Churches, Houses, Castles*, we ventured to Bontddu, south of Harlech. There, a small organ carries an identifying plate which reads 'The Positive Organ Company: Casson's Patent.' In Denbigh, the name 'Thomas Casson' appears on a stone memorial listing some who made their mark on the town. Foundry Garage, site of Tom's first factory, is as evocative as the old redbrick building in Greenland Street, Liverpool, once his father's tar and distillery works. Cae Derw, still a family home, bears a plaque on its front door, commemorating Dr Elizabeth Casson. When visiting, I was given a metal shoe, found in the garden, perhaps shed by the donkey Laura Casson led about the streets when her children were small.

At other times, this corner of North Wales seems a palimpsest, obliterating what was familiar to the Cassons and their contemporaries. When we drive out from Bron y Garth into Porthmadog, we pass the old bank building on the corner of the High Street. First built by the North and South Wales Bank, later owned by the Cassons; it now has an HSBC sign over the door. The Casson quarry closed in 1955, by then a subsidiary of the Oakeley Slate Quarries Company. The land is part of Llechwedd, once owned and worked by the Greaves family. Some slate is still worked. On the strength of the family name, we were given a private tour. We bounced along slate-strewn tracks in a four-wheel drive, between mountains of waste far more extensive than the modest ruins at Walney Scar, where William and Thomas Casson began their quarrying lives; we stood on the slopes of Diffwys, from where they surveyed their land.

Those first Cassons came to Wales to work; they witnessed the beginning of a tourism industry that now offers the main employment in Gwynedd. Today's visitors experience the landscape through more participatory activities than those who came in search of the picturesque in the early 19th century. They hike and climb, swim and build sandcastles, just as we did as children. And they experience a whole range of outdoor recreations in the mountains, the sea, the beach and the forests. At Llechwedd, now a major tourist attraction, I have watched fearless adventurers swinging between the gorges on zipwires. Portmeirion, built by a grandson of John W Greaves, thrives as a visitor venue. Each September, it stages 'Festival No 6', a multi-genre music event named after the protagonist in *The Prisoner*, the 1960s TV series that was set there. Heavy drumbeats reverberate through the neighbourhood on festival days. At a quieter time, I took tea with the owner of Plas Penrhyn, the house on the hillside above, where William Casson lived on his return to Wales. In Penrhyndeudraeth, where her husband's explosives factory once stood, there is now a nature reserve.

Many visitors besides me like to explore the past of North Wales. While early tourists were eager to identify its antiquities from their guidebooks, it's a more immersive and theatrical experience now. The growth of a heritage industry means we can see jousting in a castle courtyard, go down into the slate caverns to see scenes of quarriers and miners carrying out their work, watch slate being split for our own entertainment, poke about in replica quarriers' cottages. The first major heritage project was the restoration of the steam railways, an arduous, complicated task, dependent on an army of railway volunteers, including civil engineers as skilled as James Spooner and his son. Now, many come to play the part of engine driver or ticket collector, while others maintain the trains and the track. From Porthmadog Station, the engine puffs its way through mountains and valleys, and on its return, the disembarking passengers refresh themselves at 'Spooner's Grill, Café and Bar'. The first Cassons in Wales were emigrants who never returned to Wallowbarrow Crag. We who tread in our forebears' footsteps are fortunate, given a sense of 'place' irrecoverable to those who, for whatever reason, cannot go back to where they sprang from.

Note

[1]   Holroyd, Michael, 'What Justifies Biography?', *Works on Paper*, 2013, pp. 30-31

Bibliography

Abbreviations:

AM/MRO — Archifau Meirionydd/ Meirionydd Record Office

CCHCSF/JMHRS — *Cylchgrawn Cymdeithas Hanes a Chofnodion Sir Feirionydd/ Journal of the Merioneth Historical and Record Society*

LlGC/NLW — Llyfrgell Genedlaeithol Cymru/ National Library of Wales

NWC — *North Wales Chronicle*

Primary sources

Casson family papers: various correspondence 1874-1950, scrapbook of William Casson (1813-1877); memoir of Lewis Holland Thomas (1812-1888); 'Subscriptions to Mrs Thos Casson's Presentation Fund, by the Inhabitants of Talsarnau and its Neighbourhood, November, 1870; miscellaneous papers of Randal Casson (1850- 1914)

Casson Collection at AM/MRO

Census returns: 1841-1911

General Record Office

HSBC archives, London

Peniarth Family Estate Records, LlGC/NLW

Tanymanod and Gelli Estate Papers: No 239, LlGC/NLW

The National Archives: Catalogue of Tremadog Estate, Breese Jones Casson deposit, Gwynedd archives

Secondary sources

Aaron, Jane, *Nineteenth-Century Women's Writing in Wales*, 2010

Abel, Richard, *The Making of the English Legal Profession*, 1998

Andrews, Malcolm, *In Search of the Picturesque: Landscape Aesthetics and Tourism in Britain, 1760-1800, 1990*

Arnold, Matthew, *On the Study of Celtic Literature,* 1867

Ashmore, Owen, *The Industrial Archaeology of North West England,* 1982

Beazley, Elisabeth, *Madocks & the Wonder of Wales,* 2nd edition, 1985

Beckett, Ian F W, *Riflemen Form: A Study of the Rifle Volunteer Movement, 1859-1908,* 1982

Beale, Griffin, *William Thynne's Forgotten Partner,* unpublished

Bradley, Lonna, et al, *Ffestiniog Yesterday and Today: a history of our Village,* Federation of Women's Institutes Project, 1998

britishnewspapersarchive.co.uk

Buckley, John, *The Penny Family and Ffestiniog,* unpublished

Buckley, John, *William Turner in Ireland?* unpublished

Buckley, John, *A Society of Ancient Britons,* unpublished

Buckley, John, *Another Cumbrian at Ffestiniog,* www.windycreek.plus.com

Buckley, John, *William Turner of Seathwaite and Parkia, 1766-1853,* unpublished

Cameron, Alastair, *History of the Coniston Slate Industry,* 1996

Casson, John, *Lewis and Sybil,* 1982

Casson, Lewis, 'A Famous Welshman greets CABAN', undated cutting from a quarriers' magazine

Chapone, Mrs (Hester), *Letters on the Improvement of the Mind,* (1773), 1812 edition.

Colley, Linda, *Britons: Forging the Nation, 1707-1837,* 2009 edition

Course, A G, *The Merchant Navy, A Social History,* 1963

Croall, Jonathan, *Sybil Thorndike: A Star of Life,* 2007

Davies, John, *A History of Wales,* New Edition, 2007

Davies, William Lloyd, 'Pengwern, Ffestiniog', *CCHCSF/JMHRS,* Vol 1, 1949

Devlin, Diana, *A Speaking Part: Lewis Casson and the theatre of his time,* 1982

Dodd, A H, *The Industrial Revolution in North Wales*, 1933

Drage, Dorothy, *Pennies for Friendship*, private publication, 1961

Eifion, Allted, trans Kidd, Jack, *The Gestiana*, 2013

Evans, E D, 'Politics and Parliamentary Representation in Merioneth', *CCHCSF/JMHRS*, Vol. 3, 1958

Evans, Rev J, *A Tour through part of North Wales in the year 1798 and at other times*, 2nd edition, 1802

Felton, Felix, *Thomas Love Peacock*, 1973

Fereday, R P, *The Career of Richard Smith*, MA thesis, University of Keele, 1967, printed copy at University of Southampton

Foss, Kenelm, *Lewis Casson*, undated, unpublished memoir

Frederick, John, Earl Cawdor, *Letter to The Right Honourable Joh, Baron Lyndhurst, Lord High Chancellor of England, on the Administration of Justice in Wales*, 1828

George, William, *My Brother and I*, 1958

Gibson, A Craig, 'The Last Popular Uprising in the Lancashire Lake County', *Transactions of the Historical Society of Lancashire and Cheshire*, New Series, Vol IX

greatwarlondon.wordpress.com

Grigg, John, *The Young Lloyd George*, 1973

Gwyn, David, *Gwynedd: Inheriting a Revolution*, 2006

Gwyn, David, *Welsh Slate: Archaeology and History of an Industry*, 2015

Gwynnedd, Madog ap Owain, ed Walwyn, Richard, *Portmadoc and its Resources*, 1856, 2013

Holland, Samuel, 'The Memoirs of Samuel Holland, one of the Pioneers of the North Wales Slate Industry', *CCHCSF/JMHRS*, Extra Publications, Series 1, Number 1, 1952

Holland Grave, Mabel, *Some Welsh Children*, published anonymously, 1898

Holland Grave, Mabel, *Fraternity*, published anonymously, 1888

Holmes, Richard, *Shelley: the Pursuit*, 1974

Holroyd, Michael, 'What Justifies Biography?', *Works on Paper*, 2013

https://museumwales

Hughes, Felicity, *William Wordsworth and Wonderful Walker*, 2004

Hughes, Henry, *Immortal Sails*, 1969

Isambard Owen, Heulwyn and Hedydd, *The Caerffynnon Story*, private publication, 1973

Isambard Owen, Heulwyn and Hedydd, eds *My Welsh Heart*, Diary of Ethel Holland-Thomas [sic], 1881, private publication, 1969

Isherwood, Graham, *The History of the Oakeley Slate Quarries, Blaunau Ffestiog*, 1800-1889, www.aditnow.co.uk

Jones, E Vaughan, 'A Merioneth Murder', *CCHCSF/ JMHRS*, Vol 6,1969

Jones, Iewan Gwynedd, 'Merioneth Politics in the mid-nineteenth century', *CCHCSF/JMHRS*, Vol 5:4, 1968

justiceinspectorates.gov.uk: *A History of Her Majesty's Inspectorate of Constabulary*, 2006

Lewis, M J T & Williams, M C, *Pioneers of Ffestiniog Slate*, 1987

Lewis, M J T & Williams, M C, *Sails on the Dwyryd*, 1989

Lewis, M J T & Williams, M C, 'Archery and Spoonerism: the creators of the Festiniog Railway', *CCHCSF/JMHRS*, Vol 13, 1996

Lindsay, Jean, *A History of the North Wales Slate Industry*, 1974

Lindsay, Jean, '"Call them all rags": some complexities of the early slate trade', *CCHCSF/JMHRS*, Vol 7, 1975

Lloyd, Lewis, 'Captain Lewis Holland Thomas (1812-1888) as a Pacific Trader, 1835-1848/9, *Cymru a'r Môr/Maritime Wales*, No 14, 1991

Lyttelton, George, *Works*, 1775

Madden, Lionel, 'Beauteous Merion', *CCHCSF/JMHRS*, Vol 10, 1987/88

Marshall, J D, *Furness and the Industrial Revolution*, 1958

Mogridge-Hudson, C E, *The Manors of Wike Burnell and Wyke Waryn in the County of Worcestershire*, 1901

Moorman, Mary, *William Wordsworth: A Biography, Vol 2: The Later Years*, 1965

Morris, Jan, *The Matter of Wales*, 1986

Nicholas, Thomas, *Annals and Antiquities of the Counties and County Familes of Wales*, Vol II, 1872-5

Orbell, John and Turton, Alison, *British Banking: A Guide to Historical Records*, 2001

Owen, Hugh J, *Merioneth Volunteers and Local Militia during the Napoleonic Wars* (1795-1816), 1935

Parkinson, Canon Richard, *The Old Church Clock*, Fifth Edition, ed Evans, John, 1880 (includes reprint of a memoir of the Rev Robert Walker by his great grandson, Rev Robert Walker Bamford, originally published in the *Christian Remembrancer*)

Patsuouras, Louis, *The Anarchism of Jean Grave*, 2003

Peacock, Thomas Love, *Headlong Hall*, 1816, ed Garnett, Richard, 1891

Pennant, Thomas, *A Tour in Wales*, 1779

Portmadoc Church Magazine, June 1917, and 1932, undated

Pritchard, D Dylan, 'Aspects of the Slate Industry 11: the Expansionist Period 1', slateroof.co.uk

Probert, Rebecca, *Marriage Law for Genealogists*, 2012

Richards, Alun John, *The Slate Railways of Wales*, 2001

Richards, Alun John, *Gazetteer of Slate Quarrying in Wales*, 2007

Richards, Alun John, *The Rails and Sails of Welsh Slate*, 2011

Roberts, Glyn, 'Lewis Casson – Welsh Actor Plays Part of Welsh Prince', cutting from *Western Mail*, March 1935

Robinson, Kate, *History of St Michael's Church Ffestiniog*, private publication, 1998

Russell, Margaret M, *The Family Forest*, 2000

Smiles, Samuel, *The Life of Thomas Telford, civil engineer, with an introductory history of roads and travelling in Great Britain*, 1867

Southey, Robert, and Cuthbert, Charles, *The Life of the Rev Andrew Bell*, 1854

Toulson, Shirley, *The Drovers' Roads of Wales*, 1988

Trevelyan, G M, *A Shortened History of England*, reprint 1970

Turner, Llewelyn, *The Memories of Sir Llewelyn Turner*, ed Vincent, J E, 1903

Uglow, Jenny, *In These Times: Living in Britain through Napoleon's Wars, 1793-1815*, 2014

vcp.e2bn.org: Victorian Crime and Punishment

Wentmore, Thomas, and Prescott, Edward G, *The Charter and Ordinances of the City of Boston, together with the Acts of the Legislature relating to the City*, 1834

West, Thomas, *Antiquities of Furness*, 1805

West, Thomas, *A Guide to the Lakes*, 1778

Wilcox, Alfred, 'The Organ in the Church: interview with inventor of the "Positive Organ"', *Church Bells and Illustrated Church News*, 26 September, 1902

Williams, G J, *Hanes Plwyf Ffestiniog*, 1882

Williams, John, 'John Bellamy 1840-1919', *The Organ*, February, May, August, November, 1990

Wilson, D H, 'The Spooners up to date', *Festiniog Railway Magazine*, No 77, Summer 1977

Wordsworth, William, *The Poetical Works of William Wordsworth*, (New Edition), 1960

www.britishlistedbuildings.co.uk/wa-4699-pengwern-old-hall-ffestiniog

www.duddon.valley.co.uk, *History of the Valley*

www.lancashireinfantrymuseu.org.uk/the-royal-lancashire-militia

www.maritime.org

www.moneysorter. com

www.penmorfa.com

www.winchestercollegegreatwar.com/archive

List of Illustrations

All illustrations from family archives, unless otherwise stated.

Index

No entries for England, Wales or North Wales
For Welsh and English place names – see under town, or county before 1974, unless otherwise stated
For European place names – see under country